Y0-CCF-633

Lorette Wilmot Library
Nazareth College of Rochester

DEMCO

GUIDO CAVALCANTI
The Other Middle Ages

Guido Cavalcanti
The Other Middle Ages

MARIA LUISA ARDIZZONE

UNIVERSITY OF TORONTO PRESS
Toronto Buffalo London

DISCARDED
LORETTE WILMOT LIBRARY
NAZARETH COLLEGE

© University of Toronto Press Incorporated 2002
Toronto Buffalo London
Printed in Canada

ISBN 0-8020-3591-4

Toronto Italian Studies

National Library of Canada Cataloguing in Publication Data

Ardizzone, Maria Luisa
   Guido Cavalcanti : the other Middle Ages

   (Toronto Italian studies)
   Includes bibliographical references and index.
   ISBN 0-8020-3591-4

   1. Cavalcanti, Guido, d. 1300 – Criticism and interpretation.
   2. Cavalcanti, Guido, d. 1300. Donna me prega.   I. Title.   II. Series.

PQ4299.C2A93 2001   851'.1   C2001-902547-5

University of Toronto Press acknowledges the financial assistance to its
publishing program of the Canada Council for the Arts and the Ontario
Arts Council.

University of Toronto Press acknowledges the financial support for its
publishing activities of the Government of Canada through the Book
Publishing Industry Development Program (BPIDP).

151.1
Cav
Ard

For John Freccero

Contents

Preface

European archives are full of dust. Our love is for dust and for what such dustiness covers: pages written and lost among thousands and thousands of other pages, antique and most unreadable writing, old ideas and debates useless to us today. This book deals with issues that are part of the intellectual history of Western tradition. It does not seek to modernize such a past, but to read it because it is past. To retrace lost lines of the identity of the past is sometimes used as a tool for inventing our present and thus our future; but, in our case, it does not motivate our attitude for what is not actual. If being modern implies making a choice – excluding materials because they are extraneous to our present – then this work, as we shall see, is mostly inclusive. More than being just a discourse about Cavalcanti's poetry and ideas, this book is intended to lead the reader to think with Cavalcanti.

For Italo Calvino, Guido Cavalcanti displays the lightness of the poet-philosopher who is able to think without the weight of thinking. Although a philosopher and logician, Cavalcanti prefers not to entrust his thinking to philosophy. Because he is aware that images and metaphors are the natural language of both thinking and poetry, he chooses poetry as the mode by which to express his thought. This book seeks to understand the origin of this awareness by retracing the meaning of Cavalcanti's choice in the multiculturalism of his age.

This multiculturalism was far indeed from orthodoxy and theology, and was regarded with suspicion at the time. Largely determined by the influence of what Edward Said calls 'Orientalism,' it initiated a process of decanonization of the values basic to medieval Western culture. But the reading of Cavalcanti's poetry put forth in this book is not limited to his attack on the Western canon. In our evaluation of the culture of 'the other' found in Guido's poetry, we shall concentrate more on what Cavalcanti builds than on what he dismantles.

This book emphasizes the new space that Guido created for poetry, as well as the place he has given to the values belonging to the individual. Themes that he introduces in his poetry, like the emotions, the body's passion and desires, the animality of human nature, and the medieval discourse on the brain and imagination, appear both as a link to the present and as his legacy.

Moreover, the relationship between logic and poetry that emerges from his work opens a new way of conceiving at once poetry and knowing. Imagination, i.e., the power of making images, that Cavalcanti puts at the centre of his writing as the true activity of intelligence for human beings meshes very well with the revision of academic curricula in the field of education of the present. Thus the fact that the 700th anniversary of Cavalcanti's death is located on the border between a millennium which ends and the beginning of a new millennium appears to us as not merely a casual coincidence.

This book began as part of a large-scale work still in progress. The reason for its appearance in a separate volume is less the result of a personal decision than one dictated by happy circumstances. The importance that Ezra Pound has given to Cavalcanti was responsible for my interest in Cavalcanti during the early 1980s. But before Pound, my meeting with Professor Maria Corti in the late 1970s and my reading of her studies on Dante and Cavalcanti (*Dante a un nuovo crocevia* and *La felicità mentale*) have been crucial to my initial research.

In 1992 I spent a semester as an official guest and visiting scholar at the Pontifical Institute for Mediaeval Studies at the University of Toronto. For this I am indebted to Professor John Farge. Thanks to Father Black, the Archivist of the Pontifical Institute Archive, I was allowed to reproduce Pound's letters to Gilson and St Michael's College, now held in the Institute's Gilson Archive. Important meetings during that period were with Professor Édouard Jeauneau and Professor D.L. Black. In spring 1993, during a term as Visiting Scholar in New York University's Department of Comparative Literature, my meeting with John Freccero gave further impulse to my work. At the end of 1993, Professor Freccero founded the Institute for the Study of Science, Literature, and Art as part of the Italian Department of New York University. The Institute was inaugurated in January of 1994 under the direction of Professor Freccero. During the inaugural session, I gave a series of lectures on Optics and Poetry in Medieval Culture, one of which was dedicated to Cavalcanti's *Donna me prega*. Professor Freccero's interventions on that occasion and subsequently, his conversations and intellectual encouragement during the last six years, his reading and invaluable annotations to chapter 2 of this book (the first chapter to be written), his friendship and support for my research – all these have been crucial in the writing of this book.

I wish to thank Mary de Rachewiltz for her instigation, generosity, and friendship. My deepest gratitude is to Franca Ghitti, whose work has long nourished both my imagination and my reasoning. I am grateful to Professor Dino Buzzetti from the University of Bologna for facilitating my work; to Professor Luciano Gargan from the University of Pavia for making possible my own research at the Università Cattolica in Milan; and to my former colleague Professor Barbara Spackman for making ideas circulate. My friend and former colleague at the University of Rochester, Professor Donatella Stocchi Perucchio, has contributed to this book in various ways – not least by her belief in this project. This volume also owes a debt of gratitude to Peter Kalkavage for his editorial assistance and his patient scrutiny of my English. Margaret Morton, who makes photographs which are ideas, also deserves a special thank-you because her work has enriched my understanding of what an image is.

Graduate students of the Italian Department – Federica Anichini, Tina Chiappetta, Mimi Halpern, Elena Lombardi (now a colleague), Rebecca Wrigt – who followed my course on Cavalcanti at New York University in 1996, deserve a special thanks for obliging me to think harder with their comments and questions.

Note on Editions of Guido Cavalcanti's Texts

All quotations of Guido Cavalcanti's texts are drawn from the following editions:

Guido Cavalcanti. *Rime, con le rime de Iacopo Cavalcanti.* Ed. Domenico De Robertis. Turin: Giulio Einaudi, 1986.
Poeti del Duecento. Vol. 2. Ed. Gianfranco Contini. Milan and Naples: Riccardo Ricciardi, 1960.
The Poetry of Guido Cavalcanti. Ed. and trans. Lowry Nelson, Jr. New York and London: Garland, 1986.
Guido Cavalcanti: Rime. Ed. Ezra Pound. Genoa: Edizioni Marsano, 1932.

GUIDO CAVALCANTI
The Other Middle Ages

Introduction

According to Dante, Guido Cavalcanti leads us into a territory demarcated by John the Baptist, the fiery precursor, the *vox clamantis in deserto*. Although we have no idea what Cavalcanti looked like (to my knowledge, no synchronous portraits of him are extant), we nonetheless see him vividly depicted in Boccaccio's *Decameron* (VI, 9). There, emerging from behind the graves and leaping over them, he refuses to speak with those to whom he says, 'Voi mi potete dire a casa vostra ciò che vi piace' (Gentlemen, you may say anything you wish to me in your home). Cavalcanti thereby suggests that 'they' (the Florentine *brigata*, Betto Brunelleschi and others) were the living dead worthy of dwelling in tombs.

Logician and natural philosopher, Guido Cavalcanti, the first friend of Dante, has been depicted as a proud, solitary man by a tradition that runs from Boccaccio until at least the Renaissance. According to Benvenuto of Imola, author of a fourteenth-century commentary on Dante's *Commedia*, he was one of the 'two eyes' of Florence during the late thirteenth century (the other being Dante). Cavalcanti's eminence in his age is attested by Dante in the *Vita nuova*, which is dedicated to him. Giacomo da Pistoia, a master from the Faculty of Arts of the University of Bologna, also dedicates his *Quaestio de felicitate* to Guido. Cavalcanti is remembered for 'altezza d' ingegno' in Canto X of Dante's *Inferno*; he is mentioned in Petrarch's *Trionfi*, and in Petrarch's *Rime* (LXX) Cavalcanti is recalled for *Donna me prega*. For historians such as Giovanni and Filippo Villani and Dino Compagni, Cavalcanti is a philosopher and a man devoted to a life of study.

In the early fourteenth century, two commentaries on *Donna me prega* provide evidence of the importance which tradition accords to Guido's canzone. The more authoritative of the two was by Dino del Garbo, the

illustrious doctor from Florence (who died in 1327). The other commentary – much less important and written in the vernacular – was
falsely ascribed to Aegidius Romanus.

Del Garbo's commentary (which Boccaccio would later copy by
hand) enlarges Cavalcanti's fame. This text, which probably influenced
the portrait of Guido we see in the *Decameron,* opens a new perspective
on him. From this point onward, Guido's poetry is ascribed more to a
tradition of science than to one of literature. This perspective is no
doubt responsible for the relevant role that will be given to Cavalcanti in
the Florentine Platonic school. In the age of humanism, Antonio da
Tuccio Manetti, the biographer of Brunelleschi, organizes the first
'historical codex' (De Robertis) of Guido's work and dedicates it to Giovanni Cavalcanti, a member of Guido's family and a friend of Marsilio
Ficino. Manetti includes, along with Guido's texts, the two commentaries on *Donna me prega.* The exegesis that Ficino reserves for *Donna me
prega* in his commentary on Plato's *Convivium* is one tile of the compos-
ite mosaic that, during the age of Lorenzo de' Medici, recreates the legend of Cavalcanti. Poliziano's dedicatory letter to Raccolta Aragonese,
which emphasizes the quality of Cavalcanti's poetry, and the acknowl-
edgment to Cavalcanti in the Giuntina edition (1527), which devotes an
entire volume to him, are also influential for the sixteenth-century editions and studies of Guido and his *Donna me prega.*

This portrait of Cavalcanti, depicted over the centuries, is of great
importance. Rather than considering him a minor voice in comparison
to Dante's, tradition speaks of Cavalcanti's uniqueness. He is seen as a
representative of a medieval tradition different from the one that converges in Dante. While the proud and solitary Cavalcanti does not actually write 'God is dead,' his work nonetheless shakes the theological
foundations of medieval culture (Boccaccio's work is not fully intelligible without Cavalcanti). Dante's awareness of it, after a period of fasci-
nation, starts his gradual emancipation from, and later opposition to,
Cavalcanti. The fact that in the *Commedia* Guido appears as nothing
more than an imprint alive in the minds of a few suggests that Dante
concocts a special kind of *contrappasso* for his first friend in order to neu-
tralize the power of his thought and poetry.

Cavalcanti's uniqueness, however, does not consist solely in his dis-
belief. From Boccaccio onward, and in particular with Ficino and Poliziano, it is the quality of his poetry ('artificiosa,' as Ficino calls it) that
attracts attention. For readers in the tradition of humanism, the ingenu-
ity that Boccaccio attributes to Guido in his 'motto' to the Florentine

brigata seems to capture the essential quality of Cavalcanti's poetry. So too for Poliziano, Guido will become the poet who 'bello, gentile e pere-grino rassembra,' who is 'acutissimo' in inventions and 'gravissimo nelle sentenze.'

The focus of this book is Guido's intellectual profile. An attempt will be made to reconstruct this profile in light of the cultural climate of Bologna's Faculty of Arts in the later phase of the thirteenth century, considering the circulation of ideas between Paris and Bologna. I shall refer to this context in reading Cavalcanti's poetry in order to evaluate the kind of culture from which Cavalcanti draws.

Cavalcanti sees human life as buffeted by the winds of the passions and desires. But such passions can also exalt mankind. Passion is in fact what may allow human beings to activate the process of imagination and intelligence. The idea that the body's perfection can serve as a ladder toward the process of intellectual perfection is one of the crucial points of the culture of Guido's time that his poetry examines. The way he counteracts this idea begs to be deciphered and investigated further. Such an investigation will be one of the cornerstones of this book, which will utilize documents and texts both explored and unexplored in rela-tion to Cavalcanti. Along with the tradition that depicts Cavalcanti as a natural philosopher, this book will also focus on his fame as a logician, a fame that starts with Boccaccio, continues with Ficino, Poliziano, Lorenzo de' Medici, and is reiterated in some commentaries on Dante, such as that of the Anonimo Fiorentino and Cristoforo Landino, who probably follow Boccaccio's lead.

This book rereads Cavalcanti's poetry in the context of the philosoph-ical debate that takes place in Bologna and Paris during the later decades of the thirteenth century. It evaluates Cavalcanti not only as a natural philosopher but also as a logician, and seeks a connection between the two disciplines – natural philosophy and logic – in his poetry. This rereading will also bring into focus European 'Oriental-ism,' marked by the twelfth- to thirteenth-century introduction and dif-fusion of the Arab culture that reshaped the medieval cultural model.

Thanks to Guido Cavalcanti, poetry becomes a 'vortex.' This term was introduced by the American poet Ezra Pound to name a new type of relationship suggested by twentieth-century science.[1] It is used here to designate the new importance Cavalcanti gives to poetry and the new model of poetry he constructs in light of the learning that entered Europe between the twelfth and thirteenth centuries. The term 'vortex' may also be applied to the so-called modernism of the thirteenth century (as described by Gorce, 'Averroisme'), through which Cavalcanti empowered poetry by making it a dynamic centre that attracted different material from different fields, such as philosophy, logic, and science. This new poetry expands its vocabulary and reorganizes the laws of rhetoric in order to include psychology, physiology, physics, optics, logic, and ethics. It would have been impossible for a poem like *Donna me prega* to have been written prior to the entrance of the 'new' Aristotle and Aristotelianism.

Cavalcanti fashions a technical language for his philosophical topics. His vocabulary is constructed around specific words that embody a precise meaning. In his poetry we find words that may be understood only through a specific knowledge of specific disciplines. These are tools which are crucial in penetrating the meaning of his poetry. They will be explored in relation to *Donna me prega*, the canzone to whose analysis this book is primarily dedicated.

An important point of this work is that *Donna me prega* cannot be considered in isolation from Cavalcanti's other poems. The conceptual unity that his poetry involves is a premise for any serious reading of the canzone. From the minor poems onward, it is evident that Guido participates in a culture in which natural philosophy and medicine are related. Arabism, which some modern readers reject in Cavalcanti, has to be seen for what it is: the common learning of medical doctors of his time in which Avicenna's *Canon* and Averroes's *Colliget* interact with the old Hippocratic-Galenic tradition as well as with natural philosophy. What we term the 'other Middle Ages,' specifically in reference to Cavalcanti, is precisely this culture that sought answers to human desires and goals not in theology but in biology, natural philosophy, and in medicine. Of course, Dante too had knowledge of this culture but the crucial answers concerning man's goals and destiny are for him taken from the theological field. Thus the adjective 'other,' while it echoes Benvenuto da Imola's definition of Cavalcanti as the 'other' eye of Florence in Dante's time, also refers to the role played by 'otherness' in shaping the multicultural essence of Cavalcanti's personality. Chapter 1 focuses on Cavalcanti's method and reads some of the so-called minor poems. Here Guido organizes what I call a 'rhetoric of passion,' in which the ego is represented as acted upon by its passions and managed by its centres of sensations. The internal senses will be introduced in this chapter, and the role of imagination will be examined as a key to penetrating *Donna me prega* as well. This chapter focuses on the importance that medical science plays in Cavalcanti's poems. The interaction between natural philosophy and medicine, as it took place in Bologna in the second half of the thirteenth century, is assumed as a point of reference in reading his poems. Cavalcanti's use of the theory of *pneuma* as a medium to connect the soul and body is examined here.

By looking at the way in which rhetoric organizes the theory of love in Cavalcanti's minor poems, the chapter centres on the literal method introduced by Cavalcanti. In this method, words express functions. These functions, in turn, can be understood by looking at the bodily relations that these words bring to the page and that transform the discourse on love into a series of events that poetry records.

Chapter 2 starts by rereading *Donna me prega*. Preliminarily it does not consider the canzone as dependent on Averroism, or radical Aristotelianism, or other philosophical positions; rather it organizes its discussion around the metaphor of the 'diaphanous.' This metaphor is central for the comprehension of the canzone. For the first time, the canzone is examined in light of the theory of optics, on which Cavalcanti structures the metaphor itself. An important result here obtained through this inquiry is that the most widely accepted interpretation that reads the metaphor as showing love in the canzone as in itself obscure is refuted. On the evidence of the sources that Cavalcanti uses and exhibits, we find that love reveals itself as 'diaphanous.' While dark for man, love is in itself diaphanous. This result was obtained by taking into account the logical tools the poet has used in order to establish the being of love, as well as the new science of optics as a demonstrative metaphor. There emerges from the interpretation of this metaphor of the diaphanous a first confirmation of Cavalcanti's Averroism or radical Aristotelianism: the process of knowing originates in love, but this knowing does not belong to love itself. A series of consequences derives from this reading. These consequences will be examined here and in chapters 3 and 4. The second part of chapter 2 rereads the famous passage from *Inferno* X, in which Cavalcanti is mentioned. It also attempts to introduce a relation between the logical tools Cavalcanti utilizes in *Donna me prega* and the ambiguities that Dante puts forth in *Inferno* X in relation to Guido.

Chapter 3 will describe love by inquiring into Cavalcanti's theory of passion as it emerges in *Donna me prega*. Here the use of the singular 'passion' has a specific meaning: love appears to be considered as part of the Aristotelian theory of matter dominated by necessity. Passion thus detaches the ego from ethics because it subjects the ego to the rules of matter. This chapter structures its discussion around natural philosophy and focuses on the word 'accident,' which Cavalcanti uses in *Donna me prega* to introduce the discussion of love. While the focus of chapter 1 is the discourse on passion related primarily to medical science, chapter 3 focuses on passion in its relationship to natural philosophy. The result of the latter inquiry is of great importance: at the basis of Cavalcanti's theory of passion is the medieval theory of matter as put forth by the philosophy of Aristotle and his Arabic readers. In light of this theory of matter, the relation between *Donna me prega* and the Parisian condemnations emerges with greater clarity. Cavalcanti defines love as a created being (that is, generated); here 'created' means – we propose – that love is subject to the laws of generation and corruption that preside over the cycle of matter. This examination leads to a connecting of love and the sensitive soul (in which love is located) to the theory of the eternity of matter (as in Aristotle and Averroes). From this theory there derived the two most dangerous theories that the Parisian condemnations tried to halt: the denial of creation and the death of the individual soul. The historical commentary on *Donna me prega* written by the Florentine Doctor Dino del Garbo, will play a strong role in this reconstruction, as will other documents that testify to the Parisian debate as it relates to *Donna me prega*. The second section of chapter 3 discusses the connection we introduce between Cavalcanti's theory of matter and the theory of time that Dante puts forth in *Inferno* X.

Chapter 4 opens by considering the famous *Quaestio de felicitate* that Giacomo da Pistoia dedicated to Cavalcanti, according to the manuscript discovered and published by Paul Oskar Kristeller. The chapter investigates the *Quaestio* by comparing the thesis on happiness developed therein with *Donna me prega* and looks for a relationship between the two texts. The result of our reading is that the theory of happiness includes a debate on the role of the individual in the intellectual process as it takes place in the field of radical Aristotelianism. As we shall see, Cavalcanti's position is more radical than that of Giacomo and first appears in the poet's distinction between an intellectual and an animal happiness.

This result of our reading will be related to what arises from the analysis of love (in chapter 2) as being in itself diaphanous but dark for man. This implies the following: because man does not have intellect, he is not involved in intellectual happiness. Cavalcanti in this way enters the debate documented by Giacomo's *Quaestio*. But what distinguishes Cavalcanti is that unlike Giacomo, he puts at the centre of his theory of happiness the pleasure of the sensitive soul (*diletto*). This pleasure emphasizes the separation of the sensitive soul from the intellectual being. *Donna me prega* does not deny the possibility of a connection (*coniunctio*) with the possible intellect. On the contrary, it affirms that this connection, however difficult, can be established. Nevertheless, the individual participates in a subordinate way in the process, since he does not directly engage in intellection but merely offers the form for intellection. For this reason, intellectual happiness for Guido does not pertain to man. Given the two different *genera* of intellect and sensitive soul, a human being's happiness derives from what gives him satisfaction, namely, the body's desires. Cavalcanti utilizes tools of logic in order to show the break between these two *genera*. He then employs logic and optics to show that the pleasure of love for man consists solely in its darkness, that is, in sensuality. Chapter 4 in its second section relates Cavalcanti's position to the debate about animal power, a topic introduced in the medical school of Bologna by Taddeus Alderotto. It seems that Taddeus, while accepting the Averroistic thesis about the separate intellect, was also focusing on what is peculiar to the individual evaluating *phantasia* and memory as part of intelligence, which animal power is able to develop. According to our reading, Cavalcanti, while related to the Parisian debate, was nevertheless independent of it and looked more at the power of the individual.

One important aspect of Cavalcanti's thought that the book variously considers is what Cavalcanti designates as love. Dante's indication in *Vita nova* that Cavalcanti was an 'imposer of names' (an *impositore*) is rethought in light of this reading of *Donna me prega*. Cavalcanti defines love in the opening of the canzone by using two adjectives: *fero* and *altero*. He thus informs us – as I propose – that he intends to speak about love in two distinct ways: from one side love is animality and man's pleasure is related to it; from the other love is crucial for the process of generation of form and therefore for the process toward intellection. This is the central theme that *Donna me prega* ultimately proposes: love is a metaphor for the sensitive soul and for the animal power that initiates a process of intellection without being involved itself in intellectual knowledge. The metaphor of love, as we shall see, is developed through the metaphor of the 'diaphanous.'

The last chapter will focus on Ezra Pound's reading of Cavalcanti and of *Donna me prega* in particular. In this uncharted territory, I take up the importance of Cavalcanti's poetry for the poetry of the twentieth century and for the invention of modernity. The importance that Pound accords to Cavalcanti's *Donna me prega* has long been a point of reflection and study for the author of this book.

Cavalcanti represents an alternative line of medieval culture, a line that American modernism considered in its attempt to rewrite the Western cultural tradition by placing it on a new foundation. The fact that T.S. Eliot was interested in supporting Pound's edition suggests that not only Dante but also Cavalcanti's medieval poetry was at the centre of their interest. In fact, discourse on Cavalcanti involves a discourse on the whole notion of poetry, in which medieval culture reveals itself as a source for precisely the new kind of poetry sought by modernism. The exclusion of inspiration and romantic subjectivism, the refutation of nineteenth-century psychologism, the attempt to connect the new forms of knowledge to the language of poetry – all these are among the reasons for Cavalcanti's importance for Pound and for Eliot as well.

The extent of Pound's role in bringing Cavalcanti into twentieth-century poetry is an, as yet, unwritten chapter in the cultural history of the twentieth century. For Pound, Cavalcanti and Dante are two sides of the same coin in that they articulate complementary aspects of the culture of the Middle Ages: philosophy and science in Cavalcanti, theology in Dante. Although Dante's encyclopedia includes science and philosophy, they are theologically oriented. Dante looks to the heavens, while Cavalcanti, on his side, deliberately looks toward the earth, toward what may be experienced in this life. For Pound the 'natural demonstration' of *Donna me prega* represents the centre of Cavalcanti's importance.

The exile to which Dante condemned his 'first friend' also becomes, for Pound, metaphorical of Cavalcanti's condition. In the *Cantos*, Pound, emphatically employing the Italian language, recalls Cavalcanti from his 600-year exile. But Cavalcanti's enormous linguistic powers, which Pound exalts, constitute for him the main reason for both Cavalcanti's modernity and his exile.

Guido's work was fundamental to Pound's project of reformulating, through poetry, the processes of Western culture on a new basis. Objective conditions did not facilitate Pound's reading: Pound based his interpretation of *Donna me prega* on an old and uncorrected text of the canzone and, as is well known, his attempt at a critical edition was a failure. A paradox may explain his reading: while misunderstanding, he in fact understands. Or better, it is because he does not understand that he understands. Although wrong in the details, Pound captures in depth the message and spirit of Cavalcanti's poetry.

The importance of Pound's reading derives from the unprecedented role he gives Cavalcanti: Pound puts Guido's poetry at the centre of the Western canon and makes it the point of confluence with the

Chinese tradition. In Pound's reading, this poetry obliges the reader to work with images that are at the same time concepts; it challenges the reader to recognize the beauty of Guido's poem by deciphering its scientific, philosophical meaning. Its beauty is in its difficulty; it speaks at once to intelligence and imagination. Neither mere ornament nor addition, metaphor is something precise. The value of such poetry lies in the creation of this metaphor, which has only one meaning, and does not encourage the reader's subjective interpretation. On the contrary, it impels the reader to reconstruct the meaning the words had at that precise time period. On the one hand, Cavalcanti's reader must work like an archaeologist, reconstructing fragments of thinking through specific words. On the other, this reader must compare the metaphor with the role played by rationality in the writing of this kind of poetry.

One of Pound's claims is that this poetry was the result of a culture that did not conceive the imagination to be opposed to intelligence. For the American, Cavalcanti emphasizes the role of the body and of the imagination. Body and imagination, here considered as part of intelligence, all collaborate at different levels. For this reason, the debate on love is a debate on the human being: his power, his limits, and his desires.

As a reader of Cavalcanti, Pound proposed a project for poetry that involved his own work. In this project, poetry is the highest form of knowing. Its being lies in its ability to embrace in its language experiences of knowing that belong to different fields and that poetry empowers. But it is the reshaping of the notion of poetry – as we shall see – that is the core of Pound's reading and misreading of Guido's text.

A highly important aspect of Cavalcanti's poetry to be discussed in this book derives from the use of poetic language in light of logic. Cavalcanti deliberately introduces in *Donna me prega* logical tools because he wishes to establish the authority of certain topics. These topics will be discussed throughout chapters 2, 3, and 4. What emerges is that, with *Donna me prega*, we have a kind of poetry organized like a 'theorem' on love, whose demonstration Cavalcanti structures by means of a logic that sometimes violates the laws of grammar in order to reach a higher truth. This violation has a crucial meaning in *Donna me prega*, which aims at including within the language of poetry the break between the two spheres of intellect and matter. This break is the focus of Cavalcanti's discussion of love in the poem.

Is it possible to trace the importance Cavalcanti gives to logic to the introduction of Arabic culture into the European scene? Scholars have reflected on the fact that Arabic thought reorganized the place of rhetoric and poetics by seeing them as a part of logic. Averroes in particular and Arabic culture generally saw poetry as the weakest form of argument available for the communication process. Scholars emphasize that poetry was not important in the Islamic world and that Averroes too did not recognize the importance of Greek poetry.[2] The attack on poetry and rhetoric by Averroes is made, they say, because of the importance he gives to the demonstrative point of view. Within Arabic culture, poetry was a kind of inferior discourse for the intellectually weak. According to other studies, among philosophers like Alkindi, Alfarabi, and Avicenna, rhetoric and poetics were considered part of logic (part of the *Organon*), like the *Topics* or the *Analytics*.[3] According to Alfonso Maierù, this tradition began in late antiquity and was introduced into Western culture, thanks to the translations of Arabic texts (Maierù 'Influenze arabe').

Averroes emphasized the enthymeme as a truncated syllogism. According to a recent study, we find in Avicenna traces of metaphor used as a kind of syllogism.[4] Our reading confirms the suggestion that Cavalcanti's way of composing poetry can indeed be related to the task of the medieval philosophers, who gave the syllogism dominion over all human cognitive activities. Because poetics and rhetoric were considered as treating matters directed toward the attainment of a cognitive end, they had to be based on some kind of formal syllogistic procedure.[5] This can be connected to Cavalcanti's way of employing the science of optics (and in particular the metaphor of the 'diaphanous') in order to demonstrate his thesis on love. Cavalcanti, defining his major canzone as *ragione* or piece of reasoning, openly states its relation to logic. The peculiar tone of his poetry lies precisely in discussing love as a reasoning or argument that applies logic to natural philosophy in order to demonstrate a thesis. This employment of logical tools as applied to topics of optics (which are introduced as a metaphor for love) is one of the reasons – probably the main reason – for the impenetrability of Guido's canzone *Donna me prega*.

The sonnet Cavalcanti sent to Guittone d'Arezzo speaks openly of the importance that logic holds in his poetry: *Da più a uno face un sollegismo ... e come far poteresti un sofismo/per silabate carte?'* (Syllogism proceeds from the many toward the one ... how could you be able to make a sophism in poetry?). In this sonnet, Guittone is denigrated for not being able to write a sophism. For his part, Guido is blamed for sophism by Dino Compagni: '*e come assai scri[t]tura sai a mente / soffisimosamente*' (How much a sophistic knowledge of learning you have) in the poem Dino sends him.[6] Cavalcanti's central metaphor in *Donna me prega* was, in fact, nothing other than a kind of demonstration of what he wanted to depict: love, whose essence is accident (which is fierce and haughty), and the magnitude of the accident itself. The emphasis that medieval philosophy places on logic, appending poetics and rhetoric to the *Organon*, can explain another aspect we find in Cavalcanti: the subordination of grammar to logic. Logic was considered at once a rational and linguistic science. But logic considers language with a view to truth and falsehood, whereas grammar considers it with a view to congruity and incongruity.[7] As we have observed, Cavalcanti sometimes breaks this congruity in order to explicate truth.

Cavalcanti's method of writing is part of his legend. His new way of writing poetry is probably responsible for the interpretation the first commentators of Dante's *Commedia* have given of Guido's 'disdain,' which Dante introduces in *Inferno* X and which was interpreted as a disdain for poetry. Dante's ambiguous 'cui' was explained in terms of Cavalcanti's disdain for Virgil, who, as the symbol of poetry, would have been the target of such disdain on Guido's part because of Guido's predilection for philosophy and science. But along with these views is the language Cavalcanti uses in introducing his themes, which has generated the legend of Cavalcanti as a despiser of poetry.

As part of the legend of Cavalcanti that tradition has built, an image is offered in a novella by Franco Sacchetti, in which the narrator refers to Cavalcanti's prowess as a chess player. We assume this image, whatever its source or meaning, to be metaphorical of Cavalcanti's method of writing poetry. The geometrical board and the kind of mathematical rationality the game of chess requires is a valid image of the tools Guido has employed and which the reader needs in order to understand this sort of poetry.

But this way of writing poetry, however peculiar to Cavalcanti, had its antecedents in Italian vernacular poetry. In medieval poetry, and in Italian vernacular poetry in particular, there was a tradition that reaches its culmination in the poetry of Cavalcanti. Indeed, this poetry was modelled in part on the tradition inspired by the poetry of Giacomo da Lentini, as it emerged from the culture of the Sicilian court of Frederick II. The heritage of the Arabs and Normans, which focused on science and philosophy, was the background of Giacomo da Lentini's education. Through him this learning entered Italian poetry at its very beginnings.

Arabic and Greek thought, which shaped the *curricula studiorum* of the Faculty of Arts at the University of Naples, seems to be at the origin of Giacomo's scientific imagination. According to scholars, the Sicilian notary, a student at the University of Naples at the end of the 1220s, probably derived the themes of his poetry from that curriculum. In this poetry, presided over by the philosophy of nature, Giacomo offers a new and astonishing pronouncement of the theme of love inherited from the Provençal model. From Giacomo onward, some of the so-called Sicilian poets encompassed in their poems topics that will be encountered in the work of Cavalcanti. For example, the *quaestiones* in the famous *tenzoni* are somewhat similar to questions that Cavalcanti answers in *Donna me prega*: what is love, what originates it, when and in which part of man does it have its seat?[8]

In a poem attributed to Abate da Tivoli, we read that 'amore ha molto scura canoscenza' (Love's knowledge is very obscure).[9] So too, when Pier delle Vigne writes that 'Amore non se pò vedere' (Love is not visible),[10] he probably paves the way for Cavalcanti's discussion on love's visibility in *Donna me prega*. In addition, some sonnets ascribed to the Sicilians introduce the word 'spirit,'[11] used in a way that recalls Cavalcanti's mode. From this we may deduce that the beginnings of Italian vernacular poetry gave birth to a philosophic tradition that Cavalcanti strongly develops in his poetry.

But peculiar to Cavalcanti was the employment of a highly specific language. Scholars refer to it as a technical language, and this technicality is commonly regarded as a peculiarity of Guido's poetry. Nonetheless, a careful reading of the origins of our vernacular poetry shows that Cavalcanti's technical vocabulary did not emerge ex nihilo. Going back again to the Sicilian school, there is evidence that Guido delle Colonne introduced a technical word, 'medium' (*mezzo*), which appears in his canzone, *Ancor che l'aigua per lo foco lassi.*[12] This word no doubt testifies to Guido's dependence, whether directly or not, on Aristotle's text. The same theory of the medium (but not the word) is also present in Guido Guinizzelli's poem, *Al cor gentil rempaira sempre amore*, the manifesto of the new wave that will be called *stil nuovo*. Here the woman mediates between man and God, as the angelic intelligences mediated between God-as-Light and the cosmos, thus moving the heavens. In addition, Guinizzelli proposed an analogy between the Neoplatonic process of diffusion of light in nature and the process of love in the gentle heart. From this diffusion of light derives the notion of *gentilezza* described (through metalepsis) as the sensitivity to light of certain elements that act as mediums in this process. In order to structure this process, Guinizzelli made use of notions and specific words derived from the new Aristotelian philosophy that had entered Europe in the thirteenth century.

Present in the three Guidos of our poetry of origins – delle Colonne, Guinizzelli, and Cavalcanti – the theory of the medium will, in the work of the third Guido, acquire a central importance and a new role derived from the new sources that Cavalcanti will employ. Among these sources is the science of optics as formulated and derived from Aristotle's theory of vision in *De anima* II.

One aspect that Cavalcanti inherits deserves special emphasis – the notion of writing as a form of authority. The philosophical themes of Guido's poetry and his so-called technical language introduce into poetry the concept of writing as an authority because he writes on the basis of *auctoritates*. The unfolding practice of writing poetry that uses philosophical sources and their technical language will be peculiar to the new poetry. This new poetry, that we call *stil nuovo*, more powerfully continues what the Sicilian poets initiated. In the polemical poem that Bonagiunta Orbicciani wrote for Guido Guinizzelli,[13] the concept of writing as authority (that is, writing that was based on *auctoritates*) derived mostly, according to Bonagiunta, from a *senno* coming from Bologna. Guinizzelli heralds a method of composing poetry on the evidence of *auctoritates*. This method is probably responsible for the *sottiglianza* that Bonagiunta blames. By employing a new knowledge, Guinizzelli was able to present love as the great metaphor through which the new discourse on society, nature, and man was articulated.

The word 'nature' here must be seen in its inner relationship with the physics of Aristotle and the works connected with it. This was the Latin Aristotelianism specific to Western culture that Guinizzelli probably derived (as Dante did later) from the *philosophantes*. As is well known, Bologna was one of the centres for the dissemination of Aristotle's thought. It was among the first centres in which the new encyclopedia entered the curriculum through the Faculty of Arts and Medicine; the convents also were responsible for the dissemination of the new learning.

Cavalcanti is aware of this tradition when he enters the scene. However, a watershed development that serves to distinguish the two voices (Guinizzelli-Cavalcanti) is the Arabic rereading of Aristotle and his European followers. This Arabic influence assumes great importance for Cavalcanti. The method that Cavalcanti appropriates is the same one that Bonagiunta blames in Guinizzelli; and, like Guinizzelli, Cavalcanti sets aside Guittone's model. In addition, Guido brings about a turning point: he centres on natural philosophy by connecting it to logic.

In *Donna me prega*, the word 'accident' is introduced to indicate the field to which love belongs. Cavalcanti employs nuances of vocabulary with great awareness, defining love as an 'accident' and giving it the name *sensato*. Love is related to the 'diaphanous,' the technical meaning of which provides the suggestive and obscure metaphor on which the canzone is structured. Poetry becomes a language able to encompass the different topics furnished by the encyclopedia of the time. By connecting logic, science, and philosophy, Cavalcanti is able to answer old and new questions alike.

The turning point that Cavalcanti accomplishes in the history of poetry will be perfectly understood and taken up by Dante, who, as Dante's readers well know, shares the cultural climate of his 'first friend.' But it is also well known that Dante openly appeals to other sources as well, and that the kind of poetry he writes differs greatly from that of Cavalcanti. Dante, as is often observed, represents an *unicum* in cultural history. But it is worth noting that Cavalcanti too remains an isolated case in the history of poetry. Boccaccio at first and later the culture of humanism will place emphasis on what may be called Cavalcanti's idiosyncrasy.

The uniqueness of Cavalcanti within his culture is precisely what Pound, too, highly emphasized. Paying great attention to the rereading of Cavalcanti in the age of Leonardo, Pound integrates the medieval portrait of Guido and proposes a 'new mask' for Guido. What is important here for shaping Cavalcanti's uniqueness is not the Platonic interpretation of *Donna me prega* Ficino has given but rather Ficino's designation of Guido's poetry as *artificiosa*. The American poet creates a modern legend of Cavalcanti. He connects the persona of 'natural philosopher,' which tradition recognizes, with the *artificiosa* quality of his poetry emphasized by Ficino. Guido's fame as 'doctrina egregius numeris' (Ugolino Verino) enters as an epigraph in Pound's Cavalcanti. Pound's perspective, which is far indeed from that of Rossetti, for whom Guido was a primitive pre-Raphaelite, centres on *Donna me prega*, the canzone that Rossetti did not translate because he judged it a dull scholastic text.[14] Pound, on the contrary, centred on the canzone because, according to the new canon, he was proposing 'Beauty is difficult.' This 'difficult,' which for modernism is coincident with the beauty of poetry itself, opens up a new chapter in the history of Cavalcanti's reception.[15]

Chapter One

Love as a Metaphor:
The Discourse and the Method

E cantin[n]e gli auselli
ciascuno in suo latino[1]

A Rhetoric of Passion

Guido Cavalcanti introduces into the medieval imagination the physical
perception of a light that shines so strongly that it brings a tremor into
the air. He associates this tremor with the approach of a woman:

Chi è questa che vèn, ch'ogn'om la mira,
che fa tremar di chiaritate l'âre.

(Who is she who comes, that every one looks at her,
who makes the air tremble with clarity)

The image seems related on the one hand to the *Song of Songs*, with its
emphasis on the interrogative form (Contini, *Poeti del Duecento*), and on
the other (because of the term *tremar*) to the field of studies on light
that were conducted initially by Alhazen and subsequently by Robert
Grosseteste and Roger Bacon. A part of Roger Bacon's *Optics* (*Perspectiva*) leads in fact to a consideration of the phenomenon of tremor and
scintillation, to which Cavalcanti's image can be referred.[2] As Cavalcanti's poetry shows, however, the same verb *tremar* (to tremble) can be
associated not only with light but also with the physical phenomenon of
the passion of love. 'Trembling,' a recurrent verb in his poems and
sometimes associated with pallor, is a physiological phenomenon that

Cavalcanti emphasizes in his poetry. A specific connotation thus lies first of all in his connection of a semantics derived from medical science and physiology with a semantics derived from the philosophy of nature, of which the science of the soul is considered to be a part.[3]

In his early poems, Cavalcanti appears to set forth, in a largely problematic manner, the various ways in which love may be put into words. The topos of birds singing in their own Latin – 'E cantin[n]e gli auselli / ciascuno in suo latino' (And let the birds sing of it, each one in its own tongue) – suggests that Cavalcanti is looking at his own way of giving a voice to love. The poem *Fresca rosa novella* shows his prior adherence to the common theme of the woman as an angel: 'ché siete angelicata-crïatura / Angelica sembranza' (for you are an angel-like creature /An angelic semblance). But afterwards in the same ballad, Cavalcanti problematizes his relationship to something that appears to be beyond nature: 'ch'eo non saccio contare; /e chi poria pensare-oltra natura?' (That I know not how to describe it: And who could cast thought beyond nature?).

From the very beginning, Cavalcanti distances himself from a poetry that includes a thinking that goes beyond nature. Introducing his own 'Latin,' Cavalcanti starts by assuming that nature and colour are in themselves beauty: 'Avete 'n vo'li fior'e la verdura /e ciò che luce ed è bello a vedere' (You have in you the flowers and the greenery and what shines and is beautiful to see).[4] Alhazen's *Optics* and his theorems on beauty are employed in order to identify beauty with the natural light that enables vision.[5]

Connected to this is the problem of effability. This problem derives from the great beauty of the woman: 'tanto adorna parete, /ch'eo non saccio contare' (You appear so embellished /That I know not how to describe it).[6] Because the woman's beauty is suggested as being beyond nature and his poetry has great difficulty pronouncing what is beyond the human, the poet's 'Latin' develops an alternative path. In *Chi è questa che vèn* (Who Is She Who Comes), Cavalcanti begins by indicating only the phenomena this woman generates, without describing her superhuman virtues. The lines '... sì che parlare /null'omo pote, ma ciascun sospira' (so that no one can speak though everyone sighs) mark a turning point in his poetry. Cavalcanti introduces here, through the sigh, a language of passion that allows his *ornatus* to stay within the limits of nature.

Cavalcanti's focus is not the contemplation of beauty but what this beauty moves. His own 'Latin' will start centring on the ego, but this ego will be constructed in a way that will shape his own 'Latin.' On the surface, Cavalcanti's early poetry can be read as a recording of the experiences of an ego, but this is an ego that emphasizes the physiological character of its experience.

Specific to Cavalcanti's so-called minor poems and to *Donna me prega* is the introduction of a science of the soul, a science that Cavalcanti organizes mainly by utilizing Aristotle's *De anima* as reread in the field of Latin Aristotelianism. The tradition of medical science plays an important role as well. The interaction between natural philosophy and medicine as it took place in the work of the physician Taddeo Alderotto (who was active in Bologna in the second half of the thirteenth century), must be assumed as a point of reference in reading Cavalcanti's poetry.[7] The tradition that converges in Taddeo Alderotto (which is the old Galen's tradition, as well as that of Avicenna's *De Anima seu Sextus de naturalibus* and *Canon*) is crucial for an understanding of Cavalcanti's discourse on love. With Cavalcanti a new ego enters into the history of the *lingua del sì* as it emerges from the psychology and physiology of the time. It is this continuous interaction between the science of the soul and the medical tradition that creates the ego of Guido Cavalcanti's poetry, while the identification of the heart as the centre of the human personality shapes the content and the tone of his poetry. This connotation of the ego introduces into his poems a rhetoric of passion, the ontology of which he will describe in *Donna me prega*. According to this ontology, love will be defined as an 'accident.'[8]

The rhetoric of passion, as I am using this phrase, implies that the ego in Cavalcanti is not an autonomous subject. On the contrary, the poems represent it as acted upon by its own sensibility. The technique introduced represents this ego as subjugated by its own centres of sensation. For this, Cavalcanti utilizes prosopopeia, in which the personae are the parts of the ego's sensibility endowed with the capacity for speech. A multiple ego thus emerges – an ego that is both active and passive. Essential to this complex ego is the role assigned to the eyes. The eyes are the instruments for establishing the discourse of passion because, in studies of vision like Aristotle's and later Alhazen's, vision is itself a form of passion.[9] In addition, by introducing the visual spirit (*Rime*, sonnet XXII), Cavalcanti emphasizes spirit as the seat of vision. In so doing he seems to follow the tradition according to which the spirit of sight is the seat of visual sensation.[10] According to optical theories, vision occurs in two ways: either because the eye receives the rays emitted from an external object (intromissional theory) or because the eye itself emits a visual ray (emissional theory). Cavalcanti is no doubt aware of the theory of vision established by Alhazen, who mediated and reconciled the two theories. But by and large, he depicts vision as a power of intromission, which enters the eye and from which the lover cannot be defended. Vision is therefore one of the facets of Guido's discourse on love as a discourse of passion.

Reading Sonnet V, we see that Cavalcanti introduces vision as being responsible for wounding the heart. Love here is personified as the lord of a court where a love-trial is being held. The ritual of feudal vassalage is employed; however, the declaration of the lover as being a servant of love is not made directly, but is manifested through the eyes, which declare to the court that the ego is the woman's vassal:

> Li mie' foll'occhi, che prima guardaro
> vostra figura piena di valore,
> fuor quei che di voi, donna, m'acusaro
> nel fero loco ove ten corte Amore,
>
> e mantinente avanti lui mostraro
> ch'io era fatto vostro servidore:
> per che sospiri e dolor mi pigliaro,
> vedendo che temenza avea lo core

> (My foolish eyes that looked first on your face full of worthiness were those which, lady, indicted me as yours in the cruel place where Love holds court, and in his presence showed at once that I had become your servitor: for this, sighs and sorrows seized me, seeing that fear had my heart.)

In this sonnet, the ego is described as part of a group of love's servants who are guests in a place of restless sorrows: 'Menârmi tosto, sanza riposanza,/in una parte là v'i' trovai gente/che ciascun si doleva d'Amor forte (They quickly led me without respite to a place where I encountered people, each of whom was deeply sorrowing because of Love). The phenomena of the passions of the heart are expressed here through words like *sospiri, dolor,* and *temenza* (sighs, sorrow, and fear). The insertion of these words as part of the language of love shows that Cavalcanti's method is at once rhetorical and scientific. In order to articulate the identity of love as passion, he appears to employ a suggestion made by Brunetto Latini in his *Rhetoric.* According to Brunetto, '*inventio* is that science through which we are able to find true things, that is, reasons which are necessities – note well, necessities – to the thing itself in order to demonstrate the thing we affirm ... The good rhetorician must think about the nature of his contents, and find arguments true or veri-similitudinal in order for him to prove and make credible what he says.[11] In this sense, the invention of Cavalcanti consists in reducing the subject to a passive being, a being who is acted upon by his senses and sensations, which in turn are made to become the true personae of this process of love.

Referring to elocution (*elocutio*), Brunetto writes that *ornare* is a dignity that derives from certain words of speech: 'It is well known that ornament of words is a dignity that derives from some words of discourse thanks to which the whole discourse shines.'[12] Thus, in Cavalcanti, elocution focuses on words such as *sospiri* or *dolor,* but these words have to be seen in their inner connections and contexts if we are to understand the invention. In fact, they are introduced as word-functions of the sensitive soul and are determined by the event that he calls love. Love here is an event that originates in the eyes, is located in the heart, and is able to influence the activity of the brain. It is described as a force able to determine the personality of human beings insofar as it acts on their physiology. Thus, words like 'sorrow' or 'sighs' acquire their proper meaning only when they are understood in light of the method Guido employs, a method that blends the tools of rhetoric with those of the physician and the natural philosopher. Since the pathos of the ego as the servant of love is a physiological pathos, rhetoric here becomes instrumental in the expression of love as passion.

If we read Sonnet VI (*Deh, spiriti miei, quando mi vedete* [Ah, my spirits, since you see me]), we may enter further into the rhetoric of passion and the method Cavalcanti employs. Here Cavalcanti introduces 'spirit' as a key word for his discourse of love. He does so for two reasons: to represent the ego as acted upon by its own sensibility, and to affirm the theory of internal senses that we find in the Arabic tradition. According to this theory, spirit is not only the vehicle between heart and mind but also the seat of the sensitive faculty.[13]

According to an old medical tradition, 'spirit' or *pneuma* is a hot vapour assumed to be indispensable for the functions of physiological life. It works as a link between body and soul. Passion, according to the Aristotelian theory, is nothing other than sensibility that lives according to its own perfection, a perfection that consists in being acted upon. With this Aristotelian teaching as background, Cavalcanti introduces the drama of sensibility into his poetry. Sensibility in itself includes a dramatization because it implies an agent and an object on which the agent works – an object that is acted upon by the agent. Cavalcanti integrates this basic structure by introducing a dramatization of the powers that (according to medical science) live and are generated in the heart of man and these powers are spirits.[14] He organizes his *elocutio* by making spirits, soul, and heart his dramatis personae. The protagonist of this drama is not the ego but the powers, the dramatis personae who rule the ego:

Deh, spiriti miei, quando mi vedete
con tanta pena, come non mandate
fuor della mente parole adornate
di pianto, dolorose e sbigottite?

Deh, voi vedete che 'l core ha ferite
di sguardo e di piacere e d'umiltate:
deh, i' vi priego che voi 'l consoliate
che son da lui le sue vertù partite

I' veggo a luï spirito apparire
alto e gentile e di tanto valore,
che fa le sue vertù tutte fuggire

Deh, i' vi priego che deggiate dire
a l'alma trista, che parl'in dolore,
com'ella fu e fie sempre d'Amore.

(Ah, my spirits, since you see me in such suffering, and because you do not send forth from my mind words adorned with tears, sorrowful and dismayed, ah, you see that my heart has wounds from looks and from pleasure and humility. Ah, I beg you to give it consolation, for its powers have forsaken it. I see appear to it a spirit lofty and noble and of such strength that it makes all its powers flee. Ah, I beg you kindly to tell my saddened soul, that speaks in sorrow, how it was and always will be Love's.)

In this sonnet, Cavalcanti's *inventio* is extraordinarily innovative. A central rhetorical role is played here by the pathetic exclamation *deh* (ah), repeated four times. If we connect the *deh* to the sigh, the *deh* appears here to be introduced as the rhetorical voice of a physical event: the actual sigh. The importance of the sigh as a response to a physiological emotion appeared in Sonnet IV (*Chi è questa che vèn*), in which the emotion obstructing speech moves to sighing: 'sì che parlare / null'omo pote, ma ciascun sospirà' (so that no one can speak, though everyone sighs).' In *De anima* 1, Avicenna explains that the sigh is an instrument of the soul. The *Canon* explains the sigh as an activity decided by will ('voluntarius') and which takes place in two phases: inhalation and exhalation. These two phases are related by Avicenna to the necessity of coolness for hot vapours and for aeration.[15] The *deh* seems therefore to be a word-sigh that represents a physiological function as an instrument of responding to and resisting an emotional pressure.

According to Aristotle's *De interpretatione*, the voice-sound is a sign of the passion of the soul. According to medical tradition, the sigh is passion.[16] It could also be said that *deh* is a rhetorical way of signifying an affection because it registers only the physical event of being acted upon.[17] What Brunetto had indicated as the dignity of *elocutio*, for Cavalcanti includes an awareness of the ontology of passion. For obvious reasons, this ontology falls under Aristotle's category of 'passive.' It is this very passion as passivity that Cavalcanti's rhetoric expresses.[18]

In the sonnet, the iterative *deh* is related to spirits, and the epicentre of the sonnet is located in the word 'spirits' (*spiriti*), suggesting that *deh* is the effect of spirits.[19] We read, for instance, the suggestion that the spirits must bring comfort to the heart ('deh, i' vi priego che voi 'l consoliate') (Ah, I beg you to give it consolation). The figurative language here suggests that words of weeping are the language spoken by the heart, the seat of these emotions; words the heart sends to the mind through spirits, and the *ornatus* reproduces (parole adornate / di pianto, dolorose e sbigottite, 'words adorned with tears, sorrowful and dismayed'). But there is another meaning: because the spirits travel between the sight, the heart, and the brain, they are responsible for causing the very wounding of the heart ('voi vedete che 'l core ha ferite / di sguardo') (you see that my heart has wounds from looks). The passivity of the ego is registered and emphasized through the introduction of the spirits, which play the role of protagonist in the sonnet in order to emphasize the tyranny of sensation.

In the second quatrain, each of the two *dehs* corresponds to an exhalation that expels the overheated air, thus lightening the tension of the heart. The rhetoric of *deh* is therefore a rhetoric of physiology. The verb 'consoliate' (to give it consolation), which in the context is related to the heart, from which energies have departed, carries the meaning of a request for physiological relief from emotional compulsion – relief that only the spirits can provide.

The tercet that follows is strongly related to the preceding quatrain.

Its meaning emerges if we attend to the semantic distinction between the words 'spirit' and 'spirits.' 'I' veggo a luï spirito apparire' (I see appear to it a spirit) shapes the semantic connections through a deliberate ambiguity that obliges the reader to search for a meaning. In Avicenna's *De anima*, in which great importance is given to the theory of vision, seeing things that are not there occurs when the reason is weak and the senses are wayward. We find the same concept in Averroes.[20] But in this concentration on vision as the result of a hyperactivity of the senses caused by the powers of the heart, we may understand that the physiological reason for the illusion is determined by the spirits. They, the spirits, are the seat of sensation and are responsible for the transmission to the brain of the powers of the heart.

What emerges here is a relationship between the *ornatus* and the physiological significance of the words. The words of the spirits are the correlatives of the function they perform in connecting the soul and the body. The weakness of the ego prostrated by pain makes it impossible to send forth words from the mind. Words are but words of the senses and therefore words of pain. To this affliction to which the soul is subjugated, Cavalcanti imposes the name 'Love.' A connection is thus established between words and spirits. Because the activity of these spirits is so strong, these words are able to emerge against the unspoken words of the mind and speak a rhetoric of passion. The events of the poem can be understood only if we follow such precise relations in the text. But the result of this sonnet goes beyond every scientific premise. What makes this poem powerful is, in fact, the sense of a sight at once physical and spiritual which provides the rhythm and shapes the meaning of the sonnet. Our participation in this poetry is not at all intellectual. The feelings given voice by the poet become in turn an experience for the reader who, in giving his voice to the *deh* of the poem, becomes physiologically involved in the very event and process that the poet seeks to describe.

It appears that Cavalcanti is here establishing the kind of *ornatus* he is looking for. When he writes 'I' veggo a luï spirito apparire' (I see appear to it a spirit), he introduces the process of imagination. But this process is proposed as impossible: even though a vision appears, the heart in its weakness is incapable of activating the very process of imagination. The passage 'che fa le sue vertù tutte fuggire' (that it makes all its powers flee) conveys the sense of an unfinished process. According to medieval science, imagination belongs to the activity of the brain. It concentrates in itself the brain's activity and the strength of the spirits. But here in Cavalcanti's poem, the heart is in a weakened condition and so does not work to activate the process of imagination.[21]

The last tercet seems to suggest that a rhetoric of sorrow (*dolor*) emerges as a consequence of the failed process of imagination. The lines 'Deh, i' vi priego che deggiate dire/a l'alma trista, che parl'in dolore,/com'ella fu e fie sempre d'Amore' (Ah, I beg you kindly to tell my saddened soul, that speaks in sorrow, how it was and always will be Love's) reveal Cavalcanti as an *impositore* of the name Love (*Amore*). This is the role Dante recalls in the *Vita nuova*.[22]

The name 'Love' in fact is given here to a series of events that culminate in a kind of impossibility: love is an excess of emotion that blocks the activity of the imagination. This excess of emotion generates an *ornatus* made by words of sorrow and spoken by the 'saddened soul.'

If in this sonnet *dolore* and *sbigottimento* are responsible for the weakness of the spirits and for the *ornatus* that Cavalcanti is obliged to use, therein lies his invention: the organization of a rhetoric determined by the body's physiology. Avicenna helps us to clarify what this physiology is. According to him, *timor* (of which *sbigottimento* [dismay] is part) and *ira* (anger) are passions of *virtutis vitalis*, which has its place in the heart, the *domicilium vitae*.[23] In *De medicinis cordialibus*,[24] we read that the spirit that brings joy is strong – joy being the power of the spirits. An agent determines whether the potentiality of spirits is oriented toward delight or sadness. The spirit that is sad is subtle and dark, and for that reason is not strong. In melancholy personalities, sadness is related to the weakness of the spirit.[25] Here Cavalcanti reveals a strategy through which the preceding experiences of poetry are superseded. By applying his method to these experiences, he achieves a completely new way of expressing the traditional theme of love.

Cavalcanti's *Pronuntiatio* ('Pronunciation') has recourse to the necessary words (see Brunetto Latini) using as an argument (demonstration) the technical meanings of the words he utilizes. Latini's rhetoric and his emphasis on precise words for a peculiar goal appear to preside over Cavalcanti's vocabulary. He derives this vocabulary from medical science and psychology. The precision with which he uses his words appears similar to the importance given to terminology by medical science, as testified in the synchronous medical theory of *expositio-declaratio terminorum*.[26] The natural demonstration (*natural dimostramento*), which *Donna me prega* will organize through a technical vocabulary, starts taking its shape from Cavalcanti's early poems and their rhetoric of passion.

The battle between love and the brain's activity returns in Sonnet VII. Here we may follow the way in which the destruction of the mind takes place, and how the soul experiences the battle waged against her by the heart:

L'anima mia vilment' è sbigotita
de la battaglia ch'e[l]l'ave dal core:
che s' ella sente pur un poco Amore
più presso a lui che non sòle, ella more.

Sta come quella che non ha valore,
ch'è per temenza da lo cor partita;
e chi vedesse com'ell' è fuggita
diria per certo: 'Questi non ha vita'

Per gli occhi venne la battaglia in pria,
che ruppe ogni valore immantenente,
sì che del colpo fu strutta la mente.

Qualunqu' è quei che più allegrezza sente,
se vedesse gli spirti fuggir via,
di grande sua pietate piangeria.

(My soul is abjectly appalled by the battering it had from the heart: for if it
feels Love just a little closer to it than it was before, it will die. It stands as
one that has no strength, since out of fear it has forsaken my heart; and whoever saw how it fled would surely say: 'This man is lifeless.' Through the
eyes came the first battering that at once routed all valour, so that the mind
was killed by the blow. Whoever it is who feels most cheer, if he should be
see the spirits take flight, he would weep out of his great pity.')

The rhetoric here is concentrated on the sensibility of the body. The
ego is dismembered because it is unable to withstand the forces at war
within it. This battle is organized through medical-scientific cognition.
Avicenna explains that the animal virtues which are in the brain need
tempered humour in order to facilitate the movement of thought and
the command of the intellect. But many humours that do not obey the
command of the intellect possess movement because vapours ascend
and blend with each other. In fact, vapour and humour are not well tempered, so they obey the cogitative activity of the brain only with
difficulty. In order to gain access to intellection, accidents have to be
tempered and their internal communication must be peaceful.[27] Cavalcanti seems to name this excess of vapours the 'battle' of love.[28]
The sonnet reconstructs the battle as it originates in the eyes since it
is through them that emotions enter. This is vision, and vision may gen-

erate the excess of emotion that destroys the powers of the soul and of the brain's activity:

Per gli occhi venne la battaglia in pria
che ruppe ogni valore immantenente,
sì che del colpo fu strutta la mente.

(Through the eyes came the first battering that at once routed all valour,
so that the mind was killed by the blow.')

According to the science of Cavalcanti's time, the brain is the place of the internal senses and therefore the seat of the imaginative power, which is one of the internal senses.

While the sonnet exposes the phenomenology of love as passion, a physiological explanation of passion is provided. Through this explanation, Cavalcanti suggests a theme that will have great importance in *Donna me prega*. In fact, it is explained here, in terms of the functions of the brain, why love makes it difficult to activate the process of imagination.

When Cavalcanti writes 'che s'ella [l'anima] sente pur un poco Amore / più presso a lui che non sole, ella more' (for if it feels love a little closer to it than it was before, it will die), he wishes to say that love brings the soul to the point of death because of an excess of sensitivity. That is, the death of the soul is generated by an excess of feeling. The focus here is on the word *temenza* (fear): ('[the soul] sta come quella che non ha valore, / ch'è per temenza da lo cor partita' [it stands as one that has no strength, since out of fear it has forsaken my heart)]. This is generated by the excess of vapours. It is this fear that suggests the weakness of internal communication. In fact, in the last tercet the spirits are represented in the act of taking flight. The image of the soul that has forsaken the heart is a metaphor for the languishing spirit that cannot connect the soul and the body. This connection is a function of the spirit, which, as the poem suggests, does not work in activating the process of imagination. The death of the soul, therefore, is insinuated as being the same as the impossibility of activating the process of imagination.

In Sonnet VIII ('Tu m'hai sì piena di dolor la mente, / che l'anima si briga di partire, / e li sospir' che manda 'l cor dolente / mostrano agli occhi che non può soffrire' [You have my mind so filled with sorrow that the soul contrives to depart and the sighs that the sorrowing heart sends forth show on sight that it cannot bear up]), the soul contrives its departure because of the sorrow of the mind caused by an indefinite 'You.' This serves as a cognitive metaphor. It tells of the division between the soul and the heart (the same division found in Sonnet VII) – a division caused by languishing spirits that cannot make the connection between body and soul owing to their weakness.

According to Avicenna, death arises from the weakness of the spirit in the absence of a union between body and soul, and pain and fear (*dolor et pavor*) weaken the spirit, leading to death.[29] Therefore, the sighs that the sorrowing heart sends forth at this point ('e li sospir' che manda 'l cor dolente' [and the sighs that the sorrowful heart sends forth]), rather than being a repertoire of rhetorical declamations, are confirmed to be physiological. The reason is that the entry of air is an attempt to save, help, or reinvigorate the spirits in order for the connection to be maintained.

The physiology of passion strengthens the phenomenology of passion: the focus is on the centres of passion. Among these are the eyes, which are crucial in that they are where vision takes place. Love, as determined by the power of the 'You,' concentrates the reader's attention on feeling, a word that gives the essence of the sonnet, which tells only the drama of feeling: 'Amor, che lo grande tuo valor sente' (Love, that *senses* your great power, [italics mine]). The level of feeling increases in direct proportion to the power of the 'You.' Now Avicenna states that an excess of feeling can lead to death. 'E' mi duol che ti convien morire' (it pains me that you must die) contains the essential element: *dolor* means feeling an opposition (*contrarietatem*) (*Canon* f. 41 D 4). The pitiless woman performs the function of a *contrarium*, which acts on the sensibility by giving it pain.[30]

In the field of Aristotelianism, the sensitive soul presides over the power of movement (*virtus motoria*) and over the cognitive powers (*virtutes cognitiva*). This suggests that the ego here in the sonnet proceeds (*deambulatio*) like an automaton and feels something akin to paralysis. The symptom suggests a partial blockage that irradiates from the heart ('e porti ne lo core una ferita' [and that bears in his heart a wound]), thus impeding the body's activity, which involves the brain as the centre of the cognitive faculties. The wound is in the heart, and the blockage of sensibility is a symptom of nearness to death. But in this sonnet, the focus is on the blockage generated in the mind ('cerebrum,' Avicenna says, 'est principium virtus sentiendi et movendi' [*Canon*, f. 9 F 11]), a blockage for which the heart is responsible (Avicenna, *De anima* II, V,

176). The last stanza suggests, therefore, a correspondence between physical death and the death of intellectual activity. Love, we have seen, is an event that influences and determines the body's activity. The death of intellectual activity is presented as coincident with a corporeal death because, according to medieval Aristotelianism, the pathology of the brain's activity is an effect of the pathology of the body. The notion of the soul explains this connection. The soul, in fact, has in itself a potential for sensibility and cognition. The mind represents the cognitive activity of the soul, which, however, depends on the sensitive power. The brain's activity includes the activity of *phantasia*, which, in order to be reached, requires a balance of bodily emotions. Thus an excess of emotions is responsible for the death of the soul and its cognitive-phantastic activity. Cavalcanti's 'battle of love' is precisely this fight between heart and mind, between the biological laws of life and the cognitive power of the brain.

Imagination and Poetry

It is in relation to intellectual activity that Cavalcanti's poetry introduces imagination. For Cavalcanti, imagination is an activity that presupposes a series of bodily functions and a series of conditions in which imagination can take place. Imagination is a process. The events of the body culminate for Cavalcanti in the activity of imagination. Love and imagination appear to be correlatives and yet at the same time are opposed. The reason is that love is in itself an excess that impedes the process of the imagination.

According to Aristotelianism, the activity of imagination means the formation of an image, and imagination is nothing else that the *vis formalis*, that is, the power of generating a phantasm or form.[31] According to Avicenna and Averroes, this process takes place only in the harmony of the powers of the body.[32]

The process implied in the word 'imagination' can be retraced in the field of Aristotelianism and in the Arabic tradition, which treats imagination as one of the internal senses. In order to understand the role of imagination in Cavalcanti's poetry, it is necessary to discuss the so-called theory of internal senses that emerges from the Arabic tradition and is active in the school of Taddeo Alderotto.[33] Like Averroes after him, Avicenna thought that intellectual knowledge, in order to be attained, requires the sensory. Recognizing that the external senses do not provide secure perception, the Arabs introduced the theory of internal senses. What we perceive with our external senses is mutable, because the objects we perceive are part of the world of becoming, and also because the perceiving subject changes as it moves from one object to another.[34] The internal senses have the specific function of ensuring a stability of the perceived objects in order to be at the disposition of the subject when desired. Thanks to the internal senses, a relationship is established between what is absent – that is, not actually perceived – and the human soul. If the soul is absorbed by something else, it has no need for the absent object. But when the soul is free, it can return to the absent object in virtue of the relationship that has been established between the soul and the absent object itself.

The internal senses, therefore, establish the stream of sensible things and contribute to intellectual knowledge, preparing for reason a stable ensemble of concrete elements.[35] In the hierarchy of human powers, the Arabs, following Aristotle, distinguish three levels: the vegetative, the sensitive, and the rational. The vegetative presides over nutrition, grow, and procreation, while the sensitive presides over the powers of movement and the cognitive faculties. The internal senses, which, in their simplest form, comprehend only three faculties (the imagination, the cogitative faculty, and memory) were introduced in Arabic and Hebrew literature in order to give further power to the cognitive faculties. Two more faculties were added later: the estimative (by Alfarabi) and common sense (by Avicenna).[36] For Avicenna, the role of the imaginative faculty is to preserve the data received by common sense, even when the sensible reality is no longer present. For Avicenna, the activity of the internal senses cannot take place without the intervention of a corporeal instrument. This is the vital *pneuma*, an instrument utilized by the internal senses that is located in the heart and fills the ventricles of the brain.

From the heart, the *spiritus* or *pneuma* proceeds to the brain where it is perfected until it is able to function as an instrument for sensory and motor activities (*De anima* II, V, 8). Avicenna's conception of the *pneuma* must be located within the line of Aristotelianism and Neoplatonism. For Avicenna, *spiritus* is not the substance of the soul, as in Stoic philosophy; rather, it is an intermediary between soul and body, a subtle instrument the soul uses in order to act on the body.

In *De anima* I, Avicenna explains how the seen image influences the process of imagination. He assumes that the *pneuma* of vision is the seat of the sensitive vision. That is, the visual *pneuma* is special because it is the seat of the activity of vision. In order to understand this process, the seen image must be considered as able to condition the whole of the mental process.

These are the crucial antecedents to imagination as it appears in Cavalcanti's poetry. According to Avicenna, the process is the following: an image is transmitted through the visual *pneuma*, which is the seat of the visual faculty.[37] Then the 'sottile spirito che vede' (that subtle spirit of sight) (as Cavalcanti describes the visual *pneuma*, XXII, 12) transfers the image to the *pneuma* of the brain, where it is impressed upon the *pneuma* of common sense, which in turn transmits it to the imagination and thereafter to the memory.[38] This may explain some crucial aspects of Cavalcanti's poetry. It may, for example, explain the importance given to sight – the door without guards – as the beginning of the process of image formation from which the cognitive process starts.

This role of imagination leads us to consider that, of the internal senses, Cavalcanti mentions only imagination and memory (the latter is clearly mentioned only in *Donna me prega*). This suggests that probably he is following Averroes, who sometimes reduces the number of internal senses, returning to and restating the Aristotelian division by looking at some of the internal senses as 'subfunctions of the imagination.'[39] The same tendency to reduce the internal senses seems to preside over Cavalcanti, who appears to think of imagination as a power of the individual, probably the sole and greatest power. Imagination emphasizes the here, the now, the here-below, against the abstract common intellect which is unique for all men, according to Averroes. Imagination implies a process of image formation. The process of writing itself seems in Cavalcanti to be connected to this activity and power.

In order to understand the complexity of the process, we turn to Canzone IX: 'Io non pensava che lo cor giammai / avesse di sospir' tormento tanto' (I did not think that my heart would ever have such torment of sighs). This canzone describes the reason for love's difficulty in attaining the generation of form. The reasons for this difficulty are the same reasons for the difficulty of completing the process of imagination. De Robertis describes this canzone as 'la canzone "storica" della propria "morte"' (canzone which contains the history of his own death). But what needs to be underlined is that death here is the death of imagination. *Donna me prega* will give the notion of love's difficulty in reaching the formation of the image, furnishing the notion of matter as the unformed which opposes the formative activity of imagination. Here in Canzone IX, the reason for this difficulty is offered by blending medical and philosophical themes. This method is used in order to tell the reader of the corporeal event that obstructs imagination. At the centre of the event, we find the heart tormented by sighs as tears spring from the soul. The meeting with the lady and the words spoken by Love are a death sentence: '... Tu non camperai,/ché troppo è lo valor di costei forte' (You will not survive for her power is too strong). Virtues depart because the heart has lost all strength:

> La mia virtù si partìo sconsolata
> poi che lassò lo core
> a la battaglia ove madonna è stata:

(My vitality departed disconsolate after it surrendered my heart to the battering where my lady was.)

What is emphasized here is the central role played by the heart. From its torment, 'torment of sighs,' derives the impossibility of enduring the beauty of the woman. This affirms the impossibility of completing the process of imagination:

> Di questa donna non si può contare:
> ché di tante bellezze adorna vène,
> che mente di qua giù no la sostene
> sì che la veggia lo 'ntelletto nostro.
>   Tant'è gentil che, quand'eo penso bene,
> l'anima sento per lo cor tremare,
> sì come quella che non pò durare
> davanti al gran valor ch'è i llei dimostro.

(One cannot describe this lady, for she comes adorned in so many beauties that no mind here below can withstand her to the point that our intellect might see her. So noble is she that, when I think well on it, I feel my soul tremble within my heart, like one that cannot hold out in the presence of the great power that is manifest in her.)

The expression 'mind here below' is important. It refers to the brain's activity centred on the imagination, to which corresponds in opposition the adjective *nostro* (our) that precedes 'intellect.' This discloses the cognitive process that love could originate as a movement from the sensible (peculiar to the individual) toward the abstract common intellect. What we read here is the impossibility of image-formation, or of phantasm, which, according to the doctrine of Averroes, is the form-medium connecting the individual mind with the possible common intellect, from which the process of intellection is derived.[40]

The reason for this impossibility is given in the word 'tremble.' The soul trembles because the heart is in torment: Tant'è gentil che, quand' eo penso bene, /l'anima sento per lo cor tremare' (So noble is she that, when I think well on it, I feel my soul tremble within my heart). If we look at Avicenna, this has a clear meaning – it is a weak spirit that is responsible for the event. The wounding takes place through the eyes, that is, through the special spirit of vision in which the sensation is located. This is the *pneuma*, which goes from the eye to the brain but has as its centre the heart, that receives the wound, a wound that simultaneously strikes the eye and heart. This wounding of the heart impedes the functioning of the brain, because the *pneuma* that does the linking has been excessively weakened.

Cavalcanti's notion of the impossibility of reaching imagination now has a physiological cause, or rather a series of causes. The second stanza connects this impossibility to the mind's inability to endure the beauty of the woman. In addition, Canzone IX introduces a parallel between image and poetry and develops the theme of coincidence between the impossibility of reaching the imagination and the impossibility of writing poetry. This impossibility of writing appears in its turn as a metaphor for the impossibility of image-formation as stated in stanza 2: Di questa donna non si può contare: /ché di tante bellezze adorna vène (One cannot describe this lady, for she comes adorned in so many beauties).

The verb *contare*, which seems to include the activity of writing poetry, indicates the incapacity of words derived from the impossibility of the mind to endure the lady (che mente di qua giù no la sostene /sì che la veggia lo 'ntelletto nostro) (That no mind here below can withstand her to the point that our intellect might see her). This has a precise meaning in the process of the formative activity of imagination: it proclaims the impossibility of holding an image. The mind's incapacity to endure the beautiful woman causes the impossibility of reaching an intellectual knowledge. Cavalcanti repeats this impossibility in the third stanza. There he links it to the impossibility of giving a discourse to gentle hearts on the beauty of this woman because he lacks the strength to persist with the thought:

Quando 'l pensier mi vèn ch'i' voglia dire
a gentil core de la sua vertute,
i' trovo me di sì poca salute,
ch'i' non ardisco di star nel pensero.

(When the thought comes to me that I should speak to a noble heart of
her merit, I find myself with so little health that I dare not persist in the
thought.)

Here the identification between the imaginative process and the activity of writing poetry appears twice. Line 15 has stated that this lady cannot be described, and lines 29–32 explain that his weakness does not allow him to speak of her. This is the same weakness that does not allow the process of imagination – and therefore the process of poetry – to take place.

The third stanza proposes, through Love's speech, the complex meaning of the word 'death' in Cavalcanti's work. On the one hand, lines 25–6 (in the second stanza) suggest the corporeal death of the lover: 'Non guardi tu questa pietate / ch'e'posta invece di persona morta?' (Don't you see this object of pity that is put in place of a dead person?) But line 42 – 'per forza convenia che tu morissi' (it was perforce inevitable that you should die) – suggests that the destruction of the body is also related to the death of the imagination, and that the real death is that of the imagination. The reason for this is evident upon reading lines 33–9. It is the excess of emotion ('sofferire/ non può lo cor sentendola venire') (my heart cannot bear up on hearing her approach) which the heart cannot bear. The arrows that have passed through the lover's heart and divided Love's own are suggested as responsible for the death of the imagination:

Amor, c'ha le bellezze sue vedute,
mi sbigottisce sì, che sofferire
non può lo cor sentendola venire,
ché sospirando dice: 'Io ti dispero,
    però che trasse del su'dolce riso
una saetta aguta,
c'ha passato 'l tuo core e 'l mio diviso.
    Tu sai, quando venisti, ch'io ti dissi,
poi ché l'avéi veduta,
per forza convenia che tu morissi.'

(Love, who has seen her beauties, confounds me so that my heart cannot bear up on hearing her approch, for he says, sighing: 'I leave you no hope, because from her sweet smile issued a sharp harrow that has passed through your heart and divided mine. You know the moment you came, that I told you that once you had seen her it was perforce inevitable that you should die.')

The difficulty in completing the process of imagination returns in Ballad XIX, *I' prego voi che di dolor parlate* (I beg you who speak of sorrow). Here it is love's pain that determines that 'imaginar' cannot be completed. The same meaning can be attributed to Sonnet XXXVI (*Certe mie rime a te mandar vogliendo* [As I was about to send you certain poems of mine]), in which love, appearing as 'figura morta,' heralds the death of the activity of imagination. While these passages explain that the being of love makes it difficult or impossible to attain an intellectual life, they also explain the tone of Cavalcanti's poetry. They suggest a kind of diary of a dismembered ego spoken by its own sensations. In Sonnet XVIII we see that this diary is written by 'penne isbigotite' (bewildered quills). Cavalcanti thus confirms the connection between love, the process of imagination and the process of writing. By describing the 'quills' as 'bewildered' – indeed, as bewildered as the ego itself – he attributes to the tool of writing the same state of mind that impedes immagination: fear. Still more important is the fact that poetry appears here as the language in which the individual emotions and fears, along with sentimental and physical reasons, are found worthy of having a voice. *Phantasia* entrusts to poetry the 'lesser' reasons of the individual; however, these minor reasons are the best introduction to *Donna me prega*, in which the individual will exhibit his own reason and search for happiness.

The discourse on imagination cannot be concluded without introducing Ballad XXVI, a crucial text for understanding the role played by love and imagination in the theorem on love that *Donna me prega* will set forth. In this ballad, Cavalcanti expresses the power of love, which originates in a light full of spirits of love seen in the eyes of the beloved. This light brings a new kind of pleasure to the heart of the ego in such a way as to awaken a joyous vitality there:

Veggio negli occhi de la donna mia
un lume pieno di spiriti d'amore,
che porta uno piacer novo nel core,
sì che vi desta d'allegrezza vita.

(I see in my lady's eyes a radiance full of spirits of love, that brings a fresh
pleasure to my heart such that it awakens there vitality of joy.)

The suggestion here is that image-formation derives from this vitality.
That is, the activity of the imagination takes place because love appears
to be balanced and harmonized, thanks to the harmony of the physiological process:

> Cosa m'aven, quand'i' le son presente,
> ch'i' no la posso a lo 'ntelletto dire:
>   veder mi par de la sua labbia uscire
> una sì bella donna, che la mente
>   comprender no la può, che 'mmantenente
> ne nasce un'altra di bellezza nova,
> da la qual par ch'una stella si mova
> e dica: 'la salute tua è apparita.'

(Something happens to me when I am in her presence that I cannot express
to the intellect: I seem to see issuing from her countenance so beautiful a lady
that the mind cannot grasp her, for at once another is born of her of fresh
beauty from whom a star seems to come and say: 'Your salvation has
appeared.')

The activity of the imagination here seems to be connected, through
the phantasm, with the intelligence of the heavenly spheres. Nevertheless, what the poet emphasizes is the *difficulty* of the process: 'Cosa
m'aven, quand'i' le son presente,/ ch'i no la posso a lo 'ntelletto dire.'
In fact, the impression this woman makes on the ego hinders its ability
to describe her. This woman, however, who is called the woman of salvation (*salute*), introduces us to the salvation she brings owing to the connection she establishes between senses and intellect. The sphere of
intelligences (according to medieval theory, the star is animated by
intelligences) is introduced in line 11: 'da la qual par ch'una stella si
mova' (from whom a star seems to come).

This is what has been referred to as 'the knowledge of knowledge'
(De Robertis). The same process will be proposed in relation to love in
Donna me prega. However, because this theme will be organized in a
highly complex way in the major canzone, the minor poems help us to
understand the being of love as a double being. On the one hand it is
an excess, on the other hand it is a power toward the process of imagi-

nation and intellectual knowing. This ballad shows these two faces of love. The love in which the reasons of the body impede the process of imagination represents one of the two faces. The other face is that of love as endowed with the ability to organize the process toward *consideranza* if it proceeds in the body's balance. In this case, the body's emotions will offer the basis for the process of imagination toward *consideranza*.

The Averroistic notion of *coniunctio* presides over this poetry. Although here it is not explicitly stated, *coniunctio* establishes an accidental union of human being (through the medium or phantasm) with the separated possible intellect that is part of the sphere of intelligences. This union implies the process of imagination and its unfolding into a process of abstraction. This process is more explicitly suggested in the final lines of Ballad XXVI. There the power of the woman is said to have ascended into the heavens ('vedra' la sua vertù nel ciel salita') (you will see her essence gone up to heaven). This suggests not only that the phantasm has been generated, but also that a new abstract form has been produced in virtue of the *coniunctio*.

The more important aspect of this text lies in its description of the process of imagination as a continuous process toward abstraction. Here we may also follow the way in which this process, through the creation of the phantasm, establishes the *coniunctio* with the activity of the intellect:[41]

    veder mi par de la sua labbia uscire
una sì bella donna, ché la mente
    comprender no la può, che 'mmantenente
ne nasce un'altra di bellezza nova,
da la qual par ch'una stella si mova
e dica: 'la salute tua è apparita.'

(I seem to see issuing from her countenance so beautiful a lady that the mind cannot grasp her, for at once another is born of her of fresh beauty from whom a star seems to come and say: 'Your salvation has appeared.')

The importance of Ballad XXVI can be understood if we relate it to *Donna me prega*. But its importance also emerges from Giacomo da Pistoia's *Quaestio de felicitate* – not directly, but because the ascent from the sensible to the intellectual that takes place here through the activity of imagination and the phantasm as medium organizes themes that the

Quaestio also puts forth. (We shall return to the *Quaestio* and to this theme of the medium in chapter 4.)

Ballad XXVI shows a coincidence between Guido's theory of intellectual knowledge and the thesis Giacomo propounds in his *Quaestio de felicitate*. What the ballad puts forth as possible, however, is problematized in the major canzone and, more importantly, is rethought (as we shall see) from a more radical perspective. Cavalcanti's two texts were probably written at two different times. Both utilize the same themes, and both must be read in light of the philosophy of Averroes and the European debate on that philosophy during the second half of the thirteenth century.

The ballad puts forth and describes the process of *coniunctio*. Here imagination is a step toward abstraction. The metaphor of the star here has a precise meaning. It introduces *consideratio* (*cum-sidera*, to be with a star) as something possible for human beings. The ballad shows that Cavalcanti's early poems document an Averroistic point of view, according to which the individual participates in intellectual knowledge. The same process from imagination toward abstraction will be at the centre of *Donna me prega*. But there it will be used in order to show that *coniunctio* does *not* imply intellectual knowledge for individual human beings.

Cavalcanti's early poetry – rooted as it is in medical science and related in particular to Aristotelianism – manifests the importance that imagination occupies in his meditation. This importance will be confirmed by *Donna me prega*, which, however, shows a different stage of Cavalcanti's reflection. As we shall see in the next chapters, it will also show an evolution toward a more radical point of view. According to this view, love is a diary of a passion, in which there is inscribed a fight between bodily necessity and intellectual knowledge. Love's battle is between two different types of human desire: the desire of the body and the desire for creating a world of images and for intellectual knowledge. We have also seen that Cavalcanti employs a rhetoric of passion as the language necessary to express the difficulty, or even the impossibility, of reaching imagination. All this shows that the theme of love bears a metaphorical sense. In fact, it introduces what for the science of Cavalcanti's time was the problematic topic of 'knowledge.'

Cavalcanti draws not only on a literary tradition but also on a scientific one. Both make the result of his poetry possible. The vocabulary of Cavalcanti is determined by what I have indicated as a rhetoric of passion. In the act of writing, the poet does not really choose the words: rather the words are precisely the ones that express the network of alterations taking place in the body. Words record a bodily event. It is this event that establishes the other key words we find on the page. Such reading makes sense if we understand the physiological grid as the structure on which love's being is based. Basic to this is the function of the spirits and the internal communication that is established through them in the body and between the body and the soul. The centre of life from which the spirits radiate, is the heart: 'vitae enim principium sunt cor et spiritus' (Avicenna, *Canon*, f. 4 E 2). The spirit of sight is responsible for the initial sensible event: vision. Cavalcanti introduces into poetry what I have indicated as the theory of spirits. This theory is of great importance. Although present in some texts ascribed to the Sicilians, it was established in medieval poetry through Cavalcanti and used by Dante in his early works.

Cavalcanti's method also suggests that his writing is influenced by its subject matter. 'Noi siàn le triste penne isbigotite' (We are the poor bewildered quills) gives to the tools of writing the attributes of the lover's soul, captured by the adjectives *triste* and *isbigotite*. Canzone IX resolves the parallel between the death of the imagination and the impossibility of writing a poem, thus entrusting the role of envoy to the spirits as figures of someone dying in dismay.

In Poem XXXIV, Cavalcanti indicates his words as 'disfatte e paurose' (undone and fearful). Metalepsis functions here to relate words with states of mind. In fact his heart, like his words, is also defined as 'disfatto' (undone) because of his unhappy love. Neither beauty nor similitude is the goal of this poetry. Its rhetoric is determined by a rhetoric dictated by bodily events. Here we have a rhetoric of necessity in which poetry is ruled by the same necessity that rules matter and physiology. Love itself is a cognitive metaphor; it allows no adorning metaphor. Every poem bears witness to a level of meaning contained in love as an inclusive metaphor. This metaphor can be understood if we attend to the literal meaning of the language Cavalcanti uses. The rhetoric of passion implies that words in the text are functions. More precisely, words are sign-functions. The vocabulary that Cavalcanti introduces will become a mere repertoire in the lyrical tradition. But with Cavalcanti, this vocabulary is the language for a chain of events occurring in the body. For instance, when he uses the word 'trembling,' he has in mind a precise meaning that has to be related to other words that perform a correlated function. That is, Cavalcanti's rhetoric seeks an *ornatus* that his own inner, corporeal state imposes on him. *Deh* in Sonnet VI was the zero point of this rhetoric. It was the point at which rhetoric and physiology coincided through a word-sigh necessary to discharge the pressure of the heart. The method Cavalcanti brings into poetry thus consists of organizing the discourse on love as a recording, through technical language, of a chain of bodily events.

The process of the sensitive soul is reconstructed by Cavalcanti piece by piece. His poetry presents love as a mechanism of the body in which the soul receives an external action as an emotion and lives out reactions to that emotion. *Donna me prega* will give a name to this mechanism – *sensato* (used as a name for love), that is, the being of the senses when acted upon.

This reading suggests, therefore, that Cavalcanti's fame as a natural philosopher derives not just from *Donna me prega* but also from his 'minor' poems. In these poems Cavalcanti constructs his 'phenomenology of love.' The parallel we have traced between imagination and poetry shows that it is Cavalcanti as natural philosopher who presides over this poetry and determines both its writing and its method.

The struggle to attain imagination appears to be the same as the struggle to write poetry. That writing was considered, according to Wolfson's article, an internal sense like imagination may explain the connection Cavalcanti establishes. But the space imagination occupies in his poetry, together with the suggested identification between image-formation and the activity of writing, shows that Cavalcanti's theory of love includes a reflection on the central role of poetry in the theory of knowledge.

Poetry and Logic

We have already spoken about imagination as a part of the cognitive process. We must now take up the new connection that Cavalcanti's early poetry suggests between poetry and logic. From one side we may see that his poetry, because of the themes it embraces, functions as a medium that connects the *scientiae eloquentiae* to physics (which includes the study of the sensitive soul) and metaphysics (which studies the separate substances of which the possible intellect is part). This role as mediator between these two branches of disciplines gives poetry itself a cognitive role usually assigned to logic.

If we look at Gundissalinus's *De divisione philosophiae* and at the classification of sciences given in this work, we may see that Cavalcanti tends to assign to poetry the role given there to logic. While poetry embraces the grammar and rhetoric of *scientiae eloquentiae*, at the same time it embraces the contents of physics and metaphysics. Organized with a cognitive goal, poetry seems located between the *scientiae eloquentiae* and the *scientia sapientiae* of Gundissalinus's classification.[42] It seems to be a medium between what remained of the old trivium (in which poetry was part of grammar) and the new sciences of physics, metaphysics, and ethics. This has a precise meaning and, as said previously, we may see here an influence derived in western culture from the Arabic model (Gundissalinus was influenced by Alfarabi), in which poetics was part of logic and was conceived, together with rhetoric, as a part of the *Organon*.[43]

That poetry is a cognitive activity is confirmed in Cavalcanti's own use of metaphor. His discourse is about love. But love in Cavalcanti is a metaphor for the nature and essence of human beings. Their life, their desires, their fight for imagination and intellectual life – all these are the foci of his poetry. The way in which he employs a metaphor in order to focus on this nature and essence of human beings is of the utmost importance.

According to recent studies, Arabic philosophy introduced metaphor as a kind of demonstration and/or imaginative syllogism.[44] Cavalcanti's use of metaphor seems to coincide with what he puts forth in *Donna me prega* as natural demonstration. That is, if we assume that love is a comprehensive metaphor, this implies that the metaphor is in itself the natural demonstration of love's being. That Cavalcanti should use such a method does not mean that he does not also use tropes or figurative speech. On the contrary, he uses them in such a way as to structure them by means of precisely defined meanings – meanings grounded in a technical vocabulary.

Because love as a metaphor has a cognitive value, one must, in order to understand it, spell out the specific themes it introduces. To this end, a consideration of Cavalcanti's vocabulary is crucial. His language shows a link with the field of medicine. Medical science paid great attention to terminology (the so-called *doctrina terminorum*). Cavalcanti's method can be seen as part of this precision of vocabulary that men of science were introducing. One such man of science was Taddeo Alderotto, a physician active in Bologna and a contemporary of Cavalcanti's. Guido's method will resonate with that of another physician, the Florentine Dino del Garbo, who asserts that the *sermo* (speech) is *congruus* (appropriate) if the vocabulary is technical.[45] The connection between medical science and logic, found in Dino's *expositio terminorum*, seems to preside over Cavalcanti's vocabulary and the method used to organize it. These aspects of Cavalcanti's poetry suggest that the technicality of his language comes about because he relates poetry and knowing or, better, because he looks at poetry as a special kind of logic. *Donna me prega* will show that the reasoning contained in the poem encloses, like logic, a rational procedure. It also shows that Guido looks at poetry as being (by analogy with logic) a special kind of *scientia media.* The connection established between poetry and logic that makes poetry an instrument for knowing shows how much Cavalcanti is in step with the learning of his time, which generally considered poetry as a kind of logic and which regarded Aristotle's poetics and rhetoric as a part of the *Organon.*[46]

Dante Opposes Cavalcanti's Method

Before concluding, let us reflect briefly on a topic that relates Cavalcanti's method of his so-called minor poems to Dante's *Vita nuova,* in particular to the canzone *Donne ch' avete intelletto d'amore.*[47] As the *Vita nuova* shows, Cavalcanti's method plays an important role for Dante. Indeed, Dante himself was responsible for the eradication of Cavalcanti's way of writing poetry. In the *Vita nuova,* Dante not only indirectly confirms our reading but also reveals his reason for rejecting the themes and methods that Cavalcanti introduced. Dante does so at first because he wants to ground love not in the mechanical process of nature and its necessity, but in the inner freedom of an interior law. That this implies a new way of conceiving poetry is clearly stated in *Purgatory* XXIV. Here Dante is recognized as the poet who 'trasse le nove rime' (who brought forth the new rhymes). The canzone *Donne ch' avete intelletto d'amore* is explicitly recalled. The pilgrim himself explains what his new way implies: 'I' mi son un che, quando/Amor mi spira, noto, e a quel modo/ch' e' ditta dentro vo significando' (I am one who, when Love inspires me, takes note and goes setting it forth after the fashion which he dictates within me). Love becomes the 'dictator' of a new way of conceiving love: freedom from natural necessity. If Love dictates what Dante writes, and if the laws of rhetoric are subjected to the interior superior law of Love as written in the heart of man, then the new way of writing derives from a new concept of love. In order to establish this different way, Dante takes recourse in the mystical tradition. Beginning with *Donne ch' avete intelletto d'amore,* Dante openly speaks of initiating a 'new way.' This is evident not only in this text but also in the two following poems, *Amor e 'l cor gentil sono una cosa*[48] and *Negli occhi porta la mia donna Amore.* Here Dante seeks to erase a notion crucial to Aristotle's physics as applied to love: that of potentiality and act. Beatrice also makes gentle the hearts of those who are not naturally predisposed to love.[49] It appears that Dante's major concern in these poems is to eliminate every connection between love and necessity as basic to Aristotle's physics.

Dante also eliminates the correspondence between love as passion and the rhetoric determined by the necessity of physiology. The poetry of *lode* in the *Vita nuova* is first of all the entry into a new *dictatus*. Dante finds his own poetic voice by resolving love into a *dictatus* of an internal law that works mostly to detach his poetry from all rhetoric regulated by physical necessity. Dante, therefore, while searching for a method opposed to that of Cavalcanti, indirectly defines for us what that method is.

Donne ch' avete intelletto d'amore is usually read as including an answer to *Donna me prega*. But it must also be read in relation to Cavalcanti's ballad *Veggio negli occhi de la donna mia*.[50] The new (*piacer novo*) as a key word in Cavalcanti's ballad appears in Dante as the newness of the new. Cavalcanti had focused on the process of imagination, that is, the process of image-generation. He suggested that this image works to connect the sensible individual with the sphere of the intellect as part of separated substances. *Donne ch' avete intelletto d'amore* focuses on the woman as an angel. She is desired in heaven and for this 'Angelo clama in Divino Intellecto' (An angel entreats within the divine mind). This woman is designated as a 'meraviglia nell'acto che procede' (a marvel in the act that comes forth). She is a miracle because, by virtue of her, every separation is eliminated. Following Cavalcanti, Dante sees love as a metaphor. Beatrice as a figure of love thus includes a reflection on human nature as a whole.

Dante emphasizes the relationship between the love for this woman and intellectual activity in order to stress the unity in love of the sensitive and intellective soul. Love is neither opposed to intellectual activity, nor is it a medium for the intellectual activity posited outside the individual, because sense and intellect both coexist in the individual soul. Dante apparently returns here to the theme of courtly love without mercy, organizing the poetry of praise (*laude*), which goes beyond the theme of salutation (*saluto*). Dante announces this as a 'new matter.'[51] Beatrice, already identified with beatitude,[52] i.e., happiness, witholds her *saluto* and becomes the woman of praise. Dante locates his beatitude in what cannot be denied, and happiness is related to the activity of praising his lady. He writes that his tongue speaks under its own impulse: 'La mia lingua parlò quasi come per sé stessa mossa' (my tongue spoke as if it moved by itself).

The new language thus emerges as a language of freedom. A kind of happiness and the language Dante uses are connected. This is a poetry that focuses on the activity of thinking (*pensiero*), and love's relationship to the intellect is continuously recalled. The activity of *pensar* and *ragionar* defines the genesis of the new poetry of *lode*. While Dante rejects the division between senses and intellect, the new poetry of praise will use a language that seeks a relationship between the perfect love and the perfect word. This woman is related to *pensier* and *dolcezza*, both of which are set against death and tremor, which were specific to Cavalcanti's subject matter, and which Dante had imitated in some passages of his early work. New matter and new poetry are identified. For Cavalcanti, love, because it is a passion, is related to an incapacity of speech that may be seen as physiologically motivated: the centre of the word is in the brain. Dante, on the contrary, finds in the motive of the *lode* an inner freedom insofar as love is independent of the bondage of physiology. Love and freedom are indentified. They erase every connection with love as a necessity and the language of poetry related to this necessity.

What is crucial here is the connection between Beatrice and the notion of beatitude, as may be read in the prose text preceding *Donne ch' avete intellecto d'amore*.[53] The theme of *lode* is connected to that of beatitude. Dante shatters all necessity. By connecting love directly to the world of intelligences, he calls upon angels and makes Beatrice one of them. His poetry makes an appeal not to the truth of natural philosophy but to the truth of miracle. He thus no doubt rejects not only the themes directly found in Cavalcanti's poetry but also related topics that were central to the intellectual debate during those years.

We find these themes not only in *Donna me prega*, but also in the *Quaestio de felicitate*. In this *Quaestio* discussed, as we shall in chapter 4, at the University of Bologna during the 1290s, we find a topic that dominated the debate in those years – the so-called philosophical happiness, about which European minds such as Boethius of Dacia and Siger of Brabant wrote. We have no evidence that Dante had knowledge of Giacomo's *Quaestio*. It appears, however, that Dante counteracts those discussions by drawing on another line of thought – that of the so-called *filosofanti* of the *Convivio*. These are probably the 'annoiosa gente' (tiresome people) of the sonnet Cavalcanti addresses to Dante, *I' vegno 'l giorno a te 'nfinite volte*.[54] According to Michaud Quantin, *philosophantes* is a technical word that in the thirteenth century was probably related to the culture of the religious orders that connected the philosophy of Aristotle with the theological tradition.[55]

Donne ch' avete intelletto d'amore seems to stem from that tradition, the same tradition that entered with Guinizzelli's canzone *Al cor gentil.* There the angels-intelligences were the movers of the heavens, and the Lady was depicted as an angel because she mediated between man and God, just as the intelligences mediated between God and the cosmos. In Guinizzelli, the Aristotelian intelligences were connected with Christian teaching. In Cavalcanti's Ballad XXVI, the stars-intelligences are suggested as representatives of the world of the intellect conceived as separate. This is an initial turning point for Dante, to which chapters XXIV and XXV of the *Vita nuova* (De Robertis ed.) make a further contribution. The theory according to which 'nomina sunt consequentia rerum' reveals that the name of Cavalcanti's lady, Madonna Primavera, carries the meaning of 'she who comes before.' But the fact that Beatrice is connected to happiness in the same theory of naming leads us to understand that Beatrice-beatitude *opposes* love as passion, that is, love as it is determined by the physical necessity that Cavalcanti had described through his rhetoric of passion. Like him, Giovanna, the female form of Giovanni, is merely a precursor. And Dante's Beatrice as a figure of love clearly appears to be a comprehensive metaphor designed to oppose Cavalcanti's theory of love. At every step Dante opposes Guido's idea of love, the dismembered ego of his poetry, and his division between sense and intellect. By indicating in chapter XXV that love is an accident in substance, Dante reconstructs man as a unity. He thus seeks to correct the mistake imputed to Averroism – that the common unique intellect is not the act of the individual and is located outside the individual.

We have here a total shift of perspective. The break is evident, at least at an intellectual level. The future theme of *disdegno* in *Inferno* X begins to take on meaning here. Both Cavalcanti and Dante look at love as a metaphor that implies a reflection on the whole human being, his nature and his role. Beatrice being synonymous with love embodies this meaning. Since her name is also synonymous with beatitude, Dante identifies her with love and happiness, thus opposing Cavalcanti's theory of love, the rhetoric of passion he has put forth, and the physiological laws of necessity on which love is based. Beatrice as beatitude and as a miracle excludes not only the discussion of philosophical happiness, but also and in particular Cavalcanti's method. Against Cavalcanti's way of looking at philosophical truth, Dante rests on the truth of miracle and on theological truth. But if Cavalcanti looks to a philosophical, intellectual discussion, Beatrice cannot satisfy him insofar as she represents the renunciation of the crucial method and content of his intellectual positions.

Cavalcanti's *disdegno* must be read as his disdain for Beatrice, who is synonymous with love. But because love is a metaphor, it therefore implies not only the discussion of human nature but also the kind of poetry Dante writes which opposes Cavalcanti's poetic model. In *Inferno* X it is the ambiguous and very famous 'forse cui Guido vostro ebbe a disdegno' that once more confirms the type of discussion active in the relationship between the two poets. If, as we have seen, Dante openly relates a new way of writing poetry to a new concept of love, then the 'cui' that Dante introduces ambiguously indicates both Beatrice and Virgil. It indicates, as we shall see, Beatrice because she embodies not only transcendent love but also the possibility for a new kind of poetry, and the medieval Virgil because he was seen as the poet who implied the survival of the individual soul.

Donne ch' avete intelletto d'amore is a manifesto of the new poetry and of the values of interiority. These are themes that Dante probably brings to maturity in the ambience of the *philosophantes*. That the relationship between Beatrice and the new kind of poetry is underlined by 'cui' will be the subject of a discussion in chapters 2 and 3. At this point, it is worth emphasizing that in *Inferno* X these values are opposed to those of the Epicureans. Dante alludes here to the Averroism of Cavalcanti, whose *disdegno* would therefore imply the opposite of the values that Beatrice and the medieval Virgil both represent. If in the *Commedia* Cavalcanti is an absent-present in the minds of a few, his special *contrappasso* shows that he represents a crucial knot in a debate that goes well beyond him as an individual.

I shall return to the complexity of Canto X (vv. 52–69) in chapters 2 and 3. Here I wish to emphasize that this complexity consists of organizing crucial notions implied in Cavalcanti's theory of love through the tools of logic. For this, Dante utilizes both irony and logic. Canto X, however, cannot be understood without referring to *Donna me prega* and to the theory of love that Cavalcanti builds there. The next chapters, focusing on love as passion in its relationship to the medieval theory of matter, introduces us to themes that were at issue in Paris in the second half of the thirteenth century. That these themes were active as well in the debate between Dante and Cavalcanti will be a topic discussed in the following chapters.

Chapter Two

Vision and Logic

Vision and Logic in *Donna me prega*

In this chapter, I propose a rethinking of Cavalcanti's canzone on the basis of his identification of love with accident and on the notion of accident itself insofar as it is necessary for a comprehension of the nature of love. I will examine the following lines:

> In quella parte – dove sta memora
> prende suo stato, – sì formato, – come
> diaffan da lume, – d'una scuritate,
>   la qual da Marte – vène, e fa demora;

> (In that part where memory resides, [love] takes its state, formed like diaphanous from light on shade, that comes from Mars and dwells there.)

These lines concern the poem's primary structuring metaphor, which is derived from the Aristotelian theory of vision as set forth in *De anima* II: VII, 418a27–19a. Correctly interpreting this metaphor will enable us to understand not only the meaning Cavalcanti attributes to love but also Dante's own different idea of love.

I will initially focus on Cavalcanti's definition of love as accident in the opening lines of the poem:

> Donna me prega, – per ch'eo voglio dire
> d'un accidente – che sovente – è fero
> ed è sì altero – ch'è chiamato amore.

(A lady bids me, and so I would speak of an accident that is often fierce and so haughty that is called love.)

I will first show the connection between the word 'accident' and the word 'diaffan' (the diaphanous). In the next chapter, I will then set forth the relationship of accident to the theory of passion, in which Cavalcanti's definition of love as an accident connects the field of logic to that of natural philosophy. We shall see that in the field of physics, the word 'diaphanous' is congruent with the word 'accident.' My inquiry will show that for Cavalcanti love is neither dark nor light, but rather diaphanous, which, according to Aristotle (*De anima* II, VII, 418a27–19a), means 'transparent.' It is also a quality of matter that is for the most part changing, potentially dark and light at once, depending on the presence of another object to act as an agent, thus transforming its potentiality into act.

It is not possible, however, to render the meaning of the word 'diaphanous' in the thirteenth century simply by translating it as 'transparent.' The Schoolmen received the word 'diaphanous' from a tradition which, through the meaning of this word, had organized a theory of light and vision initially set forth by Aristotle, subsequently studied by the Arabs, and which then entered Europe with the new translations and the appearance of the new Aristotle.[1]

In fact, Aristotle introduced in *De anima* II the theory of the medium. There 'diaphanous' referred to the quality of certain elements like air and water – potentially either transparent or dark and totally dependent for their being on another object. If coloured, the object would act as an agent, transforming the potential transparency of the diaphanous into actuality. In ontological terms, we may say that the diaphanous is the being itself of accidentality.

If love is therefore defined by Cavalcanti himself in terms of 'accident' and 'diaphanous,' it is possible to establish a relationship connecting both terms. The explanation of accident appears to be the focus of the canzone itself. Here, in fact, the cognitive definition of 'accident' is organized through the language of the physics of passion, of which the diaphanous is a part.

My reading will also emphasize the fact that both the idea of love as accident and the idea of light as accident spring from Guido's poetry. This central role accorded to accident underscores the great distance that came to separate Cavalcanti and Dante at a certain point in their lives. This is evident if we consider that for Dante the relation of light to love depends upon the Platonic conception of light as a substance rather than an accident, visible and existing in itself, while Cavalcanti, following Aristotle, considers light to be an accident.[2]

In both Dante and Cavalcanti, therefore, the metaphor used to connect light and love is of great significance for explaining their distance from each other. Cavalcanti's idea of love is rooted in the world of accidentality. Emotions, passions, and movement form the basis of the theory of passion set forth by Aristotle and developed by Averroes. For Dante love, like light, is related to the world of substance.

Throughout my inquiry I shall make use of certain texts crucial for our understanding of radical Aristotelianism. This is the Averroism developed in Paris between 1260 and 1275 and condemned by Etienne Tempier in 1277.[3] The texts I will refer to are Boethius of Dacia, *Topica*, and texts contained in *Trois commentaires anonymes sur le 'Traite de l'ame' d'Aristote*, ed. Giele, Van Steenberghen, and Bazan. In addition, I will refer to Aristotle's *De anima*, *Metaphysics*, and works on logic.

In reading *Donna me prega*, it is impossible to ignore the great influence on Cavalcanti of Averroism and/or of the radical rereading of Aristotle that took place in Paris and in Bologna in the second half of the thirteenth century.[4] A crucial theoretical outline of Cavalcanti's Averroism was offered many years ago by Bruno Nardi,[5] who focused on the nature of Cavalcanti's Averroism. That Averroism appeared to be confirmed later by the *Quaestio de felicitate*, published by Paul Ostar Kristeller in 1955.[6] This was a treatise on happiness written by another Averroist, Giacomo da Pistoia, and dedicated to Cavalcanti. It has been singled out by scholars as exemplifying a common belief.

In her important book *La felicità mentale*, Maria Corti has confirmed Cavalcanti's Averroism or radical Aristotelianism, using modern critical tools and attempting to verify the meanings proposed on the basis of Cavalcanti's language.[7] She has connected the canzone to an anonymous commentary on Aristotle's *De anima*, edited by Maurice Giele, and has proposed it as both a source for the canzone and a key to certain previously impenetrable details of the text. The problem of the attribution of this anonymous commentary is debated in Giele's introduction.[8] He suggests that the author may be either Boethius of Dacia or Siger of Brabant but is inclined to attribute it to the latter. In either case, however, it is certain that the commentary is the product of the most radical Aristotelianism of the thirteenth century. The importance of Corti's contribution is that, in reading *Donna me prega*, she uses a document which testifies to the debate that took place in the latter half of the thirteenth century, that is, during the years in which Cavalcanti lived and wrote his poetry. This is the same period in which an unknown magister in Paris was pushing the Averroistic division between senses and intellect into the drastic statement that 'homo non intellegit.'[9]

Cavalcanti's *Donna me prega* is a treatise on love. Although Cavalcanti has traditionally been termed both a logician and a natural philosopher, the latter has been emphasized at the expense of the former.[10] However, in Boccaccio's novella in *Decameron* VI, 9, we read that Cavalcanti is 'un de migliori loici che avesse il mondo, e ottimo filosofo naturale' (one of the best logicians in the world and an excellent natural philosopher). It appears evident here that Cavalcanti is more notable for being 'loico' (logician) than for being a natural philosopher.

Boccaccio's novella suggests that there is a connection between Cavalcanti's fame as a logician and the answer he gives to the Florentines he meets in the story: 'Guido Cavalcanti dice con un motto onestamente villania a certi cavalieri fiorentini li quali soprapreso l'aveano' (Guido Cavalcanti with a witty speech courteously scoffs at certain Florentine gentlemen who had taken him by surprise). Here Cavalcanti uses a kind of obscurity in formulating an apparently courteous answer that conceals an enormous insolence: 'Signori, voi mi potete dire a casa vostra ciò che vi piace' (Gentlemen, you may say what you want in your own house). In light of this declaration, in fact, the Florentine knights are indirectly said to be dead because Cavalcanti considers them to be at home among tombs.[11]

One detail of the canzone that must be considered is that the definition of love as accident suggests a connection between the fields of logic and physics, that is, between the two fields in which Cavalcanti was traditionally said to excel, as 'loico' (logician) and 'filosofo naturale' (natural philosopher). Cavalcanti himself calls attention to the connection between the two fields when he introduces in the canzone the word *provare* ('chè senza – natural dimostramento/non ho talento di voler provare' [For without natural demonstration I have no intention of wishing to bring proof]) and when he connects the word 'natural' (natural) with 'dimostramento' (demonstration). Thus, when he calls for someone who is an expert in the field ('Ed a presente-conoscente-chero,' [For the present purpose I want someone who is an expert]), he is asking for someone who is learned not only in natural philosophy but in logic as well.

Whatever the reason for Boccaccio's indication of Cavalcanti as 'loico' (logician), *Donna me prega* shows that its natural philosophy is organized around certain notions derived from Aristotle's logic. The canzone itself is related to eight questions, partially related to Aristotle's *Categories* and usually read in connection with Guido Orlandi's questions set forth in a poem addressed to Cavalcanti on the nature of love.[12]

Whether it is true or not that the canzone originated as an answer to Guido Orlandi,[13] *Donna me prega* is organized around eight theses, which Cavalcanti himself indicates as 'ragione,' that is, a reasoning (De Robertis) about the nature of love. Following Aristotle's *Metaphysics*, we may say that the focus is on the ontology of love – an ontology that Cavalcanti resolves into a theory of passion.[14]

The eight theses are developed as responses to the following questions: 1) in which part does love have its seat (place), 2) what generates love, 3) what is its virtue, 4) what is its power, 5) what is its essence (*essentia*), 6) what is its movement, 7) in what does its pleasure consist (*'qualità*, and 8) is it [love] visible? The words included in parentheses return us to Aristotle's categories (place, essence, quality), thereby indicating that the theses are partially related to the modes of knowing, that is, Aristotle's categories. During the Middle Ages, these categories structured the basic laws of logic. Cavalcanti uses these categories and constructs a logic by applying them to the world of movement (*motus*) and change.

The exposition of the eight theses suggests that logic is employed to bring love into the domain of the philosophy of nature, which Aristotelian physics describes. It is this theoretical framework that allows us to recognize the basic Aristotelianism of *Donna me prega*, in which love as passion implies the passivity of the receiver.[15] By indicating the sensitive soul as the seat of love, Cavalcanti makes explicit the physical peculiarity of love, while the 'ragionamento' proceeds step by step, indicating facets of the field of passion.

According to a definition we find in Siger of Brabant and in Boethius of Dacia, a natural philosopher is one who investigates nature by means of logic. The emphasis on this connection was programmatic in the radical Aristotelianism of both thinkers.[16] Considering the *curriculum studiorum* of the thirteenth century, we see that with the entrance of the 'new' Aristotle, logic became a *scientia media* that connected, the *scientiae eloquentiae* with *scientiae sapientiae* applying theoretical knowing to Aristotle's *Physics*.[17] According to scholars, logic as *scientia media* was introduced by the Arabs and is found in Gundissalinus – who originally integrated Arabic and Latin sources.[18]

In the anonymous commentary on Aristotle's *De anima*, edited by Van

Steenberghen, an important point is made by the following question: 'whether the *philosophus naturalis et logicus* put forth their definitions in the same way' (utrum eodem modo definiant philosophus naturalis et logico).[19]

In his *Topica*, Boethius of Dacia affirms the importance of connecting logic and the philosophy of nature, judging any logic empty if it is not applied to nature: 'ex his, quae dicta sunt, duo sequuntur: unum est quod qui logicam invenit logicus non fuit sed philosophus naturas rerum et proprietates diligenter inspiciens. Et ratio huius est quae ante inventionem logicae non erat logica, ergo nec logicus; secundum est quod qui diligenter naturas rerum non inspicit et proprietates semper logicam ignorabit et omnes alias scientias' (Among the things they say one is that the person who has invented logic was not a logician but a natural philosopher looking at the properties of things. The explanation of this is that before the invention of logic, logic did not exist and neither did the logician; the other is that a person who does not research the nature of things and their properties will not have a knowledge of logic and of other sciences (pp. 4–5)).

Additionally, it is worth considering the concept of the science of the soul in the commentary on *De anima*, edited by Giele. The anonymous commentary asserts that only through operations may we know the nature of the soul because its substance is unknowable (from *Quaestio utrum De anima possibilis sit scientia*, pp. 23–4). If we consider that these operations are emotions, passions, affects – that is, accidents – we will understand that while Averroism or radical Aristotelianism was rereading the Aristotelian concept of science, it focused mostly on operations (that is, on the accidents) as the tools for knowing.

I will therefore begin by considering the meaning of 'accident' in light of the Aristotelian texts in which this concept is defined. A great debate raged in the Middle Ages around the word 'accident.' The source of this debate, according to scholars, was in Aristotle's omission of 'accident' from his *Categories*. Aristotle did, however, define the ontological and logical being of accident. Accident is opposed to that which is substance. The two terms are thus correlated, and it is impossible to understand accident without relating it to substance. In the *Physics*, in order to furnish an explanation of the process of becoming, Aristotle distinguished two forms in the being that was undergoing change: one that was the unchanging substratum and another that was mutable. Accident in this context was the moving form (*Physics* I, 7, 190a, 13–15). In *Metaphysics* V, XXX, 10025a14, Aristotle had furnished a kind of glossary wherein 'accident' is defined as an attribute related to a subject –

something not itself substantial but added to what is substantial. To summarize, Aristotle distinguished two kinds of accident. One referred to that which is fortuitous (*per accidens*); the other to whatever belongs to each thing in virtue of itself but which is not, however, contained in its essence: 'Accidens or attribute means that which applies to something and is truly stated, but neither necessarily nor usually.' In *De anima* I, I, 402a15, accident is connected to the theory of perception, and the moving form of the *Physics* is recalled. In the *Posterior Analytics* I, 4, 73a–b, *per accidens* is opposed to *per substantia*.

In Averroes's *Commentarium magnum* on *De anima*, Aristotle's accident of *De anima* I, identified with the passions, is seen as a way to know the substance of the soul. What is important for us is the presence of this debate in the works of the representatives of thirteenth-century Averroism in Paris, Siger of Brabant and Boethius of Dacia. In *Quaestio* I (Giele) we read that the 'substantia animae' is knowable through operations, and these operations are known more than the substance of the soul itself (pp. 23–4). In the same *Quaestio*, the operations are identified with the passions, and the definition he provides returns us to the definition of 'accident.'

By describing love as an accident, Cavalcanti therefore makes a highly significant gesture, thus bringing a new debate into the old topic of love. Looking at the canzone, we may find in it something that was probably obvious to the scholars of the time: that through the word 'accident,' Cavalcanti was introducing a topic of central importance to contemporary debate. He was attempting to define accident by means of physics, where physics must be connected here with the sensitive soul. The connection is strongly suggested by the *De anima*, where the study of the soul is said to be a part of physics.

The lines I will reconsider are those that have been traditionally focused on. They were cited at the beginning of this chapter:

> In quella parte – dove sta memora
> prende suo stato, – sì formato, – come
> diaffan da lume, – d'una scuritate,
> la qual da Marte – vène, e fa demora;

(In that part where memory resides, [love] takes its state, formed like diaphanous from light on shade, that comes from Mars and dwells there.)

We have learned from Cavalcanti's exposition that love is an accident.

LORETTE WILMOT LIBRARY
NAZARETH COLLEGE

What must be emphasized is that the canzone is organized around a central metaphor derived from the field of natural philosophy, namely, the theory of vision. Crucial for such a meaning is the relationship between the word 'diaphanous' and the word 'scuritate' ('sì formato, – come diaffan da lume, – d'una scuritate').

Nardi has explained the phrase in terms of an opposition. Just as the diaphanous is formed by light, so love is formed by darkness: 'Come un corpo diafano è reso luminoso dalla luce che lo attraversa e l'informa, così l'amore ... consiste in una oscurità' (As a diaphanous body become luminous because a light which passes through it makes its form, in the same way love's ... essence is obscurity). This interpretation is widely accepted today. As is well known, Nardi based his analysis of Cavalcanti's Averroism on the division between the senses and the intellect. Love is a darkness because it is confined to the sphere of sensuality.

Aware as he was of the long exegeses on the canzone, Nardi did not, however, take into account Dino del Garbo's interpretation of these lines in his important fourteenth-century commentary.[20] Contrary to Nardi's interpretation, for Del Garbo the two terms 'diaphanous' and 'obscurity' are related rather than opposed. This point is crucial since it reveals Del Garbo's thorough knowledge of Aristotle's *De anima*, which he cites. According to Del Garbo, darkness or the *obscurum* is in fact part of the diaphanous. The diaphanous is potentially both transparent and *obscurum*, and acquires its form when a luminous body transforms its potentiality into act:

> declaratum est enim in scientia naturali quod lux est actus corporis dyaphani. Et ideo dyaphanum est quod de se lucem non habet, est tamen aptum recipere et retinere lucem quae infunditur a corpore luminoso sicut apparet de aere, qui est corpus dyaphanum quod de se lucem non habet; unde ratione huius dicitur corpus obscurum, est tamen aptum recipere lucem a corpore luminoso sicut est corpus solare aut aliud corpus lucens.

> (It is declared in natural science that light is the act of a diaphanous body. Therefore, the diaphanous (*dyaphanum*) is that which of itself does not have light and yet which is apt to receive and retain the light which comes to it from a luminous body; as is apparent from the case of air, which is a diaphanous body that does not of itself have light. Consequently, it is called an obscure body and yet it is one that is apt to receive light from a luminous body such as the sun.)[21]

It is essential to understand that del Garbo did not oppose the two terms to each other. He appears to be aware that Cavalcanti here introduces the theory of vision, and that in the theory of vision (to which the word 'diaphanous' refers), to separate diaphanous from *obscurum* is nonsensical. It suffices to quote both Aristotle and Averroes in order to understand that *obscurum* is the state of the diaphanous before the fulfilment of its form. In fact, Cavalcanti in this context uses the word *formato*, as derived from form or act, in its Aristotelian meaning of a fulfilment of a potentiality ('sì formatò, – come / diaffan da lume, – d'una scuritate,' formed like the diaphanous from a light on a shade).

In *De anima* II, VII where Aristotle introduces his theory of vision, we read that darkness is not opposed to the diaphanous, but is part of it. This is evident from the following passage: 'By transparent I mean that which is visible, only not absolutely and in itself, but owing to the color of something else. This character is shared by air, water, and many solid objects; it is not *qua* water or air that water or air is transparent, but because the same nature belongs to these two as to the everlasting upper firmament. Now light is the activity of this transparent substance qua transparent; and wherever it is present, *darkness also is potentially present ... This, then, is the nature of transparent; when it is not actually but potentially transparent,* the same underlying nature is *sometimes darkness, sometimes light*' (emphasis mine).[22]

The fact that Aristotle's theory of vision presented light as an accident was underlined by some of his commentators. In Averroes's *De anima* II, 418b, 9–17, of *Magnum commentarium,* we read:

Et dixit: et diaffanum est illud quod est visibile, etc. Idest, et diaffanum est illud quod non est visibile per se, scilicet per colorem naturalem existentem in eo, sed illud quod est visibile per accidens, idest per colorem extraneum ... Lux autem est actus istius, scilicet diaffoni, secundum quod est diaffonum; in potentia autem est illud in quo est cum hoc obscuritas ... id est: corpus autem diaffonum in potentia es illud in quo invenitur ista natura communis cum obscuritate.[23]

(And said :et diaphanous is what is visible, etc. That is, diaphanous is what is not visible per se; i.e., because a natural color exists in it, but is what is visible for accident, that is for an external color ... Light is the actuality of the diaphanous because diaphanous, while in its potentiality is obscurity ... i.e., in the diaphanous body in its potentiality it is possible to find a nature which is common with darkness).

This metaphor, utilized by Cavalcanti, is therefore essential in that it places love in the domain of the accidental. If, as we read, love is presented through a metaphor deriving from the theory of vision, what is important is that in this theory both vision and light are accidents. Therefore, love is an accident generated by chance occurrences or something that intervenes. In other words, the metaphor of vision is crucial in proposing first of all that love is connected to a field of potentiality, of the being-acted-upon, which in the philosophy of Aristotle and Aristotelianism indicates the field of passion. As we will see, this implies also the disposition of *appetitus*, a potentiality that acquires its form (actuality) through the 'veduta forma.' That is, the metaphor of vision, at work on many levels, is crucial above all for explaining that the cupidity of the senses needs a 'veduta forma' in order to transform its potentiality into act, just as the diaphanous, potentially transparent, transforms its potentiality into act when a coloured or illuminated object acts on it.

It is evident from what I have said that what Cavalcanti is trying to define is the ontological being of love: 'formato, – come diaffan da lume, – d'una scuritate.' Therefore love, which has its seat in the sensitive soul where the 'virtus memorativa' preserves the images of things ('in quella parte – dove sta memora/prende suo stato' [in that part where memory resides, [love] takes its state]) is formed like the diaphanous from light (*lume*) on darkness, primarily because it starts with vision. Vision here thus works in its literal sense. However, as we shall see, it will work also as metaphor, indeed as the central metaphor on which the whole canzone is structured.

Now I will examine the following line: 'la qual [scuritate] da Marte – vène, e fa demora' ([an obscurity] that comes from Mars and dwells there). Both Nardi and Corti, having identified this obscurity with love, seek a connection with the heaven of Mars. From Mars derives an influence that stimulates the *appetitus concupiscibilis*. Corti makes reference to a series of authorities (del Garbo among them) in order to establish this negative influence from Mars. However, because of Mars, it is possible to introduce a correlation between Mars (which is the heaven of fire and the activity of cupidity that it influences) and the heat this heaven activates in the body's *complexio*. In fact, *complexio*, according to the medieval discussion that also took place in Taddeo Alderotto's medical school, may be influenced by the activity of the heavens.[24] It remains to be seen, however, whether the heat due to the influence of Mars can be related to vision's activity and therefore to the word 'obscurity' that Cavalcanti introduces.

Returning to the canzone, we may see that the metaphor of the diaphanous is adopted by Cavalcanti in order to relate love to the theory of vision and to the potentiality this theory involves. According to the metaphor, love is not obscure in itself. Obscurity represents a potentiality, and light, as a potential, represents the fulfilment of the diaphanous. The metaphor is not the result of imagination but is instead taken from the field of natural science. This suggests Cavalcanti's attempt to ground the theoretical field of love in Aristotelian physics. For it, the theory of passion receives the crucial suggestion: love comes from a potentiality, a disposition to be acted upon that is studied by physics. This potentiality is transformed if an agent changes it into an actuality. What transforms this potentiality into actuality is clearly stated by Cavalcanti: 'Vèn da veduta forma.' From Mars comes a disposition, namely, the cupidity that disposes to love. This disposition needs, however, a form in order to be transformed from potentiality into act. That the senses need a sensible in order to transform this potentiality into act was a crucial statement in Aristotle's *De anima*, and the word *sensato* (which, we recall, is how Cavalcanti names love) in the canzone holds the same meaning of the sense in act because it is acted upon.[25]

But in light of the metaphor of the diaphanous that Cavalcanti employs, this darkness (which is something potential in the same way that light is potential) requires that we explore its technical meaning as well. Is darkness here a colour-metaphor for cupidity and its excess? Or (in light of the science of vision) does it have a literal meaning? What we know is that cupidity in love enables the process toward image-formation. But we know also (according to what we read in Averroes, *Parva naturalia*) that vision takes place solely in the balance of the body.[26] If we consider that the fire of Mars influences the body's *complexio*, according to the theory of astral influence, then we may look for a relation between the obscurity induced by Mars – as Cavalcanti suggests – and a possible induced failure of the activity of vision.[27] If Mars's activity consists in promoting hotness in the bodies here below in the sublunar region, and if, as pseudo-Aegidius explains in his commentary on *Donna me prega*, Mars is responsible for perturbations because it makes the body hot and burning,[28] then we must inquire into whether this fiery activity generated by Mars may be connected with the theory of vision and the obscurity that Cavalcanti introduces.

Reading Averroes's *Parva naturalia*, we may easily understand the technicality that Cavalcanti embraces. In fact, in the section Averroes devotes to discussing *De sensu et sensato* we read the following: 'The organ of the faculty of sight is the eye. This organ is distinguished by the fact that the predominant element in its composition is water ... The organ of the faculty of sight is of this description in order that the forms of the sense objects may be imprinted upon it just as forms are imprinted upon a mirror ... This organ will perform its function only when it is in its natural complexion without anything untoward happening to it that would blur or agitate it. Consequently he whose anger is aroused ... and whose heat ascends to his head will have his vision impaired ... Inasmuch as this organ, that is the eye, can only perform its function when it has a balanced complexion ... When the heat of the eye is aroused more than is necessary ... its vision will weaken.'[29]

We learn here that an excess of heat makes vision weak. In addition in the section in which Averroes comments on *Memory and Recollection* we read that the imaginative faculty too will suffer and become impaired when the sense is impaired, and will become blurred when the sense is blurred.[30] From the perspective of these fragments, the darkness of love in the canzone is not only brought back to the field of potentiality but is also explained in relation to the theory of vision (the excess of heat being dangerous for vision) and imagination.

If we reread the line 'la qual da Marte – vène, e fa demora; we may understand from one side the effects of Mars's fiery activity on the body's *complexio,* and from the other the implications of the phrase 'fa demora.' In fact, love will be obscure if vision is weak because weak vision corresponds to the impairment of the other faculties whose seat is in the head. Located here are the internal senses – memory among them. If potentiality therefore presides over vision and over the image-formation that takes place when the body is in balance, the theory of the diaphanous in the canzone reveals the potentiality of the process. The focus is precisely on this potentiality. This principle of natural philosophy thus becomes the law itself of love and of the image-formation obstructed by the excess of desire. But in *Donna me prega,* the theory of the diaphanous works also in a more complex way. We see this if we relate it, as a metaphor, to the cognitive process and to the role human beings perform in this process. We shall see, in fact, that Cavalcanti utilizes the theory of the diaphanous also as a metaphor in order to furnish a physical demonstration of the separation between the sensitive and intellectual soul.

The metaphor of the diaphanous and the lines I have examined are strongly related in meaning to the final part of the canzone:

È non si pò conoscer per lo viso:
compriso, – bianco in tale obietto cade;
e, chi ben aude, – forma non si vede:
   dunqu'elli meno, che da lei procede.

(And [love] cannot be known by sight: once understood, white falls down
from this object and – who listens well – form cannot be seen: even less,
therefore, [love] that proceeds from form.)

Here Cavalcanti answers the last question, developing his final thesis
as to whether or not love is visible. The answer may be understood if we
attend (from our earlier explanation) to the metaphor that Cavalcanti
uses to characterize love, which he derives from the Aristotelian theory
of vision.

We find in the lines quoted above the word 'obietto.' We must first
connect this crucial word to its correlative, which appears in the phrase
'in subietto' as found in the poem's second stanza. In this stanza, Cavalcanti exposes the process through which the form lives once it has been
impressed in the memory. The line 'Vèn da veduta forma che s'intende' (derives from a seen form that become intelligible) explains that we
are in the process of the creation of the phantasm and its intellection.
The condensed language suggests a well-known theme for Cavalcanti's
'expert reader.' Let us consider lines 21–8:

Vèn da veduta forma che s'intende,
che prende – nel possibile intelletto,
come in subietto, – loco e dimoranza,
In quella parte mai non ha possanza
   perché da qualitate non descende.
resplende – in sé perpetüal effetto;
non ha diletto ma consideranza;
sì che non pote largir simiglianza.

([Love] derives from a seen form that is intellected, that takes up place
and dwelling in the possible intellect as in a substance. In that part [love]
never has any power. Since it does not derive from quality, it shines in itself
as a perpetual effect; it does not have pleasure but rather contemplation;
and thus it cannot create likeness.)

These lines organize the process that love activates. The sensitive soul participates in this process by creating a phantasm from which the separated possible intellect (which does not belong to human beings individually but is common to them all) abstracts the form of intellection. On the one hand, we have the expression 'in subietto,' which specifically indicates that love-phantasm is an accident for the possible intellect. On the other, there is the perpetual 'resplende' of intellect, which is 'in sé.' This refers to the fact that, according to Averroism, intellect is a separate being and is not part of any individual. It is evident that here the term 'resplende – in sé perpetüal effetto' (shines in itself as a perpetual effect) is opposed both to accident and to the diaphanous. The reason is that the latter two belong to the realm of mutability, while the perpetual effect is the actuality proper to the separate intellect. This separate intellect has 'consideranza' and does not participate in the world of qualities proper to matter.

In this section, we encounter the expression 'in subietto,' which is correlated to the word 'obietto' in line 64. The two sections (lines 21–8 and lines 63–70) are correlated because they focus on what is highest and lowest in love's process. For the correlation between 'in subietto' and 'obietto,' we are indebted to Corti. The phrase 'in subietto' means that the possible intellect acts as subject on the 'veduta forma' during the process of abstraction. 'Forma' is therefore the accidental object of this act of abstraction.

Once the process of abstraction is concluded, love loses its luminous whiteness ('compriso, – bianco in tale obietto cade'). For the meaning of 'compriso,' etc., Corti furnishes the following explanation: '*comprehensus* dall'anima sensitiva ... in balia dell'anima sensitiva l'amore perde la sua bianchezza luminosa, si fa privo di colore' (comprehensus from the sensitive soul ... possessed by sensitive soul, love loses its luminous whiteness, becomes deprived of colour).[31] This information derives from her interpretation of 'veduta forma che s'intende,' as we find it in lines 25–8. According to this interpretation, the activity of 'resplende' (shines) must be referred to the "forma," which is intellected, 'che prende – nel possibile intelletto ... loco e dimoranza.'[32]

Whether or not we accept this suggestion (to which we shall return in chapter 4), it appears evident that love lives through a phase of luminosity. Consequently, as Corti writes, love loses its lightness once the process of abstraction is concluded. However, inasmuch as she had previously maintained (following Nardi) that love is darkness and is opposed to the transparency of the diaphanous, Corti's assertion introduces a new factor.[33] Reading the line 'compriso, – bianco in tale obietto cade,' she now states: '*compriso*, cioè *comprehensus* dall'anima sensitiva, l'amore in sè bianco, luminoso perchè generato dalla *forma intellecta*, cioè dal soggetto universale contemplante ... cade giu'nell'anima sensitiva ...' (*compriso*, that is, *comprehensus* from the sensitive soul, love white in itself, luminous because generated by the intellectual form, i.e., from the universal subject contemplating ... falls down in the sensitive soul).[34]

Hence we see therefore that love's process passes through a phase of luminosity. Therefore, if, according to Corti, love is luminous at a certain stage of its process, it must not be defined as darkness but instead as diaphanous, that is, as both dark and luminous – as a potentiality that encompasses both the dual process from darkness to transparency and light, and the reverse from light to darkness. In fact, according to the text, when 'forma' is already 'intellecta' ('bianco in tale obietto cade'), what emerges is again the obscurity of love.

Therefore, according to Cavalcanti's metaphor, love is diaphanous during the process of abstraction and returns to darkness when this process reaches its end. Love, therefore, is made from a potentiality that becomes actual once it is a 'veduta forma' because from it starts the process toward intellection. When the process of abstraction is concluded and the 'veduta forma' is abstracted, love returns to being only the 'obscura' sensuality inspired by Mars. It loses the 'bianco' because, in the metaphor of vision, 'bianco' and light are synonymous. Both are metaphors for the process of abstraction that Cavalcanti condenses in the 'veduta forma che s'intende' (seen form that is intellected).

Let us turn now to the following lines:

> E non si pò conoscer per lo viso:
> compriso, – bianco in tale obietto cade;
> e, chi ben aude, – forma non si vede:
> dunqu'elli meno, che da lei procede.

(And [love] cannot be known by sight: once understood – white falls down from this object, and, who listens well, form cannot be seen: even less thereby [love] that from form proceeds.)

In order to understand the meaning of the last section, we must now connect it to the question to which Cavalcanti is responding here. We read this question in line 14: 'e s'omo per veder lo pò mostrare' (Whether one can show it to be visible). That is, is love for man visible or not?. The answer is peremptory: 'E non si pò conoscer per lo viso.' It is impossible to know love by means of sight (i.e., to see love). Cavalcanti's answer encloses a technical sense that refers us back to the theory of vision. Through it he explains that because human beings do not participate in the luminous phase of love but only in love's darkness, love is not visible to them. Again it is the metaphor of vision to which Cavalcanti appeals. Once the process of abstraction is concluded, love loses that which is 'bianco,' namely, its light or splendour. 'Forma,' he says, is not visible if not illuminated. Therefore, love that derives from 'forma' is not visible. Love, we may say, would be visible if men were able to participate in the phase of intellection in which the form ('che s'intende'), having its dwelling ('loco e dimoranza') in the perpetual light of the possible intellect, is illuminated.

It is important to note here that Cavalcanti sets up the relationship between love and the theory of vision by introducing a kind of sophism. I use this term to refer generally to an 'enigmatic' proposition, 'which from a logical viewpoint presents certain difficulties in virtue of its ambiguous or faulty formulation.'[35] The obscurity of these lines (64–6) derives from the fact that Cavalcanti here mixes assertions that appear both true and false.[36] According to the Aristotelian theory of vision, it is in fact true that a form is not visible if not illuminated. It is also true that love generates the form and is associated with the process of form. But what is difficult to understand is that love is not visible because form is not visible. And in light of the physics of vision to which Cavalcanti refers his sophism, the very question of love's visibility is nonsensical. According to some scholars, at the end of the thirteenth century sophisms were applied to physics in order to clarify difficulties deriving from the new science.[37] Whether this is true or not, it is evident that in the canzone, what I indicate as sophism has the goal of putting forth a problem in order to resolve it: the intended obscurity is instrumental. Indeed, in order to understand it, the reader must understand not only the theory of vision but also the profound correlation between the theory of vision and the metaphor of the diaphanous.

In lines 63–8, it seems that Cavalcanti is setting forth a specific theory that goes beyond the texts of Aristotle or Averroes on *De anima*. The fact that he is introducing the term 'bianco' as a synonym for light suggests that he is referring (directly or indirectly) to Alhazen, whose *Optics*, translated into Latin late in the twelfth or early in the thirteenth century,[38] devoted a chapter to explaining that colours and light work together to organize vision, and that white is like light.[39] In addition, Cavalcanti says that once the form is without whiteness ('bianco ...

cade'), the form is not visible. Two lines later, he makes another assertion that love is situated in an obscure medium that cuts off light ('For
di colore, d'essere diviso,/assiso – 'n mezzo scuro, luce rade' [Lacking
in colour, separate from being, set in a dark medium, light is erased]).

These assertions are basic to the science of vision for two reasons:
1) in order to obtain vision, we need an illuminated object; and 2) it is
necessary to have a transparent medium, whereas an opaque body cuts
off vision.[40]

What appears gratuitous is Cavalcanti's affirmation that love is not visible because the form loses its whiteness. On the basis of what law does
the unilluminated form render love invisible' The only possible explanation of the matter in terms of the science of vision is furnished by
relating love to the diaphanous.

In this case, it is evident that love, being diaphanous, needs an illuminated, coloured form in order to be visible, and therefore, if the form
loses its light ('bianco'), the love – like the diaphanous – can no longer
be visible. A perfect equation is established here between the physics of
vision and the theory of love. We know that love proceeds from 'veduta
forma,' that vision at first establishes the process of imagination but the
meaning of 'dunqu' elli meno, che da lei procede' (even less, thereby,
[love] that from form proceeds) has to be taken in the sense that Cavalcanti has established at the outset: if love is like the diaphanous, we
know that the diaphanous is not visible without having been illuminated
by a coloured object. It is only by virtue of the analogy with the diaphanous that the last *quaestio* acquires its meaning. Apparently organized as
a sophistical trick, in reality it displays evidence of the theory of the
diaphanous, which points to the central meaning of the canzone.

This deliberate obscurity, therefore, is Cavalcanti's expedient to
ensure that the reader comprehends the definition of love in terms of
the central metaphor of the diaphanous. Again, it is the metaphor of
vision that enables us to penetrate its meaning. The plenitude of love is
in the diaphanous, which includes the luminous phase of 'forma intellecta.' However, man knows only the sensual part of love, its darkness.
Even if he has seen the form ('vèn da veduta forma'), he does not see
the abstracted form ('che s'intende'), that is, the illuminated form.
'For di colore' means that love, once divided from its true being
('d'essere diviso') – which resides in its diaphanous being – remains situated in an 'obscure' medium that cuts off the beam of light. Love
returns to a state of mere cupidity, and we know that it is 'obscure':
'd'essere diviso' means that it is not act, but only potentiality, which
potentiality corresponds to the obscurity of the diaphanous. Here, love

is only 'obscure.' And herein, writes Cavalcanti, resides the pleasure of love. We may say that however important the role performed by love through the phantasm in the activity of the possible intellect, the only source of individual pleasure is in this cupidity, which is influenced by Mars and provides man, who is of course an animal, with the satisfaction of his appetites.

'Amore' is proposed in the canzone as the highest human activity. Precisely because of this capacity of constructing phantasms, love offers the forms for intellection – an intellection which, in Averroism, belongs only to the separate intellect. The canzone shows, however, that although man is excluded because intellection does not belong to him, love participates in it in a subordinate way insofar as it offers the 'veduta forma' and incites the luminous process of intellection.

The metaphor of the diaphanous works, therefore, to emphasize the true being of love. On the one hand, it is cupidity – a tendency toward the 'veduta forma' lived by the sensitive soul. On the other, it is a creation of the phantasm, which is subsequently abstracted by the possible intellect, which is separated and does not belong to man. This is to say, through the phantasm love participates in two orders: the sensitive ('obscurity') and the intellectual (light), although for man, only the darkness of sensuality is offered to his life. The canzone suggests that the accident called love lives a higher reality than that of man, who generates it. Love, in itself diaphanous in its actuality and participating through that metaphor in two realities, is lived and known by man only as obscurity; for this reason love is not visible to man. The separation between the sensible and the intelligible is inscribed by Cavalcanti in the metaphor of the diaphanous and in the impossibility of man's participation in that which is luminous about love and is related to the life of the intellect. If we consider the attention that Averroes pays to the ontological being of the medium, we may understand that through this metaphor, it was easy for the Schoolmen of the thirteenth century to understand this dual nature of love, a duality that spoke indirectly of another duality, that between sense and intellect.

As the scholars of medieval optics, David Lindberg and G. Federici Vescovini, remind us, the medium was for Averroes a being of a double nature. It was at once spiritual and corporeal. This was evident above all in Averroes's *De sensu et sensato*, in which he discussed the Aristotelian theory of vision.[41]

Cavalcanti reconstructs the logic of accident through physics. His physics is the physics of passion, of a changing substrate opposed to the perpetual unchanging world of the intellect. Love belongs to the world of generation and corruption ('elli è creato'),[42] and so obliges man to look in a 'non formato loco'; that is, as we shall see, the world of potentiality, change, and passion. A logic of passion emerges from *Donna me prega*, which discusses accident and causes a logic of accident to emerge from physics.

A Note on Dante's *Inferno* X

In light of what has just been said, the reasons for Dante's opposition to Cavalcanti are evident. From the *Vita nuova* onward, Dante creates a complex texture that seeks to destroy the structure of Cavalcanti's theory of love and to forge in love the unity of human intellect and senses. Dante's attempt at a subtle critique of the theory of accident and of the idea of looking at love as an entity in itself is evident in *Vita nuova*, chapter 25: 'potrebbe qui dubitare persona degna ... che io dico d'Amore come se fosse una cosa per sé, e non solamente sustanzia intelligente, ma sì come fosse sustanzia corporale: la quale cosa secondo la veritate è falsa; ché Amore non è per sé sì come sustanzia, ma è uno accidente in sustanzia.'[43] Love, writes Dante, is not a being for itself. It is neither an intelligent nor a corporeal substance, but an accident in substance that brings about the unity of body, sense, and intellect.

In this affirmation, Dante reveals himself as the best reader of Cavalcanti's idea of love as a being superior to man, organizing accidentality as a kind of substantiality. Dante's opposition was just the beginning of his gradual emancipation from Cavalcanti, which is written more in the *verso* than in the *recto* of Dante's work and is in any case outside the boundaries of this study.

Before concluding, however, I would like to make a few observations connecting this theory of accident to Boccaccio's novella and Dante's *Inferno* X. In light of Boccaccio's novella, the importance of this love-theory rooted in the theory of accident contains several implications. If love is an accident and is correlated to a series of accidents, it is in Giele's commentary on *De anima* that we encounter the central question of whether *anima* itself is an accident: 'queritur utrum anima sit accidens' (Giele, pp. 65–6). The answer is affirmative, but ambiguous: 'videtur quod sic nam est actus entis in actu ergo accidens'; that is (as we read in the next *quaestio* a few lines further) *anima* is part of the world of potentiality: 'anima est potentia corporis sicut visus est potentia organi.' If we consider Dante's line from *Inferno* X – 'che l'anima col corpo morta fanno' – we see a connection between the theory of accident and the theory of the death of the individual soul.[44]

It is furthermore possible, if we attend to Boccaccio's novella, to establish a relationship among this novella, Canto X of Dante's *Inferno*, and *Donna me prega*. In Boccaccio, Cavalcanti insolently attributes to the living the strange attribute of being dead: 'Signori, voi mi potete dire a casa vostra ciò che vi piace,' where 'casa vostra' are the tombs, or *arca*, the same ones in which Dante's meeting with the Epicureans in Canto X takes place. A more complex meaning of this insolent remark is suggested by a rereading of *Inferno* X. A connection could be established between Cavalcanti's answer to the Florentines and Dante's answer to Cavalcanti's father. Both passages use a language that is densely obscure and reminiscent of Cavalcanti's penchant for sophisms. Here, as is well known, Cavalcanti's father asks Dante: 'Se per questo cieco/carcere vai per altezza d'ingegno,/mio figlio ov'è, e perché non è teco?' Dante's answer seems deliberately obscure: 'E io a lui: "Da me stesso non vegno:/colui ch'attende là per qui mi mena/forse cui Guido vostro ebbe a disdegno."' The obscurity appears similar to Cavalcanti's inclination to organize sophisms. If we accept that the first meaning of 'sophism' during the Middle Ages was that of an intentional obscurity, we may see that the intentional sophism of lines 65–8 of *Donna me prega*, the obscurity of the answer in Boccaccio's novella and Dante's obscurity are similar and possess different degrees of obscurity.

Why, then, has Dante introduced this obscurity? In Canto X, as John Freccero has emphasized, several lines are made to correspond with rhymes in *Donna me prega* – a fact that obliges us to look for a direct connection with Cavalcanti's canzone.[45] We may say that with respect to *Donna me prega*, the sophism of lines 63–9 has a meaning because it obliges the reader to go back to the crucial metaphor of the diaphanous in order to understand the canzone. In the same way, we may say that the obscurity Dante encloses in the passage in which Cavalcanti is indirectly recalled makes perfect strategic sense. It is, in fact, because of this obscurity that this canto has been designated as the *canto di Cavalcanti*. The absent one presents himself through the obscurity; that is, Cavalcanti's presence emerges through the enigmatic quality of Dante's language. My claim here is 1) that Dante organizes Cavalcanti's emergence in order to contradict him; 2) that this contradiction is organized through logical tools that focus on a correspondence (through contrariety) with Cavalcanti's *Donna me prega;* and 3) that this correspondence works to reverse Cavalcanti's theory of love and the implications of that theory.[46]

We turn our attention to the following tercet and specifically to its last line:

E io a lui: 'Da me stesso non vegno:
colui ch'attende là, per qui mi mena
forse cui Guido vostro ebbe a disdegno.'

(And I to him, 'I come not of myself. He who waits yonder, whom perhaps your Guido had in disdain, is leading me through here.')

Here Dante uses logical tools to catch his reader's attention. We may say that the last line puts forth what in logic is indicated as a problem. What appears to be a problem of interpretation may be seen as a problem Dante himself has deliberately posed. We know also that in order to be resolved, a logical problem requires an analysis of its parts. It is evident in the lines we are analysing that there are at least three problems of interpretation: the meaning of the verb 'ebbe,' the pronoun 'cui' (that is, an oblique Latin case, a dative, which requires the reader's special attention if it is to be understood), and the difficulty of ascertaining the precise meaning of 'forse.' If 'forse' refers to 'cui,' then the uncertainty refers to the destination of Dante's journey through the various realms. But if 'forse' refers to the verb 'ebbe,' then it is possible that Guido had nourished disdain for the values embodied by the 'cui.'

All these difficulties have puzzled Dante's readers. However, if we consider that these lines are organized through the tools of logic, the reader is faced with the task of resolving these obscurities in order to understand the central meaning to which they point. A connection, therefore, may be established between *Inferno* X and the deliberate obscurity of *Donna mi prega* – especially with reference to the sophism Cavalcanti uses to clarify the difficult discourse of love, which is diaphanous in itself but obscure for human beings.

Dante's use of logical tools was probably evident to the learned readers of his time, who were able to detect Dante's insertion of a *syncategorema*, a word that was introduced into propositions which presented logico-linguistic difficulties.[47] The adverb 'forse' (perhaps) is, in fact, a word that, in medieval logic, was designated as a *syncategorema*.[48] That is, it belonged to that class of words, the meaning of which is incomplete or indefinite – words that have meaning only in relation to *categoremata* – and whose position changes the meaning of the sentence according to what is referred to. Usually the *syncategorema* occurred in propositions whose logical relationships were in question. The *syncategorema* was inserted in order to distinguish what is true from what is false.[49]

Dante's introduction of this sort of word serves to alert his reader that in these lines a logical problem is being introduced in order to clarify something.[50] Because the *syncategorema* was dependent upon a *categorema*,[51] it is evident that the strategy that governs its introduction in the sentence concentrates the reader's attention on the *categorema*. That is, the position of 'forse' reinforces the centrality of the *categorema* 'cui' or, alternatively, of the *categorema* 'ebbe,' in order to obtain a meaning for 'forse.' The result is the following: because of the introduction of 'forse,' the 'mi mena [forse] cui' and its content are organized as a logical alternative to '[forse cui] Guido ... ebbe a disdegno.' Both appear to organize opposite fields insofar as they compel the reader to make a logical choice.

If we accept that the 'cui' is a deliberate obscurity that includes a reference to Beatrice (to the values she represents and which include also those of Dante's Virgil, as some scholars today agree[52]), then the obscurity can be explained if we focus on the logical tools Dante uses to introduce them.[53] I begin by examining the word 'ebbe.'

We may read in Dante's usage of 'ebbe' an intentional obscurity that Cavalcante, Guido's father, is called upon to underline. As is well known, the misunderstanding here is generated by Dante's use of the past tense of the verb 'ebbe': 'cui Guido vostro ebbe a disdegno' induces Cavalcante to suspect that his son Guido is dead. However, 'ebbe,' once read in connection with 'cui,' has to be interpreted as a preterite action in relation to the thing itself. That is, 'ebbe' could be related to the distant past in which Dante and Cavalcanti were friends and Cavalcanti felt disdain for values that Dante was introducing in his poetry. This meaning of 'ebbe' would be perfectly clear without Cavalcante's misunderstanding. It is, however, obvious that Dante, in using this preterite verb-form, is seeking to *create* this misunderstanding. Therefore, the question asked by Cavalcanti's father functions in order to create the misunderstanding. Dante's 'ebbe' poses a problem of interpretation that Dante has devised by correctly using the verb 'ebbe,' but at the same time aiming to generate an obscurity. In the same years, the 'logica modista' of Boethius was focusing on the divisibility of operative processes in nature, distinguishing in the *praeteritum* a greater or smaller distance from the present: 'aliquando autem actus verbi praeteriit perfecte.' However, this 'praeteritio non multum distat a praesenti, aliquando autem actus verbi praeteriit perfecte, cuius praeteritio multum remota est a presenti.'[54]

'Ebbe,' therefore, could express something that is past in Cavalcanti's life: 'est enim tempus in verbo modus quidam significandi designans sub qua differentia temporis realis cadit res verbi.'[55] The action of the verb 'ebbe' here in Canto X refers to the time in which Guido held Beatrice (and/or the values she represents) in disdain. This is a time that has long since passed, not because Cavalcanti's life is past but because that period of Cavalcanti's life is now part of the past (the death of Beatrice also could explain the aorist form). And this meaning would be perfectly clear had Cavalcante not been deceived by it. What Romanticism has seen as the lines that trigger the father's desperation could be given a different interpretation – one probably closer to the spirit of the poem, once we see the planned misunderstanding as the expedient that is able to concentrate the reader's attention primarily on the 'cui.'

The pronoun that presumably refers to the object on which Cavalcanti exercised his 'disdegno' reveals itself through logical analysis as the counteracting subject. Because of its obscurity, the semantics of 'cui' implies a double difficulty. The first derives from its being a pronoun and not a noun, which thus demands to be deciphered, and the second from the use of the Latin dative case. Aristotle, in *Sophistical Refutations* (14 173b 35–174) writes that paralogism can be introduced when a term is used in such a way that it can be referred to different cases. In that same work (14 173b 25–34) we also read of apparent solecism introduced through terms in which genus is equivocal. It seems plausible that 'cui' can be referred to this passage: it is a pronoun whose genus cannot be identified, and its case appears to be problematic.

In the same years that Dante was writing the *Inferno*, Thomas of Erfurt, a Modist logician, was writing about the construction of the dative case. In the construction of the dative he distinguished a 'proprietas of principii' and a 'proprietas termini': the first expressed by a construction like 'Socrati accidit,' and the second one by the construction 'faveo Socrati.'

Returning to Canto X, we see that the two constructions are both present: 'mi mena cui,' where 'cui' is used as *terminus*, and 'cui ebbe,' where 'cui' has the meaning of *principium*, that is, according to Thomas's analysis, 'a different grammatical potentiality.'[56] We do not know whether Dante knew of Thomas of Erfurt. Because, however, we possess a partial knowledge of the work on logic in Italy during that period, we may suppose that analysis of this kind was also being carried out in Italy. In light of the importance that 'cui' possesses in the two lines of Canto X, it appears that the word order of the construction focuses on 'cui' as both *terminus* and *principium*: in relation to the verb 'ebbe' as *principium*, and in relation to the journey as *terminus*. In light of this analysis, Dante has deliberately inserted the dative 'cui,' resorting to a series of obscurities in order to focus the reader's attention: Beatrice (i.e., the set of values she embodies) as both *principium* and *terminus* is opposed to Cavalcanti. Cavalcanti is recalled at the same time in which Beatrice is recalled and focused upon as a point of opposition. But according to the logical analysis, not only does the construction of the sentence point to Beatrice as *principium*, it also sets up an opposition (through 'cui' and 'ebbe') between a substantial form and an accident.

It is worth considering that, while a verb (an accidental form, in terms of *modistae* [Freccero])[57] is used to express the obscurity related to Cavalcanti, a pronoun is used to indicate Beatrice (her values) – pronouns being parts of speech that indicate the permanence of things.[58] It is also worth noting that what is accidental in 'cui' (the case) is resolved in 'cui ... ebbe' by making it the *principium* of the construction. If we accept that Dante is using speculative grammar here,[59] it is evident that the *modus significandi* has the function of relating *dictio* – that is, *significatio* – to the realities and to the ontological meaning of these realities. Dante uses the opposition between substance and accidents set up by the 'modistae,' who distinguished between 'partes orationis:' those expressing stability and permanence (*nomen/pronomen*), and those expressing the concept of becoming (verb). He uses them as the *modistae* do, seeing in them the correlatives of realities and looking for their ontological meaning.[60]

If the theory of accident marks the distance between Dante and Cavalcanti, the obscurity of 'cui' and 'ebbe' works to create a correspondence through oppositions. In *Donna mi prega*, obscurity was necessary in order to define the being of love, which through the diaphanous expressed the accidentality of love and the meaning of that accidentality. In Dante, the obscurity focuses on values that Beatrice represents. The meaning she holds here as logical *principium* of construction and substance works as the foundation for an opposition. 'Ebbe' is the grammatical tool to express the world Cavalcanti has assigned to love – that of movement, accident, and becoming – in a word, matter. 'Cui,' on the contrary, refers to the world of stability, permanence, and substance – in a word, form. To put forth this opposition, Dante uses the logical tools of speculative grammar, just as Cavalcanti had used physics and logical tools. Both Dante and Cavalcanti seek the ontological implications of their tools. For Cavalcanti, the absolute is located in the field of accidentality and matter, of which the human soul is part; for Dante, the absolute and the human soul are related to the permanent world of substance and form.

Chapter Three

Love as Passion

The Medieval Theory of Matter in *Donna me prega*

A text largely responsible for Cavalcanti's fame as a natural philosopher
is the important commentary on *Donna me prega* written by Dante's contemporary, the Florentine doctor Dino del Garbo, who died in 1327, six
years after Dante. In his commentary – a crucial text for reconstructing
the meaning of Cavalcanti's major canzone – del Garbo asserts something that should not be taken for granted, namely, that the theme of
Donna me prega is passion.[1] In addition, it is interesting that, for del
Garbo, to identify this theme of passion with love is to give it a name *ad
placitum.*

Del Garbo introduces love as passion by explaining it in light of the
ways Cavalcanti has set down in his poem. He therefore gives a brief
explanation of the meaning of the word 'accident' – the word Cavalcanti introduces in the opening of the canzone as a name for love:[2]

Donna me prega, – per ch'eo voglio dire
d'un accidente – che sovente – è fero
ed è sì altero – ch'è chiamato amore:

('A lady bids me; and so I would speak of an accident that is often fierce,
and is so haughty, that is called love.')

According to del Garbo, love is an accident because it is not a substance
(i.e., something that is for itself) but manifests itself in a subject as an
appetite or a desire. It is an accident because it can either take place or
not. This accident, he explains, is defined as 'fero' because its being is

an excess, and as 'altero' because the effect it causes in the body is 'magnum.' A few lines later, he also asserts that he will not take into account the reason why Cavalcanti calls this passion 'love.' In fact, del Garbo writes that, according to the Philosopher (Aristotle), names are imposed *ad placitum*.[3]

Commenting on the line, 'ché senza natural dimostramento,' del Garbo explains that Cavalcanti derives his demonstration of love from the principles of natural science.[4] Without actually saying so, however, del Garbo thereby suggests that there exists a discourse of passion in *Donna me prega* that is related to natural philosophy. Because he also says that to label the accident 'love' is to give it a name *ad placitum*, he suggests that in order to penetrate the meaning of the connections established, it may be useful to use the tools of logic. In fact, it is in a section of Aristotle's *Organum, De interpretatione* (I, 1–2 16a20), that we find the theory of *nominatio ad placitum*.

Del Garbo therefore paves the way for a consideration of passion as the content of *Donna me prega*, in which love is just a name for passion. Because of Cavalcanti's fame as a natural philosopher, we may consider that Cavalcanti's *impositio nominis*, rather than being *ad placitum*, derives from the ontological meaning of love on which he wants to focus. We may therefore conclude that Cavalcanti identifies love and passion. The reason is that for him the very being of love resides in passion.

By focusing on passion, del Garbo invites us to consider the relationship between passion and accident. He also compels us to look at the two adjectives Cavalcanti uses to define accident. In light of this, the accident as 'fero,' ferox (fierce) can be related to the field of passion to which del Garbo points. The adjective 'altero' (haughty), on the other hand, opens the way to a more complex investigation that I will discuss in the following chapter.

Del Garbo's commentary contains two important seeds. The first is the relationship he suggests between the word 'passion' and the natural philosophy Cavalcanti uses in the canzone. The second is his suggestion of a relation with the field of logic. The connection between passion as derived from Aristotle's physics and Cavalcanti's widely acknowledged fame as a natural philosopher (a view that clearly emerges from del Garbo's commentary) is confirmed by Boccaccio. In both the *Decameron* and the commentary on *Inferno* X, Boccaccio (who was the transmitter of del Garbo's text, which he copied by hand) speaks of Cavalcanti as a natural philosopher.[5] Boccaccio does something else of great importance: he transmits not only Cavalcanti's fame as a natural philosopher (a fame widely acknowledged) but his fame as a logician as well.[6] In Boccaccio too the legend of Cavalcanti's atheism ('se trovar si potesse che Iddio non fosse') (if it should be possible to find that God does not exist) is recorded as a popular belief.[7] The word 'trovar' (find) that Boccaccio introduces here seems to echo the word 'provare' (to demonstrate) that we find in *Donna me prega* for 'natural dimostramento' ('ché senza natural dimostramento/non ho talento di – voler provare'), which del Garbo connects with natural philosophy.

All this suggests that as a natural philosopher, Cavalcanti puts forth philosophical truths as opposed to theological beliefs, and that in doing so he applies the tools of logic. Whether or not we regard Boccaccio's perspective as derived, in part, from his reading of Dante's Canto X, Boccaccio's text paves the way for a connection among Cavalcanti's natural philosophy, logic, and the errors which Bishop Stephanus Tempier condemned in Paris during the same years in which Cavalcanti lived. That natural philosophy contained in itself philosophical truths which were in opposition to the truths of faith brings us to the heart of the debate that the entry of the 'new' Aristotle and his Arabic commentators generated in Europe.

During the thirteenth century, the meaning of the expression 'natural philosopher' was not generic. It had a precise sense in an age characterized by the rediscovery and reading of Aristotle's philosophy. A natural philosopher was someone who studied nature or, in Aristotle's term, *physis* (physics). Physics was a new science steeped in the works of the 'new' Aristotle which entered Europe from the late twelfth century, e.g., the *Physics*, the *Metaphysics*, etc. Physics here was broadly understood and included not only the *Physics* of Aristotle, but also other works related to nature as *De generatione et corruptione, De caelo, De anima, Meteorologica, De animalibus*, and *Parva naturalia*.[8]

Aristotle had discussed the various fields that the natural philosopher must investigate. Because of the coincidence between natural philosophy and physics,[9] Cavalcanti's fame as a natural philosopher was coincident with that of a *physicus* for whom the science of the soul was a part of physics. Of particular importance for us is Aristotle's assertion in *De anima* (I, 1, 403a27–30) that it is the task of the natural philosopher to investigate the soul. This assertion follows Aristotle's view that the affections of the soul are all connected with the body (I, 1, 403a16), that passions are forms in matter I, 1, 403a20–5. Because of the connection between the sensations and the body, it is the specific task of the physicist to investigate the soul either generally or in the particular aspect described. The definitions of the soul that a physicist and a dialectician furnish are different. That of the physicist is related to matter, that of the dialectician to form or notion (*De anima* I, 1 403b2–3). In the *Metaphysics* (VI, 1 1026a5–7), Aristotle asserts that it is among the duties of the physicist to broaden the inquiry to certain aspects of the soul that are inconceivable apart from matter.

From this, we may draw three conclusions about the soul from Aristotle: first, that the soul is related to natural philosophy; second, that this relationship is based on the consideration of matter; and therefore third, that a part of the soul is related to matter. Because this part includes the sensible soul, it is evident that a theory of matter presides over sensibility (*sensatum* in Aristotle's word), and that in this respect, man is similar to the animals. In *De sensu et sensato* (I, 436b10), we read that sensation belongs to 'animal qua animal' and therefore to the animal part of man, which is the sensitive soul.

It is in relation to the theory of matter that the word *passio* acquires its organic meaning in Aristotle's philosophy. And it is in light of the word 'accident' ('accidente – che sovente – è fero'), matter being the cause of the accident (as Aristotle says in *Metaphysics* VI, 2 1027a14–15) that we understand that love is manifestly connected by Cavalcanti to Aristotle's sensible substance and therefore to matter, and that passion is related to this theory.[10] At the centre of *Donna me prega*, therefore, is a theory of love as passion – a theory that emerges from Aristotle's theory of sensible substance. But how can we relate this theory to Cavalcanti's reputed atheism?' To do so, we must first give an account of the theory of passion in the thirteenth century and how this theory is linked to atheism and to the Parisian condemnations of 1270 and 1277.

The tradition that identifies Cavalcanti as a natural philosopher is not extraneous to what I am mapping out as a theory of passion. This theory, as I have said, is part of Aristotle's natural philosophy and was emphasized in Arabic thought. Scholars have widely discussed and agreed that the philosophy of nature contained in the works of Aristotle was primarily responsible for the prohibition of Aristotle beginning in 1210.[11]

While readers agree that Cavalcanti's *Donna me prega* presents love as passion, the real meaning of this term is generally unexplored. Scholars usually follow Dino del Garbo's lead on this issue. Del Garbo, however, does not fully explain the meaning of the word 'passion,' even though he uses it with great frequency. He introduces his reader to Cavalcanti's 'scientifico modo et veridico tracto ex praeceptis scientiae naturalis et moralis' (Bird, p. 160). He also makes some observations that are essential to understanding natural philosophy in the canzone and its relation to the science of the soul. But mainly he seems inclined to explain passion in terms of medical science as the passion of *appetitus* (appetite), as a pathology of the senses as *bestialis amor.* He takes for granted certain relations between medicine and natural philosophy that were well known to his contemporary readers.

However, a modern reader needs more if he is to understand the meaning of the word 'passion.' This meaning emerges when we relate it to Cavalcanti's fame as a natural philosopher. In order to understand what this fame entailed, I will furnish a short introduction to what the word 'passion' included in the thirteenth century. This will allow us to reconstruct the discussion of passion as it took place in the thirteenth century (as the condemnations testify) and to reconsider *Donna me prega* in light of this discussion.

The word 'passion,' which derives from the Latin word *passio* as found in the Latin translations of Aristotle, derives in turn from the Greek *páskein,* to be acted upon or affected. Aristotle's concept of passion is deeply rooted in his theory of matter, matter being passive. Páskein is one of the categories of Aristotle (*Categories* 9, 11b) and therefore is part of Aristotle's theory of sensible substance, since categories belong exclusively to the sensible being.[12] In *De anima,* passion enters as part of the theory of perception or of sensible knowledge (sensation).

The inner meaning of 'sensation' in Aristotle, in fact, was connected with an activity of receiving, a sensible knowledge acted upon by external influences. According to Aristotle, when influences from the physical or intellectual world are operative, the object on which they work is in the condition of *páskein. Páskein* is the condition that the sensible faculty suffers. The word *páthos,* affection (which derives from *páskein*) has the meaning of something that is in an affective state. To be in *páthos* implies the concept of passivity. Aristotle's theory of perception as contained in *De anima* II was solidly organized around the theory of passion. In *De memoria et reminiscentia* and *De sensu et sensato,* Aristotle had worked on the same topic, building a theory of perception or sensible knowledge in which perception includes passion. That is, perception is a largely passive condition that receives influences and reacts to them. Perception, therefore, was connected with the Aristotelian theory of alteration. In *De anima* II, 415b24–6, we read: 'for sensation is held to be change of state [an alteration] and nothing feels which has not a soul.' An important indication on the extent of Aristotle's theory of passion is given in the *De anima* II, 416b32–417a, where Aristotle connects sensation with physics, thus referring his reader to the theory of passion (and action) as set forth in *De generatione et corruptione*: 'Let us discuss sensation in general. Sensation consists, as has been said, in being moved and acted upon; for it is held to be sort of change of state [alteration] ... we have already stated in our general account of acting and being acted upon.'[13]

In order to understand Aristotle's theory of passion, it is necessary to emphasize that the general theory is not given in *De anima*, contrary to what the word might suggest to the modern reader. Rather it is found in *De generatione et corruptione*, the book in which the theory of matter is discussed. Chapter I, 7 of *De generatione et corruptione*, in fact, contains a theory of passion. Here we may read the central tenet of passion, insofar as passion is ascribed to the things that have their form in matter (I, 7, 324b5–7). We find the important assertion that matter, precisely because it is matter, is passive (I, 7, 324b17–20). Passion forms part of the general theory of alteration – a central tenet in Aristotle since in nature nothing is born from nothing. The material cause of generation and corruption is therefore in matter, which can assume one form or another. According to Aristole, generation is just a transformation that appears as generation because it is imperceptible to the senses. Generation and corruption are two different aspects of the transformation of a single substance. Some of these transformations are called generations; others are called alterations. Alteration for its part occurs when there exists a persistent and perceptible substrate. In *De generatione* (I, 4), Aristotle considers alteration as a change of quality, and the new quality (alteration) belongs to the persistent substrate (319b6–20).[14]

The material cause that makes generation possible is what can be or not be, that is, the changing substance (accident) (*De generatione* II, 9 335a33–335b6). It is characteristic of matter to be moved, and matter is absolute potentiality. Matter per se, as we may define it, is the changing substrate that seeks its form.[15] It follows from this that the theory of passion belongs to Aristotle's theory of matter, and that passion is part of the cycle of the generation and corruption of matter, which cycle takes place because of matter's passivity. But we must also understand that this theory of passion, because it is part of the Aristotelian theory of matter, is connected with and derives (as we shall see) from Aristotle's theory of the eternity of the world. According to this theory, *genesis* (generation) is merely a transformation since nothing new can be generated: what appears as new is only a product of transformation.

To sum up, for Aristotle the material cause of generation and corruption is what can either be or not be, that is, the changing matter of physics (accident). Indeed, it is the property of matter to have *pathos* and to be moved (*De Generatione* II, 9 335b29–30). Therefore, Cavalcanti's designation of love as an accident enables us to understand that the word in itself was, for an expert thirteenth-century reader like del Garbo, related to the passion that matter experiences. Aristotle's explication in *Physics* I can be fruitfully related to Cavalcanti's theory of love: 'Matter as matrix or womb in the genesis of things ... the very nature of which is to *desire.*'[16] In addition (and this is the crucial point), *Donna me prega* relates love as accident to the notion of generation, which for Aristotle (and emphasized by Averroes) is part of the theory of the eternity of matter.[17] When in fact Cavalcanti writes that love is created ('elli è creato') [love] is created, he intends to inform the reader that love – which implies the generation of the phantasm – is rooted in matter, that it is determined by the laws of matter and is part of the cycle of generation and corruption, presided over by the influence of the stars (Mars, in the canzone).[18] 'Created' here, however, includes the generation of image, wants to insert this generation into the general principles of natural philosophy and into the biological process. 'Created' must be read in the context of Aristotle's assertion that nothing new in the world of generation and corruption can be generated and that the apparently new is just a product of transformation. The word is more properly understood in light of Averroes, who asserts that eternal generation may be identified as a process of creation because it is continuously changing.[19]

The dangers of this theory of matter for Christian faith (a theory recalled through the assertion that love is created, i.e., generated)[20] are evident: the eternity of matter indirectly recalls the theory of the eternity of the world and denies the biblical notion of creation. Cavalcanti obviously did not want to either affirm or deny any theory of the eternity of the world. He simply asserts that love is an accident and that it is created. But from this assertion, if we connect it with 'ed ha, sensato, – nome,' there derives the conclusion that the sensitive soul, in which love is located, is rooted in what is generated, that is, in the sensible substance as part of physics (with its cycle of generation and corruption eternally occurring), as in the Aristotelian theory of *genesis*, radicalized by Averroes.

But up to this point nothing sounds outwardly heterodox in the canzone. Heterodoxy will, however, emerge when Cavalcanti, in establishing the intellect as separated and common, identifies love as the metaphor used to put forth the theory that it is just matter that presides over human beings.

Summarizing, we may say that in *Donna me prega* we may follow the theory of passion through a pathway that Cavalcanti condenses in words like 'accident' (love as an accident), or in a verb 'è creato' ([love] is created). Cavalcanti's imposing on love the name of 'sensato' ('ed ha, sensato, – nome') not only implies that love is located in the the sensitive soul; it also implies, if indirectly, that love and the sensitive soul are related to the theory of matter – to matter's eternally recurring cycle of generation and corruption.

Once understood in this relation to the theory of matter, love thus appears indirectly related to the two main errors that prevailed in Paris in the thirteenth century. One asserted the theory of the eternity of the world, while the the other proclaimed the theory of the death of the individual soul. That *Donna me prega* was associated with the latter is well known to readers of *Inferno* X, where Cavalcanti is mentioned in a context in which Dante speaks of people 'che l'anima col corpo morta fanno' (who make the soul die with the body). My claim here is that if Cavalcanti's *Donna me prega* suggests the theory of the death of the individual soul (as is well known), it is because his discussion of love as passion is rooted in the Aristotelian theory of matter and its eternity, which in Averroes's rereading implies the death of the individual soul.

If we refer passion to its peculiar field within the medieval theory of matter, it is evident that its meaning goes well beyond the field of love, and that it brings love into the heart of the debate that was active in Paris. This theory of passion, as it emerges from Aristotle's theory of matter, may be held responsible for the opposition put forth in those same years between the laws of matter and the field of the moral and free choice of human beings.

That these themes were the focus of intellectual debate emerges from the condemnations that took place in Paris in 1270 and 1277 during the time of Cavalcanti's poetic activity. The *Chartularium Universitatis parisiensis*, dated 10 December 1270, lists the thirteen articles condemned as errors: 'Isti sunt errores condemnati et excomunicati cum omnibus qui eos docuerint vel assuerint' (these are the errors condemned and excommunicated, and with them are condemned and excommunicated those who have thought and assumed them). The following articles, which are connected to what I am calling a theory of passion, are listed in the condemnation under the numbers 3, 4, and 9:

3 'That the will of man wills or chooses out of necessity' (quod voluntas hominis ex necessitate vult vel elegit);

4 'That all that goes in here below falls under the necessitating influence of the celestial bodies' (quod omnia quae hic in inferioribus aguntur, subsunt necessitati corporum celestium);

9 'That the free will is not an active but a passive power and that it is moved in a necessary manner by the appetite' (Quod liberum arbitrium est potentia passiva non activa et quod necessitate movetur ab appetibili).[21]

As can be seen, these articles contain as a key word the lexeme *necessitas*, connected in articles 3 and 9 with will (*voluntas*) and free will (*liberum arbitrium*). Because the first of the thirteen condemned theses brings us to the heart of Averroism and its theory of the unique intellect ('Quod intellectus omnium hominum est unum et idem numero,' that, the intellect of all men is numerically one and the same), scholars view these propositions as derived from the influence of Averroes's thought. Weisheipl connects the condemnation to the Averroism of Siger of Brabant and Boethius of Dacia,[22] and also recalls Thomas Aquinas's *De unitate intellectus*, which opposes Siger's theses condemned in 1270. Van Steenberghen asserts in *Maitre Siger de Brabant* that the condemnation of 1270 is only partially aimed at Siger of Brabant.[23] Instead, he suggests that the articles 3 and 9 quoted above, for example, are derived from Arabic materialism and are extraneous to Siger's position as it appears in his first writings.[24] Here Van Steenberghen refers his readers to a scholar of Averroism, M.M. Gorce.[25] In an article published in 1930, 'La lutte "contra Gentiles" à Paris au XIIIe siècle,' Gorce initially summarizes Renan's general discourse on Averroism, which proposed that Greek and Arabic thought and science entered Europe through the name of Averroes. He also discusses the condemnation, comparing the theses with Siger's position in Paris. For the purposes of our discussion, it is less important to establish whether the condemnation was directed against Siger of Brabante than to identify a theory of passion on the evidence of the condemned theses.

An important tool for reconstructing such a theory is offered by Gorce in this article, and in 'Averroisme,' a long entry written for the *Dictionnaire d'histoire et de géographie ecclesiastique*. Although Gorce's work antedates the more recent studies on Parisian radical Aristotelianism, it is nonetheless important because it takes into consideration the 1270 condemnation, the sources of which the same Mandonnet neglected to consider.[26] In order to examine them, Gorce makes a connection with Thomas Aquinas's *Summa contra Gentiles*, and, in recalling some passages of Aquinas's work, relates them to the condemned articles. According to Gorce, Aquinas's *Summa* offers the tools for reconstructing not only the reasons for the condemnation but also the structures and topics of the intellectual debate that the condemnation tried to halt. Gorce's connections are not always fully convincing.[27] However, it is worth considering his thesis that Aquinas's opposition to 'Gentiles' counteracted all the teachings of Greek and Arabic philosophers that entered Europe from the end of the twelfth century onward.[28] In order to give an account of the condemnation, Gorce also takes recourse to the synchronous *Errores philosophorum*, as written by Giles of Rome (Aegidius Romanus).

What is important for us in Gorce is his reconstruction of the errors derived from Arabism and Hellenism, a thesis that van Steenberghen accepts as well.[29] The word 'Averroism' – which would include more than just the theories of Averroes – will be treated as synonymous with the philosophy of the Gentiles.[30] Gorce stresses a recurring point in the thirteenth-century polemic against Aristotle: its opposition to the danger allegedly deriving from Aristotle's physics and from the reduction of the world to merely astral physics. Here Gorce emphasizes the role played by natural philosophers, as he writes that Thomas Aquinas, in order to oppose the thinking of natural philosophy which was assumed to be responsible for philosophical errors, had recourse to a Christianized Aristotle.[31] Gorce therefore introduces a series of quotations from the *Summa contra Gentiles* in order to show Aquinas's opposition to such theories. Gorce cites what he sees as Aquinas's opposition to the theses contained in articles 3 and 4 in the condemnation of 1270. On article 9, he quotes the *Summa contra Gentiles* as follows: 'Quidam occasionem errandi sumpserunt putantes quod nulla creatura habet aliquam actionem' (Certain people committed the error of assuming that any creature or person performs any action').[32]

Rather than following the connections Gorce establishes with the condemned theses, we may follow Aquinas's *Summa contra Gentiles*, since it contains (in order to refute them) the theories that were at the basis of the condemned articles. Regarding the same article 9, Gorce recalls chapter 85 of Book III of the *Summa*, where Aquinas opposes the theory of astral determinism; that is, the theory for which natural necessity influences mankind's choices.[33] In other words, the field of ethics is assumed to be part of the determinism of matter. What emerges is the relationship between the theory of matter and man's activity, in which ethical actions are determined by physics. Odon Lottin and E. Gilson have emphasized that it was a common assumption from the beginning of the thirteenth century, under the influence of Aristotle, to associate freedom with immateriality.[34] Van Steenberghen also recalls that Siger of Brabante defines necessity in the world of nature as derived from matter.[35] The effect of determinism on the field of ethics also emerges from Albertus Magnus, who, in his *De XV Problematibus*, takes into consideration the condemned propositions of 1270.[36] Albertus, opposing thesis 9, makes an observation that is a useful introduction to Cavalcanti's theory of passion (p. 41): 'Quod vero nono dicuntur liberum arbitrium esse potentiam passivam et non activam et ideo de necessitate movetur ab ipso appetibili, omnino absurdum est et contra principia ethicorum philosophorum' (In the ninth article it is said that free will is a passive, not active power. Therefore, it is necessarily acted upon by the object of appetition. However, this is absurd and contrary to the principles of ethical philosophers).

In rejecting this theory, Albertus places responsibility for it on the old theory of Theophrastus, who equated the passions of the soul with the passions of physics. Albertus accuses these theories of destroying ethics on the grounds that they had subjugated free will to the laws of physics. This accusation is of great importance for the discussion of passion in *Donna me prega* because it is evident that passion cannot be isolated from the whole of the debate.

The condemnation of 1277 confirms this reading. In particular, some propositions that were condemned help us better understand the relationship between the theory of passion and so-called determinism. For them I will follow R. Hissette who, in his important work (*Enquête sur les 219 articles condamnés à Paris le 7 mars 1277*), distinguishes (p. 313) four kinds of determinism: 1) 'generic determinism' (propositions 62, 101, 150); 2) 'psychological' (this kind of determinism lists eleven propositions); 3) 'astral' lists eight propositions); 4) 'determinism of passions' (propositions 167–9).

In proposition 168 (determinism of passions) we read that one of the theses condemned asserted that a man who acts under the impulse of passion acts under constraint: 'Quod homo agens ex passione coacte agit.'[37] If we connect this article to the articles condemned in 1270, we see that determinism is part of the general theory of passion. Hissette is highly uncertain about the sources of this proposition. Because it recalls the proposition condemned in 1270, we may look at the sources Gorce indicates in the philosophy of Alkindi and Algazel as he finds them in

Giles of Rome (Aegidius Romanus), *Errores philosophorum.* Looking at Giles, however, we find that this theory of determinism is both much more complex and more dangerous. It appears impossible to confine it to Alkindi's and Algazel's philosophy, as Giles suggests. It is perhaps more useful to follow Giles's reconstruction of the errors of philosophers.

Giles starts by considering the errors of Aristotle. What is essential here is the theory of the eternity of the world.[38] This theory contains the crucial error of believing that what is *novum*, what appears as created, is determined exclusively by the laws of nature, that is, not by a creator God. It is evident that the crucial teachings of Aristotle's philosophy of nature are under attack here. Giles criticizes this philosophy because it results in an assault on the Christian theory of creation: 'he erred in holding that nothing new can proceed directly from God, as is clear from Book II *On Generation* where he says that as long as a thing remains the same, it always produces the same.'[39] And again: 'He believed that nothing new can proceed directly from God but that every new thing occurs by way of motion and through the operation of nature.'[40]

It is Giles's word *novum* that refers us to *Donna me prega*, in which love (as already noted) is said to be created. In light of this debate, to assert that love 'is created' has a specific meaning: it implies that love is determined exclusively by the cycle of nature. In addition, this peculiar definition of love as created – which is strategically connected in the canzone with the 'sensato': 'elli è creato – (ed ha, sensato, – nome') – links sensations and the sensitive soul with the theory of matter. The suggestion is that both are acted upon by the influence of Mars. In any case, the phrase 'elli è creato' ([love] is created) would supply an answer to a specific question Cavalcanti puts forth in the beginnning of the canzone: 'Chi lo fa creare,' (What generates or creates love?). The answer 'elli è creato' implies something specific: that love is part of the world of matter and therefore is ruled by its laws.

This theory, for a natural philosopher, implies the eternity of matter ruled by laws of action and passions, laws that are recalled by Giles himself when he refers to Aristotle's *De generatione.* Crucial here is Giles's conclusion that all mistakes of the Philosopher depend on a central error: 'Careful investigation will show that all his errors follow from this principle of his, that nothing new comes into being except as the result of preceding motion' (Omnes tamen errores depend from nihil novum in esse progreditur nisi per motum praecedentem).[41] In the chapter devoted to Averroes, Giles reiterates the crucial error of conceiving the world as eternal ('The Commentator reaffirmed all the errors of the Philosopher with greater obstinacy ... [he] opposed that the world had a beginning').[42] In the chapter in which he refutes Averroes's mistakes, proposition 9 denounces, among the other mistakes of Averroes, the assertion that some things come to be as a result of an inner determinism in matter that is derived from 'necessitate materia' independently of the order of divine providence.[43]

Giles's accusation that every error derives from conceiving matter as eternal appears useful in reading Cavalcanti's *Donna me prega*, where, in fact, love is said to be created. It is in this ambiguous assertion, which recalls creation in order to indicate generation, that the theory of passion in man is introduced by Cavalcanti as a theory dependent on the world of generation and corruption. In addition, as previously said, Cavalcanti connects 'elli è creato' with 'sensato' as a name for love – a name that implies the being of senses acted upon.[44]

This means not only that the sensitive soul is the place and the identity of love, but also that love, given its place and identity, is determined by the principles of matter. The laws of matter are here laws of passion, and the laws of passion belong to the sensitive soul since this is part of physics.

The theory of matter implied in Averroes the disappearance of the individual. According to the Commentator, the individual does not have an individual intellect, which alone among the parts of the soul – as Thomas Aquinas pointed out in *De unitate intellectus contra Averroistas* – seems to be incorruptible and immortal.[45] Averroes denies the survival of the individual because he thinks that the individual possesses only the generative and the sensitive soul, which are subjugated to matter and its cycle of generation and corruption. In fact, the theory of matter, while it affirms the eternity of the genus, at the same time in Averroes and in radical Aristotelianism, involves as a consequence the disappearence of the individual soul, which is subjected to the cycle of matter of which it is a part. The extent to which the theory of passion that I am mapping out was emphasized by Averroes is therefore evident once we consider that the detachment of the sensitive soul from intellect that takes place in his philosophy left the individual living a life wholly determined by matter. In focusing on Averroes's notion of a separate intellect, Giles in fact emphasizes that in Averroes man's species is the sensitive soul and not the intellective ('On this account he was forced to say that man belongs to the species man not through the intellective soul but through the sensitive soul').[46]

Love as passion, once seen in its relation to the theory of matter, explains the extent to which these teachings were interwined with Cavalcanti's fame as an atheist and indirectly with the intellectual debate, of which the articles of condemnation of 1270 and 1277 are a document.

It is now time to explore the way in which this theory of determinism or passion interacts in *Donna me prega* with the field of ethics, that is, to what extent (as Albert the Great writes) determinism destroys ethics. We start by considering the line in which Cavalcanti asserts that the 'accident' love, which 'is created' (i.e., lives the laws of sensible substance) and is named 'sensato' (*'sensatum'*) is not a virtue. The reason, he says, is that it derives from the power that is the perfection of the sensitive soul – a perfection that is not rational but sensitive and that blocks the activity of judgment. Here the reader reaches a new level of meaning: love, because it is a passion, is detached from human choice. It is evident that we must first search out the sources of this affirmation in Aristotle's writings on ethics. Here we read that virtue as man's activity involves first of all purpose, a choice (*E.E.*3.1.1228a23–4), which implies a free will. We read also that virtue is an instrument of the intellect. By grounding love in the laws of matter, Cavalcanti opposes the animal power of love to virtue as free choice and intellectual power. In order to explain his meaning, he openly opposes love to rational virtue and says that love is not a virtue but comes from that virtue which is the animal power:

Non è vertute, – ma da quella vène
ch'è perfezione – (ché si pone – tale),
non razionale, – ma che sente, dico.

('[Love] is not a virtue, but comes from that (power) which is a perfection (for so it is posited), not the rational do I mean, but the sensory.')

Crucial here is the use of the word 'vertute' (one occurrence explicit, the other implied) to indicate the two opposite fields: the field of rationality and free choice (rational virtue), and the field of animal power ('virtus animalis') – 'perfezione ... non razionale, – ma che sente, dico.'[47] And because rationality is an activity of the intellect, we may understand that love heralds – because its nature is 'non razionale' – an opposition between the sphere of sensibility and that of intellect. Such opposition signals a division between two different genera: the intellectual and the sensible, where sensibility is part of the sphere of matter.

Summarizing, we may say that the organization of the canzone suggests that for Cavalcanti what is called love originates in the being of matter itself, a matter that is always potential. This fact was established by Aristotle and emphasized by Averroes, who, in his *De substantia orbis*, furnishes the general theory of matter: 'its essence is to be only potential.'[48] This potentiality in turn implies that matter is an appetite for being acted upon.

Donna me prega seems to bestow on love the peculiarity of matter itself. The first stanza immediately introduces the reader to an essential notion: love – since it is identified with accident, that is, with what can either be or not be – is identified with matter as potentiality, from which potentiality derives its peculiarity of seeking to be acted upon. Love as passion is deeply rooted in this theory.

Cavalcanti also uses the tools of language to emphasize the potentiality of matter as a condition of being acted upon. The predominance of passive forms in this passage of *Donna me prega* puts forth a strategy of meaning as it emerges in 'elli è creato' ([love] is created), followed by 'ha, sensato, – nome,' that is, its [love's] name is sensibility ('sensatum'), the senses acted upon by the sensible object. In attributing to love the name 'sensato,' Cavalcanti finds a specific category (*kategorein* means to attribute a name) for love.[49] Through this category, love becomes the very being of sense, where sense, like matter, desires and longs to be acted upon by an external agent. Love, like matter, is a potentiality, the very nature of which is desire.

To grasp more fully the pattern woven around this theory of passion, let me recall another passage of *Donna me prega* in which the obscurity of love is said to be the result of the influence of the sphere of Mars.

> In quella parte – dove sta memora
> prende suo stato, – sì formato, – come
> diaffan da lume, – d'una scuritate
> la qual da Marte – vène, e fa demora.

('In that part where memory resides, [love] takes its state, formed like diaphanous from light on shade that comes from Mars and dwells there.')

This last line, which introduces Mars's influence, is crucial for understanding how love is rooted in the theory of matter. In medieval philosophy, the heavens exercise their influence on the movement of matter. The sun is the first influence. But since Mars is peculiarly the heaven of fire and heat, and since heat is responsible for the perennial movement of matter,[50] it appears that Cavalcanti wishes to connect the fiery activity of Mars and the heat of the matter that it influences with the being of love. It is in light of the influence of Mars that the being of love as 'created' acquires its proper meaning. Love is part of the theory of matter acted upon by astral influence. This general theory is brought into the canzone in relation to the 'sensato.' The sensible soul ('anima sensitiva') is a generated being and therefore subjected to the principles of matter: this is without doubt the crucial connection to be grasped here.[51] The poem's account of love as passion continues in stanza 4:

> L'essere è quando – lo voler è tanto
> ch'oltra misura – di natura – torna,
> poi non s'adorna – di riposo mai.
>   Move, cangiando – color, riso in pianto,
> e la figura – con paura – storna;
> poco soggiorna; – ancor di lui vedrai
>   che 'n gente di valor lo più si trova.
> La nova – qualità move sospiri,
> e vol ch'om miri – 'n non formato loco,
> destandos'ira la qual manda foco
>   (imaginar nol pote om che nol prova),
> né mova – già però ch'a lui si tiri,
> e non si giri, – per trovarvi gioco,
> nè certamente gran saver nè poco.

('Love's mode of being is when desire is so strong that it goes beyond nature's measure, because [love] is never at rest. It moves making the colour change, turning laughter into tears, and through fear it puts the image to flight; it stays a brief while; moreover, you will see that it is to be found mostly in people of worth. The new quality [love induces] provokes sighs, and it obliges man to gaze at an unformed place, arousing one's anger that gives off fire (who has not felt it cannot imagine it), and that one cannot turn elsewhere for relief: of course one's mind has neither much nor little learning.')

Peculiar to this stanza is the notion of love regarded in its essence. Here Cavalcanti in fact provides an answer to two questions he had put forth in the opening of the canzone: '[qual sia] l'essenza' (what is the essence [of the accident called love]), and 'ciascun suo movimento?' (what is the movement of love?). If these two questions, along with the answer Cavalcanti gives, are to be understood, they must be seen in terms of their connection with one another.

Guido starts by saying that the essence of love consists in its being an excess of desire – a desire beyond natural measure:

L'essere è quando – lo voler è tanto
ch'oltra misura – di natura – torna,

('Love's mode of being is when the desire is so strong that it goes beyond nature's measure.')

'Oltra misura – di natura' (beyond nature's measure) introduces us to the description of this excess. It is in this description that we find the essence of love. This essence is revealed in the sentence that follows: ('poi non s'adorna – di riposo mai') because [love] it is never at rest). This very brief assertion allows the learned reader to trace what is said to the word 'accident' itself. Reading Averroes's *De substantia orbis*, we may understand that the essence of love in *Donna me prega* is obtained by applying to it the being that pertains to prime matter, which, being 'the nature of the potential,' is never at rest. Ontologically, love is rooted in the universal laws of matter.[52]

The fact that love is described as a will beyond the measure of nature ('ch'oltra misura – di natura – torna'), however, requires further attention. If love is a movement of desire without rest, then the law of matter here appears related to the theory of the generation of animals.[53] A section of Averroes's *De generatione animalium* helps us. Here we in fact read that what procreates is 'quid in semine infinitum.'[54] Del Garbo's commentary, which uses the word 'infinitum' to explain 'oltra misura,' seems to confirm this reading.[55] Love is part of the theory of matter. But its ontology derives from the generative spirit or 'semen,' which is acted upon by the influence of the stars and in particular by Mars's heat. According to Aristotle and Averroes, the heat of the generative spirit responds to this heat in proportion to the virtue of the element of the stars.[56] The essence of love in the canzone shows that the sensitive soul is subjected to the generative soul, whose laws are determined by the appetite of generative spirit.

The essence of love leads us to the sixth answer as it is given in stanza four. This answer responds to question 6: what are the movements of love ('e ciascun suo movimento'). Guido says that love's movement produces an alteration that makes one's colour change, turning laughter into tears: 'Move, cangiando – color, riso in pianto' (It moves, making the colour change, turning laughter into tears).

This line grounds love's movements in the theory of alteration as explained by Aristotle in his *De generatione et corruptione*. The learned reader is sent to this text via a technical expression – nova qualità ('La nova – qualità move sospiri'). This new quality is, in alteration, the quality of the persistent substrate (*De generatione* I, IV, 319b).[57] In order to make perfectly intelligible the view that connects love as passion with the theory of matter, Cavalcanti writes that this alteration or 'new quality' that moves man to sighs, obliges him to look at an 'unformed place' (non formato loco):

> La nova – qualità move sospiri,
> e vol ch'om miri – 'n non formato loco,
> destandos'ira la qual manda foco

> ('The new quality [love induces] provokes sighs, and it obliges man to gaze
> at an unformed place, arousing one's anger that gives off fire')

'Non formato' is highly specific. Its meaning is obtained when we realize that 'non formato' is the opposite of the formative power ('vis formalis'), which is the activity of imagination or *phantasia* as 'vis formans.'[58] Love's opposition to the formative process refers us to a passage of Averroes's *De substantia orbis*, in which Averroes summarizes the general theory of matter as being that does not have form ('non habere formam') and whose nature is that of potentiality.[59] But here this general law of physics is brought into the field of the sensitive soul. What belongs to this 'animalis virtus' is the formative activity of imagination (*phantasia*), which the nature of matter obstructs. The resistance of matter to the formative process of *phantasia* appears to be a struggle between the laws of matter and the beginning of an intellective process that matter itself incites and at the same time obstructs. Love between the 'non formato' and the 'informans' (form-giving) of *phantasia* offers evidence that *Donna me prega* shows love as a double being. On the one hand, love is a power of generating the image (animal power); but on the other, because it is rooted in animal power, love is an excess that acts against the fulfilment of that potentiality.

The way in which the nature of this excess is suggested is most precise. Relating love to 'sigh,' Cavalcanti suggests that the 'new quality' is an alteration that generates an excess of heat. In medical terms, a sigh occurs when the body needs to discharge an excess of heat. This heat is introduced in the line: 'destandos'ira la qual manda foco.'[60] Fire here is in fact an excess of heat.[61] 'Ira' is commonly related to an excess of heat. But the origin of this heat is most precise: 'ira' is the 'vitalis virtus' associated with the 'virtus' concupiscibilis.'[62] It is the heat of the generative power, in other words, that produces 'ira' or anger.

A crucial relationship emerges here through the connection between the 'non formato' ('La nova – qualità move sospiri, / e vol ch'om miri – 'n non formato loco' (The new quality [love induces] provokes sighs and it obliges man to gaze at an unformed place) and anger ('ira'), which arouses and gives off fire: 'destandos'ira la qual manda foco.'

Cavalcanti writes that this 'ira' or anger is in fact associated with 'foco' and that this fire is the cause of the impossibility of the formation of the image. A fragment of Averroes's *Epitome of Parva naturalia* helps us to understand what this association implies. Here we read that anger generates an imperfect vision. According to Averroes, if we are to have perfect vision, no agitation must intervene in the visual act. Consequently, he whose anger is aroused and whose eyes redden and whose heat ascends to his head will have his vision impaired.[63] Averroes further suggests that what impedes formative activity is precisely the being of matter. Matter itself is rooted in heat, which, while securing the continuous process of generation,[64] is responsible for generating in the human body the excess of heat that may obstruct the activity of sight, from which the process of imagination starts. The influence of Mars consists of increasing this activity of heat that presides over bodies in love. The lines in which Cavalcanti introduces this theory of the influence of Mars assert that love's obscurity ('sì formato, – come / diaffan da lume, – d'una scuritate') derives from Mars ('la qual da Marte – vène, e fa demora') and dwells in that part of the sensitive soul in which memory lives.

This obscurity (which in the canzone is also a metaphor for the power of matter) in stanza 4 is related to vision itself, which cannot take place when vision is made weak through anger. And because vision is essential to the imagination, anger therefore can obstruct the formative activity of imagination – an activity that aids the process toward intellection. If, therefore, matter works too powerfully, this process cannot take place, as Guido explains in the third stanza:

Di sua potenza segue spesso morte,
se forte – la vertù fosse impedita
la quale aita – la contraria via:

('Death often follows on [love's] potency if the power should be
obstructed that furthers the contrary course.')[65]

As we have seen, Cavalcanti's *Donna me prega* contains a physics of passion that sets up an opposition between the field of the intellect and
that of the heart. Love is not vertue but instead derives from sensibility.
It is an affection of the senses acted upon according to a process that
starts from a form that is seen ('veduta forma'). Love is determined by
the influence of the sphere of Mars. It is part of the potentiality of matter; it is, in other words, a condition of being acted upon. Love is part of
the natural process of generation. But, in particular, love's essence lies
in the generative power of the animal. It is determined from the infinite
desire produced by the generative spirit. Matter as responsible for the
infinite process of generation in nature defines the being and the power
of love.

Love, however, is a power that in a balanced condition of the body is
also able to generate a medium, the phantasm. In this chapter I have
spoken of the first aspect, that is, love in its relation to the theory of matter. In the following chapter, I will discuss love in its relationship to the
formative activity of 'phantasia.' The second stanza of *Donna me prega*, in
fact, takes into account what the power of love includes and generates
when it works in a balanced condition of the body. As we shall see,
stanza 2 focuses on the 'vis formalis' or 'inchoatio formarum,' that is,
what the senses can produce or generate when they are acted upon.

Summarizing, we may follow the themes of *Donna me prega* as follows.
These themes take us back to the theory of passion as derived from the
definition of love as an accident.

1 Love is influenced by the heaven of Mars (astral influence).
2 Love, being created (i.e., generated), is part of the theory of generation and corruption, which theory in turn refers to the theory of matter and the laws of generation and corruption that Aristotle and
  Averroes put forth in *De generatione et corruptione* and in *De generatione
  animalium*. The relation between a general theory of physics in its
  connection with the specific physics and operations of the generative

and sensitive souls seems to be at the focus of *Donna me prega*: 'natural dimostramento' (natural demonstration).[66]

3 Love's name is 'sensato,' that is, sensibility.

4 Love induces alteration in human bodies. Cavalcanti introduces this alteration through a technical expression: 'new quality.' This 'new quality' – the quality of the persistent substrate – brings us to the heart of Aristotle's theory of alteration.[67]

5 Love is opposed to ethical virtue ('non è vertute') and rooted in the field of matter ('ma da quella vène/ch'è perfezione ... non razionale, – ma che sente, dico'). Love, as animal power, replaces ethical choice with physical necessity.

6 Love's essence lies in the generative spirit or sperm. Its movement is infinite. It obliges human beings to look at the realm of matter, which is never at rest. The generative power of love, here described as part of the infinite process of natural generation, connects the theory of love in *Donna me prega* to the thesis of the eternity of matter.

In light of these relations, Boccaccio's assertion of Cavalcanti's popular fame as an atheist seems to derive from a correct understanding of the theoretical framework of *Donna me prega*. Passion and error are connected because they are derived from the same theory. Both are rooted in the theory of matter and its eternity. For Averroes and his followers, this theory implies the death of the individual soul. Love as a metaphor for man's being implies man's necessary relation to and limitation by the general principles of nature, of which he is part. If (as we shall see) in *Donna me prega*, love is a metaphor for the activity of the sensitive soul, then because this soul is detached from the intellective soul, the laws that rule Aristotle's physics are the same laws that rule human life.

This account of passion brings us to the relationship between natural philosophy and medicine, a relationship emphasized in the school of Taddeo Alderotto, who considered the study of the human body (which is the object of medicine) to be subordinate to natural philosophy.[68] This relation is confirmed if we return to the initial topic with which I began my discussion on love, where love, according to del Garbo's interpretation, was a passion. It is not improbable that del Garbo's assertion that the name 'love' is given *ad placitum* echoes the relationship between medicine and logic that was active in Bologna during the late thirteenth and fourteenth centuries. In a recent study on medieval logic, Dino is recalled and quoted for the attention he pays to the use of terminology.'[69] We know that attention to names was specific to del Garbo, as it was to the school of Alderotto, and that this attention derived from the necessity of summoning logic in order to determine the crucial epistemological connection between natural philosophy and medicine.[70] We also know that del Garbo, like Taddeo Alderotto, paid great attention to the *expositio terminorum*. For this reason, it may be possible to find a connection between this attention to terminology and del Garbo's emphasis (in his commentary on *Donna me prega*) on the theme of passion to which, *ad placitum*, Cavalcanti gives the name 'love.'

If we consider the connection between logic, medicine, and natural philosophy, we may deduce that in *Donna me prega* the terms that define love as 'accidente' (accident) and as 'sensato' (sensate) looked at emphasizing its being as determined from the sensitive soul as a province of natural philosophy. In fact, while 'accident' belongs to both fields, 'sensato' belongs only to the animal body. But while 'accidente' and 'sensato' are technical terms that Cavalcanti relates to love, they help us in designating to what *ad placitum* Guido gives the name 'love,' according to del Garbo's suggestion of love as a name for passion. Moreover, it is not just 'accidente' and 'sensato' that lead us to the being of love. Cavalcanti also introduces two adjectives to determine the being of the accident called love: 'fero' (ferox), and 'altero' (fierce and haughty) Because of them, we must first examine the possible relation linking the two attributes of love. In light of the relation between medicine and natural philosophy, love as 'fero' (ferox), and as something rooted in the sensitive soul can be traced to the debate on animal power ('virtus animalis'), which was active in the school of Taddeo Alderotto. In this case this ferocity of love could be in some way related to a haughty being ('altero'), if we accept that the latter coincides with the natural process that love may initiate and unfold, i.e., with the formative power of *phantasia*.

In asserting that love's name is given *ad placitum*, del Garbo thereby suggests that Cavalcanti was making an *impositio nomen*. It remains to determine whether or not Cavalcanti was, in his canzone, deliberately organizing a theory of *impositio*; and, if this turns out to be the case, what such an *impositio* reveals.

A testimony of Cavalcanti's penchant for *impositio* is given by Dante in chapter 24 of the *Vita nuova*. Here, Cavalcanti is suggested as an 'imponitore del nome' for having imposed on his woman the name 'Primavera.'[71] The fact that Dante interprets this name as 'the woman who comes before' (*Prima-verrà*), when seen in the context of Dante's idea of love, suggests that Dante (who is an *imponitore* too), condenses in the name of Beatrice his own concept of love that opposes Cavalcanti's idea of love.[72] But because love, in Cavalcanti, was a metaphor for introducing a discussion on the soul, it is a debate on the soul that takes place between Dante and Cavalcanti. This is a debate to which the theory of names should also be related if we look not just at Dante's names in the Vita nuova, but also at Guido's *impositio* in *Donna me prega.*

If we accept that Cavalcanti's *impositio* of the name 'love' is, according to del Garbo, *ad placitum,* and if the theme of *Donna me prega* is passion, we may conclude that passion and love in Guido are coincident. The reason is that, for him, passion reveals the ontology of love as rooted in matter.

A recently published collection of studies on logic in Bologna allows us to connect the different positions of Guido and Dino with the debate on *modi significandi.* Gian Carlo Alessio's article, 'Il commento di Gentile da Cingoli a Martino di Dacia,' introduces us to the debate on *modi significandi* and its presence in the work of the Bolognese Gentile da Cingoli in the last decade of the thirteenth century. What he writes about the distinction between *modus significandi activus* and *passivus* suggest, for instance, that Cavalcanti's indication of passion as love is a *modus significandi activus,* in which the intellect understands a thing through its property and proceeds to impose *vox* in order to signify this thing by means of its property.[73] Dino, however, indicating that love is passion, uses what in the discussion is indicated as a passive nomination. He does so in order to give a name that corresponds to the thing he wishes to signify.[74] We may see in this discrepancy a transition from a premodal logic, which asserts the freedom of *impositio* (as in Cavalcanti), to a modal logic (of Boethius of Dacia, for instance), in which 'impositor a proprietate rei regulatur' (he receives his law from the specificity of the thing itself.[75]

If, therefore, the *impositio nomen* and technical terminology can be seen as part of Cavalcanti's attitude toward logic, and if a discussion involving logical tools is active in the relationship between Cavalcanti and Dante from the time of *Vita nuova,* logical tools indeed could preside over the obscurities of *Inferno* X.

Before concluding, I would like to return to Canto X to discuss the ambiguities that Dante places in this canto in relation to Guido Cavalcanti when he is remembered by his father. I discussed this passage in chapter 2. There I introduced logical tools and proposed that Dante had used elements of speculative grammar in order to oppose central contents of *Donna me prega* that Guido includes in a logical account. I now return to this discussion in light of the theory of matter I have proposed as basic for the theory of love as passion in *Donna me prega.*

Matter and Time in Dante's *Inferno* X

In light of what has been said about matter and passion in this chapter, we may pursue a further discussion of *Inferno* X. Hell is the locus of torment for those who subjugated themselves to the laws of matter. Dante introduces his reader to this subjugation to matter through the metaphor of the wood ('selva') at the beginning of the *Inferno.* Whether or not the 'selva' can be connected with matter, Dante's meaning acquires a greater dimension in light of Cavalcanti's theory of passion rooted in matter and the synchronous debate in Paris.[76] However, because this discussion lies outside the present context, I will limit myself to Canto X, beginning with the theory of time that Dante inserts there. In particular, I will focus on the relation between the theory of time and the theory of matter, which I introduced in the previous section, a theory that, in the philosophy of Averroism or radical Aristotelianism, is also related to the death of the individual soul.

In considering the canto devoted to those 'che l'anima col corpo morta fanno,' I shall focus on a possible connection between the theory of time that Dante puts forth in Canto X and the denial of the immortality of the individual soul (which is punished here):

Suo cimitero da questa parte hanno
con Epicuro tutti suoi seguaci,
che l'anima col corpo morta fanno.

(In this part Epicurus with all his followers, who make the soul die with the body, have their burial-place.)

As I have already proposed, in the passage of Canto X in which Guido is mentioned, two ambiguities are deliberately put forth with the aim of attracting the reader's attention. The first is the verb 'ebbe,' which as a remote past tense, induces Cavalcanti's father to believe, erroneously, that his son is dead. The second lies in Dante's use of the pronoun 'cui.'

As many scholars have noted, the line 'forse cui Guido vostro ebbe a disdegno' contains obscurities. My point here is that these are deliberate ambiguities, which logical tools can help us to resolve. In Aristotle's

Sophistical Refutations we read, for instance, that the pronoun can be used as a tool for introducing deliberate obscurities. In this work Aristotle speaks also of apparent solecism introduced through terms that are neither feminine nor masculine but neutral. In addition, he writes that paralogism can be introduced when a term is used in such a way that it can refer to different cases (*Sophistical Refutations*, 14, 173b25–174a). It seems probable that 'cui' can be related to these passages of Aristotle, especially in light of the fact that it is a pronoun, that it is used as a neutral term, and also because its case is ambiguously interpreted.

It is thanks to this ambiguity that the reader of *Inferno* X is introduced to a highly important knot that obliges him to search for a meaning. Such meaning suggests not only that 'cui' can be referred to both Beatrice and Virgil (who are, as already mentioned, representatives of the same values of interiority that Dante wants to put forth), but also that both these figures stress an opposition to Cavalcanti's poetry and its contents. In addition, once read with the tools of a speculative grammar (as I suggested in chapter 2), 'cui' works to organize a field of opposition to 'ebbe.' Both therefore work to emphasize an ambiguity that, once understood, will reveal a meaning. The sense of opposition between that which is related to permanence (according to speculative grammar) and to stability (since 'cui' is a pronoun) and what is related to accidentality and time ('ebbe') acquires a further meaning once we insert 'ebbe' in its own context, that is, in the theory of time on which *Inferno* X focuses.

Earlier, I said that 'ebbe' is inserted in this canto as a strategic tool, which Dante emphasizes through the aorist form 'ebbe' that appears in the line: 'forse cui Guido vostro ebbe a disdegno.' Here the aorist form, although it expresses an action that has taken place in the past, does not necessarily imply that the agent of this action is dead (see chapter 2). I therefore suggest that the aorist ('ebbe') is used in order to call our attention to some specific meaning. Our attention is captured because Cavalcanti's father is deceived precisely by the verb form, that is, the past tense the pilgrim has used and, because that past is thought to imply that Guido, the son, is dead: 'Come?/dicesti 'elli ebbe'? non viv' elli ancora?' (What? Did I hear you say he 'had'? He is not still alive?).

If from one side Cavalcante's words stress the past form 'ebbe,' from the other they organize a metaphor in order to express his answer about Guido's death – an answer that echoes *Donna me prega*. The lines 'non viv' elli ancora?/non fiere li occhi suoi lo dolce lume?' ('He is not still alive? Does the sweet light not strike his eyes?'), which have been read as consonant with *Donna me prega*, require that we search for a connection between Cavalcanti's major canzone and this particular passage of Canto X.[77]

I have already underlined the fact that, as a verb, 'ebbe' is related to the world of change, movement, and becoming, a world which in Aristotle is the being studied by physics. A crucial aspect emerges here if we consider that *Inferno* X is devoted to the torment of those who did not believe in the immortality of the individual soul: 'che l'anima col corpo morta fanno' (who make the soul die with the body). That this belief, put forth by Averroism or radical Aristotelianism, was related to the theory of the eternity of matter has been the subject of discussion previously in this chapter. Here it is sufficient to recall what was previously said: Averroes denied the survival of the individual after death because he thought that the individual has only the sensitive soul, which is subjugated to matter and its eternally recurring cycle of generation and corruption. Averroes, in fact, guaranteed the survival of the common intellect because this, as he says in his *De anima*, is detached from matter and its cycle and belongs to a genus different from that of the sensitive soul. He put forth the view that human beings are eternal *as species* but perishable as individuals.

What is crucial here is the relationship between the theory of the death of the individual soul and the eternity of matter. For Averroes, this eternity guaranteed the eternity of the human genus while at the same time implied the mortality of individuals. In fact, according to the Commentator, while the world as a whole is ungenerated and incorruptible, parts of the world are continually changing. In the cycle of matter, the generation of one substance presupposes the destruction of another. What persists here is not a particular subject in the same form but matter that was elsewhere.[78]

Aristotle's theory of matter is strongly connected with his theory of time. Time for him is nothing other than a measure of the movements of matter. And because matter is eternal, time too is eternal. Time is a measure of the changes that occur in matter. Following Aristotle, the existence of time presupposes the existence of movement and hence of a moving body. Since time is the measure of movement, if it can be established that matter is eternal, then it would follow that time too is eternal. For Aristotle, therefore, the dimensions of 'before,' 'now,' and 'after' are vital aspects of any language involving change and movement.

Averroes followed Aristotle's theory. Like the Stagirite, he thought that 'now' is not a period of time but a limit that marks the end of one period of time and the beginning of another. There is, then, time on both sides of the 'now,' and there could not be a first 'now' with no time before it, nor a last 'now' with no time after it. Therefore, there is no beginning or end of time (*Physics* VIII, 1, 250b–252b).[79]

That Dante had knowledge of Aristotle's theory of time emerges from the *Convivio* IV, ii, 6, where he refers to it.[80] In Canto X, the theory of time is introduced in connection with the sinners who denied the immortality of the soul. This suggests a close relationship between the two themes, which I will attempt to trace.

It is important to emphasize that the denial of the immortality of the individual soul in the field of radical Aristotelianism is dependent on the theory of matter in the same way that time in Aristotelianism is related to matter. In Canto X, the misunderstanding created by 'ebbe' emerges from the fact that the damned have no knowledge of the present, even though they do know the past and the future. For his part the pilgrim does not know what they know. The focus is therefore on their lack of knowledge of the present, as we see in the following lines:

El par che voi veggiate, se ben odo,
dinanzi quel che 'l tempo seco adduce,
e nel presente tenete altro modo.
'Noi veggiam, come quei c'ha mala luce,
le cose,' disse, 'che ne son lontano;
cotanto ancor ne splende il sommo duce.
Quando s'appressano o son, tutto è vano
nostro intelletto; e s'altri non ci apporta,
nulla sapem di vostro stato umano'[81]

(It seems if I hear right, that you see beforehand what time brings with it, but have a different manner with the present. 'Like one who has bad light we see the things,' he said, 'which are remote from us: so much does the Suspreme Ruler still shine on us; but when they draw near, or are, our intelligence is wholly vain, and unless others bring us word, we know nothing of your human state')

According to what we read in Aristotle (*Physics* IV, 11–12, 219b–21a), time is not thinkable apart from the 'now,' and the 'now' is a kind of middle point uniting in itself both a beginning and an end – a beginning of future time and an end of past time.[82] For Dante, the dead have no knowledge of the present. This suggests that they do not have perception of the 'now' – a fact that indirectly calls to mind the theory of time that Aristotle deduces from physics and the motion of sensible substance. The cognition of the damned here evinces the Aristotelian theory, while simultaneously introducing an additional element related to it.[83] According to Aristotle, it is the 'now' that produces time by acting as a boundary between the past and the future. The fact that the damned for Dante have no knowledge of the present, even though they know the past and future, thus functions at one level to deny that they have any notion of time at all. But this awareness on the reader's part can come about only if he inserts this discussion into its proper context, that is, only if he grasps the connection between time and matter that shapes Aristotle's theory of time.

My claim here is that the enigmatic 'ebbe' links the discussion of time with the theory of the death of the soul, and that this connection takes place through the theory of matter and its accompanying necessity. According to Aristotle, time is eternal because matter is eternal. Something, therefore, of the necessity of matter enters into the concept of time. For instance, according to scholars, the principle of potentiality and act, crucial for physics, once related to time generated the principle that every possible will be.[84]

It may therefore be the case that the theory of matter's eternity is the link between the two crucial themes of Canto X: the belief in the death of the individual soul that is punished here and the theory of time.

If we look at the debate that took place in Paris in the second half of the thirteenth century, we may relate Dante's use of the aorist form 'ebbe' to the discussion of the future as antecedently necessary as it emerges in particular from an article among those condemned in 1277:

> Quod nihil fit a casu, sed omnia de necessitate eveniunt, et quod omnia futura, quae erunt, de necessitate erunt, et quae non erunt, impossibile est esse, et quod nihil fit contingenter considerando omnes causas ...

> ('Because nothing happens by chance, but everything happens of necessity, and because future things which will happen, will happen of necessity, and things which will not be – it is impossible they be – nothing contingent happens if we consider all causes ...')[85]

Traces of this debate are also found in a *quaestio* discussed by Siger of Brabante: 'utrum omnia futura necessarium sit fore antequam sint' (if it is necessary that future things will be before they be).[86]

What emerges from these elements is a possible relationship between those topics in which the future events are discussed in terms of necessity, and Dante's introduction of the past tense 'ebbe.' This relationship can be maintained if we connect 'ebbe' to the theory that asserts that future events necessarily will be before they are.

It would be difficult to claim that Dante was explicitly referring to this debate without knowing how much the content of this article (which we find condemned in Paris in the seventies) was related to a discussion that was peculiar to the Middle Ages since the time of Severino Boethius and which is usually referred to as the debate on the future contingent. At its beginning, this debate mainly involved logic and the Aristotelian principle of bivalence.[87] According to Calvin Normore, the object of this debate was to determine whether there is an objective difference between past and future. Traditionally, 'the problems of future contingents arise because there seem to be various principles which connect every statement about the future with a corresponding statement about the past in such a way that it is impossible for one of the statements to be true and the other false. If any such principle is accepted, our intuition about the objective difference between past and future may have to be revised ... the problem of future contingent arises only if the future is antecedently necessary.'[88] Because, according to Normore, the debate on the future contingent arose from Aristotle's *De interpretatione*, chapter 9, and from *Metaphysics* VI, 3,[89] we may assume that the discussion on such topics had involved logic and metaphysics. In the condemnation of 1277, the problem of the future was discussed in terms of necessity; Hissette lists the article 102 which I have quoted above as part of those devoted to necessity and contingency.

We find traces of this debate in Aquinas's commentary on Aristotle's *Metaphysics* VI, 3, in which Aristotle discusses accident and accidentality. To predict the death of someone who is living is something like a corollary that Aristotle introduces in his discussion on accident in order to show that accident cannot be reduced solely to the theory of generation and corruption, and must not be seen only as part of the necessity that presides over matter and the future. Accident says Aristotle, is also chance. I recall this crucial passage of the *Metaphysics* (VI, 3, 1027b), in which, from the theory that the future is determined by the past, Aristotle deduces the death of someone who is living; however, the cause of his death is also by chance: 'Therefore everything that will be, will be of necessity; for example, one who lives shall die; because some part of the process has already been completed, as the presence of contraries in the same body, but whether he will die from illness or violence not has yet been determined, unless something else will have happened.'[90]

Aquinas's commentary on this passage is important for us. Like Aristotle, he asserts that accident is governed by chance and not simply by necessity. It is therefore impossible, he argues, that all future events should happen of necessity.[91] In addition, in order to give an example of how necessity is distinguished from freedom, Aquinas recalls the death of an animal, which death 'is the result of its being composed of contraries as he [Aristotle] mentions in the text.' Aquinas thus comments on this peculiar passage of Aristotle and applies it to an animal. According to Aquinas, necessity rules the world of matter, to which an animal belongs, while the rational soul is free from necessity.[92] It is worth recalling the example Aquinas gives: 'Thus it is possible to hold as true now the antecedent of a conditional proposition in whose antecedent clause there is a past cause and in whose consequent clause there is a future effect. And thus since all future effects must be traced back to such present or past causes, it follows that all future events happen of necessity.'

At this point, he introduces the example I mentioned above as he reads it in Aristotle: 'For example, we say that it is absolutely necessary that one now living is going to die, because this follows of necessity in reference of something that has already come to pass, namely, that there are two contraries in the same body by reason of its composition; for this conditional proposition is true, "If a body is composed of contraries, it will be corrupted."' This last conditional clause is essential if we are to understand Dante's 'ebbe': if we accept that this verb is related to the theory of the necessity of the future, then, by using it, he makes Cavalcanti's corruption necessary. Corruption as necessary, according to Aquinas, applies only to the death of an animal to whom necessity applies. In light of Aquinas's text, which states that something that has happened in the past will of necessity happen in the future, Dante's 'ebbe' applies to Cavalcanti the necessity that shapes the being of the animal, as Aquinas suggests here and again at the end of the same chapter.[93]

The debate on the future contingent was traditionally associated with Aristotle's theory of truth. In light of this theory – as summarized by Calvin Normore – we may say that: 'a sentence is true if things are as the sentence says they are. On one interpretation of this view, a sentence *is* true only if the things that *now are* verify it.' In light of this interpretation, 'ebbe' is manifestly false. But since the debate on the future contingent was connected to Aristotle's theory that the possible will necessarily be (that is, if something is possible, then it will at some point be actual), the same assertion is true because it is antecedently necessary.

According to Hintikka, the future contingent is connected with the 'now' because what now appears false 'in light of Aristotle's principle of plenitude is not false, because if it is possible it will happen means that in the future it will be true.'[94] Therefore in Dante Canto X the *aporia* of the present (Freccero) is the condition for the intentional obscurity that Dante introduces. Because what now appears false is not false because it will happen, it is this absence of the present that allows for both the obscurity and the irony on which it is based. 'Ebbe' as an aorist form makes a future antecedent because this future is necessary, and presents something that has not yet happened as if it had happened in the past. The clarification given in the final part of the canto, where Dante says that Guido is still alive, works to confirm this reconstruction.

In light of what I have proposed, the irony on which Freccero has insisted in his reading of this passage of Canto X finds its crucial reason here: irony works to emphasize the paradox contained in this theory, a paradox that becames visible once applied to the individual.[95] But if we pay attention to the distinction Aquinas has introduced between the world of necessity and the world of freedom (the former being applicable to the animal), we may penetrate the reason why Dante uses this paradox and the meaning he wants to introduce through it. In light of the debate on the future, we may say that 'ebbe' looks at focusing on necessity and matter. The death of Cavalcanti – which is false if read in relation to the 'now' – is true if we organize a syllogism like the following:

1) Future events necessarily will be before they are;
2) In the future, Guido will die necessarily;
3) Therefore, Guido's death is antecedently necessary.

The paradox here focuses on determinism and necessity. In light of necessity, Cavalcanti's death is antecedently necessary. In his commentary on *Metaphysics* VI, 3, Aquinas, who distinguishes between what applies to the animal (necessity) and what applies to the rational soul (freedom), offers the essential key to interpreting the paradox. If the theory of matter presides over the condemned article 102, and if we accept that Dante is referring to the debate on the future contingent as it is shaped in the thirteenth century after the entrance of the new Aristotle and his Arabic commentators, we must then conclude that Dante introduces in the canto devoted to those who believe that the soul dies with the body the problem of necessity, which is part of the theory of matter. By employing a paradox, he rejects matter and its necessity, a necessity that presides over physics and was the same necessity that Cavalcanti had focused on in *Donna me prega* when he discussed love and its ontology.

But Dante's paradox shows that a special kind of *contrappasso* is organized for his best friend. This friend is a living dead man, or better, a dead man still living. The paradox is obtained if we apply to him the necessity that rules animal life. The death of the soul as part of the theory of matter appears confirmed here, together with the correlation between this canto and *Donna me prega*.[96] Boccaccio's obscure sentence in the novella dedicated to Guido – the sentence in which Guido's insolence in treating living people as dead, is inserted in a landscape that recalls that of Dante's Hell (Canto X) – may in some way be the result of his reading of Canto X.

The criticism that has focused on the crucial importance of 'ebbe' in Canto X of *Inferno* and on Cavalcanti as the absent one who imposes his reason appears confirmed.[97] Dante uses one of the issues of the debates of the seventies as a paradox. What is under attack by Dante here is natural philosophy and rational knowledge as the only source of truth. All the values that oppose these themes and methods explain the word 'disdain.' Cavalcanti's disdain includes both Beatrice and Virgil. It is disdain for a poetry and a notion of love built on the betrayal of philosophical rational truth. Important too is the fact that the 'cui' emphasizes an ambiguity deliberately put forth in order to include not only Beatrice but also Virgil, who, according to medieval tradition, celebrates the immortality of the individual soul in his poetry. Beatrice and a kind of poetry that celebrated the immortality of the individual soul are opposed as alternative values to Cavalcanti and the followers of the death of the individual soul. The Parisian debate allows us to understand the framework in which the Dante-Cavalcanti dialogue takes place. Virgil, who from antiquity has been regarded as opposed to the physicist Lucretius, is related to Beatrice. In the same way, Averroism is revealed as part of an old error assumed by Epicurus and his followers. The death of the individual soul as part of the theory of matter is here suggested and reconfirmed.

Chapter Four

Pleasure and Intellectual Happiness: Guido Cavalcanti and Giacomo da Pistoia

Giacomo da Pistoia: Quaestio de felicitate *as a Document of the Debate on Happiness*

During the 1950s, Paul Oskar Kristeller found in the library at Stuttgart a treatise written by Magister Jacobus de Pistoia and dedicated to Guido Cavalcanti. This treatise was the *Quaestio de felicitate.* Kristeller assumed it to be a document of radical Aristotelianism, as had Martin Grabmann before him, who had found the same text in another codex in the Vatican Library. Unlike the Stuttgart codex, the Vatican manuscript did not contain a dedication to the Tuscan poet Guido Cavalcanti. The text was published by Kristeller in the 1950s as part of a collection of studies in honour of the famous scholar Bruno Nardi, since Kristeller had found in this treatise a confirmation of Nardi's reading of *Donna me prega.*[1]

It was the dedication to Cavalcanti that, for Kristeller, confirmed the importance of the relationship between the Faculty of Arts in Bologna (where the *Quaestio* was discussed) and the Tuscan *dolce stil novo,* and hence of the importance of using philosophical tools to read thirteenth-century poetry.

This suggestion has been emphasized in recent years by Maria Corti and is used and quoted in her works on Dante and Cavalcanti. In her book *La felicità mentale,* Corti briefly reconsiders Giacomo da Pistoia's text.[2] She proposes that *Donna me prega* bears traces of Giacomo's influence on Cavalcanti.[3] According to Corti, the text was written between 1290 and 1300 and was one of the documents circulating radical Aristotelianism in Bologna. She reiterates what Kristeller also proposes: that at the basis of Giacomo's treatise is the *De summo bono* of Boethius of Dacia, a famous Parisian scholar suspected of radical Aristotelianism. Corti identifies the theme of intellectual happiness in *Donna me prega* with the *perfectum bonum*, of which she finds an equivalent in the canzone's phrase 'buon perfetto.'[4]

Corti proposes that Giacomo influenced the structure of *Donna me prega*, and that the canzone was conceived probably as an answer to the *Quaestio de felicitate*.[5] Another scholar, D. De Robertis, challenges the importance of Giacomo's *Quaestio* for *Donna me prega*, asserting that the relationship between Giacomo's treatise and Cavalcanti's canzone is difficult to ascertain.[6]

This chapter rereads Giacomo's text with the aim of understanding how, according to Giacomo, it is possible for man to reach happiness, and (crucially) if and how this *quaestio* can be connected to *Donna me prega*. What follows is an attempt to reconsider a few lines of *Donna me prega* in light of the suggestions derived from Giacomo's text. In this reading, I shall not emphasize the *Quaestio de felicitate* as a source of *Donna me prega*. Instead, I will consider it as the document of a debate in which, as Kristeller understood, poets as well as philosophers participated.

According to Kristeller, the *Quaestio* contains a confirmation of Bruno Nardi's reading of Cavalcanti's canzone. As is well known, Nardi was the first to organize the theoretical framework of the canzone by reading it in light of Averroism. Love, in his interpretation, is opposed to the life of the intellect. According to Nardi, love in the metaphor of the canzone – structured around the diaphanous – is therefore dark, and this darkness is located in that part of the soul where memory lies. Unaware of the technical meaning of diaphanous, Nardi reads in that metaphor an opposition between dark and diaphanous and identifies this darkness with love.[7] Since I have explained this metaphor in chapter 2, in this section I will simply verify my interpretation in light of the theory of happiness, with a few important additions.

The reading of Giacomo's *Quaestio*, once compared to some passages of *Donna me prega*, confirms my previous hypothesis that love, while dark for man, is in itself diaphanous – a technical word that Cavalcanti introduces with great skill, encoding in it a complex meaning. In addition, this chapter attempts to explain why a sophistical reasoning presides over this metaphor. That *Donna me prega* is organized as a sophistical refutation is, in light of my inquiry, the central reason, as we shall see, for its construction. My reading therefore appears to confirm the reason for Giacomo's dedication. Cavalcanti was one of the intellectuals who took part in the debate on happiness. While it is difficult to ascertain whether the canzone was written as an answer to Giacomo's *Quaestio*, it does appear evident that it is constructed in order to oppose the thesis of intellectual happiness. The fact that Cavalcanti uses poetry instead of philosophy for his sophistical refutation makes his discussion unique.

In his introduction to the *Quaestio*, Kristeller on the one hand introduces the text into the intellectual debate of the period (presumably the end of the thirteenth century), and on the other hand offers a summary of the themes of the text. According to Kristeller, Giacomo opposes the life of the intellect to the life of the senses, advising *medietas* and temperance. By exposing the theory of *continuatio* through a medium, he also explains the necessity of the sensual life so that man may participate in the process of nature that culminates in intellection.

I will begin by considering the kind of happiness Giacomo illustrates in the treatise as well as the two aspects of being Giacomo considers, namely, the intellectual and the physical. I will propose that Cavalcanti's canzone apparently shares a similar viewpoint with Giacomo's treatise. The importance of the latter largely resides in the fact that Giacomo exposes some aspects of radical Aristotelianism that are crucial in understanding the role that love performs in the canzone. Love is, in fact, seen as an obscure passion and at the same time as a medium – as the 'veduta forma [che s' intende]' – between the two different genera of sense and intellect. This difference of genus is the basic point of radical Aristotelianism common to both Giacomo and Cavalcanti.

Giacomo's treatise is organized as a scholastic *quaestio* – a series of arguments in support of a thesis, and another series of arguments designed to refute the objections raised.[8] According to Kristeller, the main source of the ideas presented in the treatise is Aristotle's *Nichomachean Ethics*, which the author quotes and mentions. There are also references to other works of Aristotle, such as *Physics, Metaphysics, De anima*, etc. The sources of the text are mostly identical to those that Giacomo indicates; however, as Kristeller notes, some of the references are incorrect. The author also cites Averroes and Avicenna. In order to determine the author's position in the thirteenth-century ethics, Kristeller compares Giacomo's position on happiness with that of Aquinas and concludes that, while some elements could be attributed to a common dependence on Aristotle, there are some differences.

The first crucial difference is that, unlike Giacomo, Aquinas denies that perfect happiness involves a kind of contemplation of separate substances. It is also important, as Kristeller points out, that Aquinas distinguishes between the perfect happiness that can be reached only in a future life and the imperfect participation in happiness that may be attained during the present life. Giacomo, for his part, does not make such a distinction and maintains that happiness is proper to *this* life. Implicit therefore in Giacomo's position is a connection with Boethius of Dacia, who, like Giacomo, considers human happiness as something that may be attained by the philosopher in this life.[9]

The six properties Giacomo sets forth as essential for the kind of happiness he is investigating are worthy of examination:

1 'Prima est quod ipsa est summum bonum possibile homini advenire' (Happiness is the *summum bonum* which is possible for man to reach).
2 Happiness is the highest goal of human life ('quod ipsa est ultimus finis humane vitae'). That is, happiness is the *summum bonum* and the ultimate goal of human life.
3 Because of this, happiness 'totaliter quietat humanum appetitum.' That is, it satisfies every human desire ('recte et naturaliter dispositum'). Happiness is the complete satisfaction of human desire.
4 Happiness is a kind of good that is completely sufficient unto itself ('quod est bonum per se sufficientissimum'), and this sufficiency derives from the fact that human beings desire that which they need, and for that it suffices.
5 This good is uniquely a good for man ('bonum proprium ipsius hominis') and is not shared by animals or plants.
6 This good must be a property of and an operation carried out by man ('Sexta et ultima proprietas et condicio est quod est bonum possessum et operatum ab homine').[10]

The logical sequence of the treatise must be underlined, since Cavalcanti's fame as a *loico* and a *filosofo naturale* could help explain the reason for the dedication. There is a common inclination to employ the tools of logic in order to reach knowledge. But while Giacomo's goal appears to be ethics, Cavalcanti's goal appears to be the science of the soul as part of the philosophy of nature. When he introduces ethics, he shows, in fact, that the law of ethics is opposed to the principles of nature of which the body's passions are part. Thus, when he introduces the 'buon perfetto' (the perfect good, i.e., intellectual happiness), he does so in order to state that love is different from it because of 'sorte' (destiny, necessity): 'che da buon perfetto tort'è/ per sorte.'

Cavalcanti begins his discussion with natural philosophy, of which animal being is a part, and then proceeds to inquire whether and how animal life, which is different in genus from intellect, can enter into a relation with intellect. Giacomo begins by considering the highest grade of being to be the intellectual. He asserts that 'bona corporis are propter bona anime,' and that the sensitive soul is 'propter intellectiva.' He proceeds to show that however essential it may be to the life of the intellect, the animal being is fundamentally opposed to that life. In order to connect the two different genera, he has recourse to the Averroistic theory of *continuatio* or continuity, that is, the gradation in nature. Through this theory, the Commentator had made an accidental unity between the different levels of reality. This connection had been entrusted by Averroes to the medium as an accident that temporarily connects different levels of reality.

What must be emphasized here is that the intellect, however separate, i.e., independent, enters into an accidental connection with the lower level through the medium. Through this connection, Giacomo offers the theory of nature's gradual ascent, which takes place through a medium. This theory is introduced in the *Quaestio*:

natura duplicem modum servat in educendo materiam ad nobilissimam formam que est anima intellectiva. Primo enim removet contrarias dispositiones impedientes, secundo ordinate procedit incipiendo a prima forma et veniendo ad formas intermedias gradatim. Primo enim inducit ipsam formam elementi, et mediantibus formis elementorum, inducit formam mixti, sicut dicit Commentator tertio Celi et mundi, et mediante forma mixti introducit formam vivi, et mediante forma vivi introducit formam sensitivi, qua mediante introducit formam nobilissimam que est anima intellectiva. Et introducendo formam mixti unam formam introducit mediante alia. Et breviter iste videtur esse processus nature que gradatim procedit de extremo ad extremum per medium, sicut dicit Aristoteles septimo de historiis animalium. [11]

(Nature works in two ways in order to lead matter toward the noblest form, which is the intellective soul. At first it removes the inclinations that oppose this process; then, it continues, starting from the first form and gradually going toward the intermediate forms. Initially, it leads the form of the elements, and through them, generates the form that is mixed, as the Com-

mentator says in *tertio Celi et mundi*, and through the mixed form generates
the living form, and through the living form generates the sensitive form,
and through it, introduces the noblest form, which is the intellective soul.
And in introducing the mixed form, it introduces one form through the
other. In brief it may be seen that this is the process of nature, which gradually proceeds from one extreme to another through a medium, as Aristotle says in the seventh book of *De historia animalium.*)

Giacomo introduces the process of nature as a gradual ascent that
takes place through a medium. In this process, the theory of the
medium is useful in connecting the different levels of the natural process and therefore the three souls that Giacomo distinguishes (generative, sensitive, intellective). In order to emphasize how this theory is not
orthodox, I introduce the criticism of this theory as recalled in
Aquinas's *Summa contra Gentiles* (II, 58). Here Aquinas opposes the theory that diverse souls are within us: 'Si igitur anima intellectiva, sensitiva,
et nutritiva sunt diversae virtutes aut formae in nobis, ea quae secundum
has formas nobis conveniunt, de invicem praedicabuntur per accidens'
(Accordingly, if in us the intellective, sensitive, and nutritive soul are
diverse powers or forms, then the things that appertain to us according
to those forms will be predicated of one another by accident).
Aquinas deduces (ch. 58) that if three souls are in man as different
forms, a man is not a single being but rather a plural being. In addition,
if the soul is not one in itself, it is necessary to introduce something to
unify the different parts:

Si igitur ponantur in homine plures animae sicut diversae formae, homo
non erit unum ens, sed plura ... Item adhuc redibit praedictum inconve-
niens ut scilicet ex anima intellectiva et corpore non fiat unum simpliciter,
sed secundum accidens tantum ... Adhuc. Ex duobus aut pluribus non
potest fieri unum si non sit aliquid uniens.

('Consequently, if several souls as many distinct forms are ascribed to man,
he will not be one being but several ... Also the impossibility noted above
will again arise, namely, that from the intellective soul and the body there
results a thing that is one, not unqualifiedly speaking but only accidentally
... And again, the one cannot be made from two or more, without something to unite them.')

Upon comparing this text with Giacomo's, we find that the *Quaestio* takes the position that Aquinas opposes: the *anima*, having plural forms, needs a medium to unify them. What Giacomo's theory implies may be better understood by reading chapter 59 of Book II of the *Summa contra Gentiles*. Here Aquinas openly refers to Averroes in discussing the following: 'Quod intellectus possibilis hominis non est substantia separata' (that for man the possible intellect is not a separate substance).[12]

What is under attack here is the theory that the possible intellect is separate and is not, therefore, the act of the body. I quote: 'ex his autem motus est Averroes et quidam Antiqui ut ipse [Averroes] dicit, ad ponendum intellectum possibilem, quo intelligit anima, esse separatum secundum esse a corpore, et non esse formam corporis'[13] (Now for these reasons Averroes was moved, and, as he himself says, some of the ancients, to hold that the possible intellect, by which the soul understands, has a separate existence from the body, and is not the form of the body).

Aquinas criticizes Averroes's theory, according to which this intellect, even separated, continues with us in a way determined by the same intellect. This way, explains Aquinas, is reached through 'forma intellecta in actu,' and everything connected to this 'forma intellecta' is connected to the possible intellect, and in turn connected to us through phantasms. In this way, the possible intellect continues with us.

What Aquinas opposes here is the connection and the medium through which the connection takes place, that is, the 'formam intellegibilem intellectui.' The object of this discussion and the very thing that Aquinas rejects is useful to explain what Giacomo and Guido accept and share: the theory that the intellect is a substance that is separate from that of the body and is not the act of the body. Because of this separation, Giacomo, as we have seen, introduces the theory of medium and Cavalcanti, as we shall see, the process of form to be intellected.

Love as the *virtus*, that is, the animal power that enables the natural process to unfold gradually through the medium, i.e., the phantasm or form, propounds a theory of the medium in *Donna me prega* in which the level of sensuality is apparently essential in attaining the highest level of the intellect. Through the 'veduta forma [che s' intende],' the process of form is identified with love.

Cavalcanti's position therefore presents certain similarities to Giacomo's *Quaestio*. Here, in Giacomo, the expression 'mediantibus' in fact indicates the *media* that operate the connections between the three different souls (generative ['forma vivi'], sensitive, and intellective). A medium (and/or form) has the peculiarity of participating in the different levels in order to connect them. The process of nature is a continuum culminating in the *coniunctio* in virtue of the medium or phantasm that allows the connection between the sensible soul and the intellectual. This continuum is therefore at the centre of Giacomo's *Quaestio,* and *coniunctio* is what Giacomo indicates as basic for happiness.

It is therefore important to compare the main theses proposed by Giacomo with *Donna me prega* in order to see whether, in Cavalcanti's canzone, we find a connection with some of the themes presented in the *Quaestio.* As we shall see, Cavalcanti introduces the same theory of *coniunctio* that Giacomo does. He does so, however, in order to criticize it.

Happiness, writes Giacomo, consists of 'operatione illius partis animae in qua est sapientia tamquam in subiecto.' This happiness lies in a contemplative operation of the intellect. Here, Giacomo recalls Aristotle's *Nicomachean Ethics.* Happiness in its highest form is an operation of the speculative intellect, and this happiness is an activity of the intellect (*intelligere*), which in Giacomo's text is written with a caesura, so that it may be understood as an act of 'intus/legere.'

Giacomo proceeds to a discussion of the peculiarities of this activity of speculative intellect, explaining that it must have as an object that which is the highest in nobility and intelligibility. What is therefore important is the object of contemplation, a contemplation that must be continuous and therefore exercised to the highest degree. And because its nobility derives from the object on which this activity operates, this object must be God or separate substances.

The process of nature in Giacomo has as its aim this intellectual happiness, which takes place through *coniunctio.* This process and *coniunctio* are also at the centre of *Donna me prega.* But Cavalcanti, as we shall see, focuses on this process and on *coniunctio* in order to refute the thesis of intellectual happiness. Apparently, the 'veduta forma' that will be intellected in *Donna me prega* is introduced as the medium that connects the sensitive and intellective souls, which, as Giacomo also affirms, differ in genus (the genus of the intellective soul being different in its substance from that of the sensitive soul). Under this aspect, Cavalcanti seems therefore to follow the thesis of intellectual happiness.

However, in *Donna me prega* – as I will show – the *coniunctio* does not allow intellection for the individual. Because Cavalcanti does not accept that man intellects in the *coniunctio, Donna me prega* refutes Giacomo's belief in man's intellectual happiness. *Donna me prega* underlines the distinction between the genus of the sensitive soul and that of the intellective soul by introducing two different words – 'diletto' (suggested as the happiness of the sensitive soul) and 'consideranza' (line 27) (as the happiness of the intellective soul). These two words are used in order to emphasize that to every genus there corresponds a different kind of happiness. This distinction introduces an aspect of Cavalcanti's originality in approaching the common theme. According to Cavalcanti, corporeal 'diletto' is in fact not a negative being at all but, on the contrary, the only kind of happiness that the individual can experience. From this we may establish that while the debate focuses on intellectual happiness, Cavalcanti introduces another happiness as the proper happiness for love: pleasure ('diletto').

I will begin by examining a section of stanza 2 of *Donna me prega*, in which Cavalcanti devotes several lines to the activity of the intellect: '[possibile intelletto] ... da qualitate non descende:/resplende – in sé perpetüal effetto;/non ha diletto – ma consideranza;' ([the possible intellect] ... does not derive from quality; it shines in itself as perpetual effect; it does not have pleasure but rather contemplation).

Here, in just a few lines, Cavalcanti condenses the theory of the possible intellect as separate: 'in se' means that it is for itself, operating in 'consideratio,' which is continuous and always in act ('perpetüal effetto'), and this activity is opposed to the world of physics ('da qualitate non descende'). 'Qualitas' is one of the Aristotelian categories, which define the sensible substance of physics.

In the lines I have quoted, we may read the theory of the possible intellect, which is separate from physics and also belongs to a different genus. It is evident, therefore, that its activity is suggested as a being substantially different from the animal power that originates the activity of love, so that while love forms part of physics (because it belongs to the sensitive soul), the intellect is for itself separate. The word 'consideranza,' which Cavalcanti introduces, therefore contains an important meaning: it suggests something that Cavalcanti's *conoscente* understands with ease. Cavalcanti in fact opposes the 'consideranza' of the possible intellect to the 'diletto' of the sensitive soul. In Averroes's *De anima* (a text Giacomo refers to), the word 'consideratio' is related to the activity of the intellect. 'Consideratio,' writes Averroes, belongs just to what is 'in actu (et quod est in actu est simile ad considerare),' and is useful for indicating the world of intellect, which is always in act and does not depend on sensation: 'et ideo homo potest intelligere cum voluerit sed non sentire quia indiget sensato.'[14]

Cavalcanti's word 'consideranza' invites us to look at the world of pure actuality as a world of continuity ('perpetüal effetto'). This continuity is opposed to physics and sensation, which Cavalcanti essentially indicates when he defines love as 'an accident.' Cavalcanti's 'consideranza' includes this activity of contemplation of separate substances for the possible intellect. 'Consideranza' involves an extremely precise terminology. According to scholars, the meaning of the word 'considerare' during the Middle Ages was derived from the Latin *cum-sidera*.[15] As is well known, in Book XII of the *Metaphysics*, Aristotle introduces the eternal substances or intelligences as movers of the heavens. The word 'consideranza' involves an activity of contemplation of separate substances, as well as the notion that the possible intellect is separate. Its activity consists of an act of intellection of what is separate since its being and activity are *cum sidera*. And because the active intellect was conceived as a separated substance too, the possible intellect considers the agent but also considers those abstract things (species) that participate in the nature of the intellect.[16] 'Consideranza' therefore introduces the sphere of abstract knowledge as the perfect knowledge that belongs to what is per se, i.e., is detached from the sensible.

But what is the nature of the possible intellect? Giacomo states: 'viso autem quid est ultima felicitas hominis et in quod consistat ... unde et commentator in tertio de anima dicit ipsum esse novum genus materie' (p. 453). Reading the passage of Averroes's *De anima* mentioned by Giacomo, we find that the nature of the intellect is 'quasi' that of light.[17] *Donna me prega* follows the same line. In stanza 2 we read, in fact, that the possible intellect 'shines,' and that its light is always in act ('resplende – in sé perpetüal effetto').

At this point, it is relatively easy to understand that in Cavalcanti love, rooted as it is in the field of accidentality, is in itself opposed to the light of intellect that is perpetual and always actual. In addition, because this intellect knows only abstract things, 'consideranza' introduces the perfection of the abstract sphere as a being in itself opposed to the imperfect world of sensual cognition – the world to which love belongs.

But crucial questions arise. The first has to do with the relationship between the Averroism of Giacomo (which is radical, according to Kristeller) and that of Paris (also radical), which asserts that 'homo non intellegit.'[18] Giacomo's *Quaestio* apparently proposes a more moderate point of view wherein 'homo intellegit,' that is, man engages in the activity that is most important to him.

Could it be said that Giacomo's position is not Averroistic? And is there a relationship between the positions of Cavalcanti and Giacomo?

The answer to the first question is an easy one. Giacomo is indeed a radical Averroist. However, Giacomo's assertion that man possesses intellectual activity even though the intellect is separate (which appears in a crucial section of the *Quaestio*), shows that Giacomo's position is different from that of Parisian radical Averroism, according to which man does not intellect.

Reading the Averroistic commentary on *De anima* II (which Giele has listed as radical in *Trois commentaires anonymes*), we may understand that the theory present in Giacomo is part of an Averroism that accepts the following: however much the intellect is separate, man thinks, that is, he exercises an activity of thinking insofar as the medium brings about the accidental connection. This seems also to be the position of Boethius of Dacia in his *De summo bono*. This, however, is a position that the radical text published by Giele opposes because in the *coniunctio*, pure intellectual activity does not belong to man but to the possible intellect alone.[19] According to Giacomo the passage from one level to the other takes place through a medium. It is this medium that guarantees that man's sensitive soul will be connected to the higher level of *consideratio*, the medium that brings about the connection. That is, on one side this possible intellect copulates with phantasms generated by the sensitive soul and abstracts them; on the other, this intellect has an activity of contemplating separate substances. Form acts as a medium that connects the sensitive soul to the separate intellect. Only through form does the individual human enter into a relationship with the possible intellect and perform an intellectual activity.

Grammar and Knowledge in Donna me prega

In light of what has been said, we may give an answer to the other question related to *Donna me prega*: what is Cavalcanti's position on the issue of happiness?

Cavalcanti's answer to the theory of happiness and his own way of considering the theory of *coniunctio* may be read in those lines of his canzone that interpreters have found to be the most problematic:

> Vèn da veduta forma che s' intende,
> che prende – nel possibile intelletto,
> come in subietto, – loco e dimoranza.
> In quella parte mai non ha possanza
> perché da qualitate non descende:

resplende – in sé perpetüal effetto;
non ha diletto – ma consideranza;
sì che non pote largir simiglianza.

([Love] derives from a seen form that is intellected, that takes place and
dwelling in the possible intellect as in a substance. In that part [love] never
has any power. Since it does not derive from quality, it shines in itself as perpetual effect; it does not have pleasure but rather contemplation; and thus
it cannot create likeness.)

These lines relate love to the process of form and to the theory of
coniunctio. In order to explain the process of form, Cavalcanti follows
the same theory Averroes had introduced (and Giacomo follows), that
is, the notion of continuity as the accidental connection established
between the common possible intellect and the multitude of individuals, through the intelligible form, which is ambiguous. It is located on
the one hand in the possible intellect and presents identical properties
of eternity. On the other hand, it has as its subject the sensible image,
and under this aspect it is transitory. Through form, there is therefore a
connection between the material and intellectual, but this connection
does not take place between the same kinds of substance.[20] This was a
point of debate in the thirteenth century[21] that emerged from Averroes's *De anima* III, where we read the following: 'necesse est etiam ut
intellecta in actu habeant duo subiecta, quorum unum est subiectum
per quod sunt vera, scilicet forme quae sunt ymagines vere, secundum
autem est illud per quod intellecta sunt unum entium in mundo, et
istud est intellectus materialis' (It is necessary that in the act of intellection there be *two subjects*, one of which is the subject for which we have
true things, that is, forms that are images, and the other is the subject
through which the intellected things are the common being of the
world, and this is the material intellect [emphasis added]).[22]

Returning to the lines I quoted from Cavalcanti's canzone, we may
easily understand them if we respect the two subjects that Averroes has
put forth. In fact, Cavalcanti, following this line of thought, puts forth
two logical subjects in this section of *Donna me prega* and obliges his
reader to follow his changes of subject in order to get the meaning he
wants to introduce. Lines 21–8 (quoted above) use the change of subject as a tool in order to show that the subject changes because the substance changes. This is the meaning that may be obtained: Love derives
from a form that has been seen and thence intellected. This form takes

place in the possible intellect as an accident ('in subietto'). It has no power in that realm (the realm of the possible intellect) because it (the possible intellect) does not derive from quality, i.e., it is not subject to alteration. It (the possible intellect) shines within itself with continuity; it has no pleasure but rather an intellectual activity ('consideranza').

These lines inform the learned reader that the change of subject that takes place at line 25, 'perché da qualitate non descende,' (since it [the possible intellect] does not derive from quality) is the means by which two different orders of being enter into connection through the phantasm, as a form to be intellected. On the one hand, the phantasm, because it has been generated by the sensitive soul, belongs to it; but at the same time, because it is intellected from the possible intellect, it belongs (accidentally) to the possible intellect itself. However, as we shall see, a subtler distinction needs to be made if we are to understand Cavalcanti's position.

Cavalcanti displays great mastery in not explicating the logical subject of 'non descende.' This subject is the possible intellect, which, according to what we read, does not derive from quality, the latter being a category that belongs to the sensible substance. The passage powerfully introduces the process of form itself. Indeed, in the first four lines the subject is the sensible form; but in the next three lines, the subject is the new genus of the possible intellect, to which the abstract form is assimilated.

How Cavalcanti develops his own point of view is of the utmost importance. I return therefore to stanza 2 and to the break this stanza exhibits by introducing two subjects in the process.

In stanza 2 of *Donna me prega*, grammar is subordinated to the philosophical meaning. Of interest here is that Cavalcanti emphasizes the very thing that enables the reader to distinguish the being of intellect from the being of love. He organizes – through the 'form' – an apparent continuity through different levels and exposes its content, breaking the continuity of grammar in order to expose the break that takes place in the process he is describing. The laws of rhetoric are subject to the laws of ascent from physics to metaphysics. Because the logical subject here is love, he follows it through the correlated object, which is the form. The being of love is the being (process) of form itself. Because the genus of the intellect differs from that of the sensitive soul, he breaks the grammatical continuity by introducing two subjects. While apparently reproducing the tenets of Averroistic *coniunctio*, in reality they work to emphasize the break as derived from the two different genera that enter into a connection that is purely accidental. This break is the sign of a *sottiglianza* (subtlety) used in order to explain the process, which at a certain level belongs to physics and beyond that level to the separate substance of the possible intellect.

In this regard, it is worth examining Cavalcanti's use of grammar in the following line: 'Vèn da veduta forma che s'intende' ([Love] derives from a seen form that is intellected). Grammar here is used ambiguously in order to respect the order of the process in which the seen form which belongs to the sensitive soul, is understood by a subject (the possible intellect) that is given here without being determined. The relative pronoun 'che' (the phantasm) is here a grammatical subject of a passive verb form. In other words, the subject suffers an action that is exercised on it ('che si intende: quae est intellecta').[23]

It is crucial to both Averroes and Averroism that in the process of intellection (which starts from imagination), imagination belongs to physics, that is, to corporeal sensibility, while the act of intellection belongs to the intellect. But because physics and intellect represent two different orders of being, Cavalcanti takes recourse to grammar to show that through the relative pronoun 'che' (that) – grammatically a subject but used as being acted upon in the act of intellection – a relationship is established between two different orders of being. In this relationship, even though it is the phantasm that makes the link, the activity of intellection is not performed by it. In fact, we know that in the process, the form is intellected by a different subject – the possible intellect, which is of a different genus from that of the sensitive soul. It is this sensitive soul that generates the form to which the phantasm belongs. We understand, then, that the pronoun 'che' ('che s' intende') is introduced as having the function which is peculiar to the phantasm – that of connecting the two subjects that enter into the *coniunctio* (the sensitive soul and the intellective soul). But at the same time the passive form of the verb 's'intende' emphasizes the subordinate role of the sensible since the act of intellection is performed by the separate being of intellect.

Line 22–3 continue to describe the unfolding of the process: 'che prende – nel possibile intelletto, /come in subietto, – loco e dimoranza (that takes place and dwelling in the possible intellect as in a substance). Here, the relative pronoun 'che' performs an action; 'che' is a pronoun for the form that takes place in the possible intellect as 'in subietto,' that is, as an accident. This is the technical meaning of 'in subietto,' according to Aristotle and Aristotelism.[24] 'Loco' and 'dimoranza' point to the temporary status of this presence because it is 'in subietto.' The form has no power there.

'In quella parte mai non ha possanza' makes evident that here the reference is to the sensible qualities of form. Hitherto, the subject of the discussion had been the pronoun 'che' for form. Abruptly, in the following line ('perchè da qualitate non descende'), an additional explication is furnished in which 'perché' works as a causal preposition. The verb it introduces, 'non descende,' does not refer to the form-phantasm but rather introduces the sphere of the new genus, that of the separate intellect, to which the abstract form belongs. It is this new genus that functions as a new subject.

Cavalcanti disorients his reader in order to explicate the process of the form itself. The change of subject is introduced in line 25 as a strategic tool. The sensible qualities of the phantasm have no power in the possible intellect: this phantasm has been solely an object of the possible intellect. For its part, this new genus of the possible intellect becomes the new subject. The reason for this is explained in the following three lines. Here we read the destiny of the form itself (now abstract) that the learned reader knows is now included in the sphere of the possible intellect. The intellect (as well as the abstract form) belongs to the sphere of continuity; it has *consideranza*; that is, it considers the separate entities. In the act of intellection, it is not the phantasm that intellects but the new genus of the possible intellect.

The final line of stanza 2 – 'Sì che non pote largir simiglianza' – introduces a problem of exegesis. The ambiguity of this line is worthy of further consideration. In order for it to be understood, we must see what this phrase has to be referred to, what its logical subject is. Here the reader is compelled to decide. A natural philosopher will connect 'simiglianza' with 'qualitate.' In fact, in Aristotle's *Categories* 11a 15, we read: 'Things may be said to be like (or similar) or to be unlike each other only with respect to quality; for one thing may be like another with respect to quality ... and nothing else. Thus, it is a property of quality that things are said to be like or unlike each other with respect to quality.' This tells us that the sensible form has no power in the sphere of intellect ('in quella parte'). That is, its sensible being (quality) cannot enter into a relationship of likeness with the intellect since the intellect belongs to a different genus. In other words, it is not the sensible form that performs the activity of intellection. However, because the reader can also understand that the intellect does not allow a likeness of itself in the sensible, the line, 'Sì che non pote largir simiglianza,' shows that this additional ambiguity is introduced deliberately in order to focus on a precise meaning, i.e., the difference between the sensible form and the intellectual genus. It is in fact made explicit here that the process of form is not that of *continuatio*.

Love and Happiness

The previous analysis shows that at the centre of the process that speaks of the *coniunctio*, Cavalcanti deliberately focuses on the process of form as useful for designating the break between the sensitive qualities of the phantasm and the abstract being of the intellect through which the act of intellection is performed. This break has a precise meaning: the act of intellection does not belong to the sensible qualities of the phantasm. The break between the sensitive soul and the possible intellect is not just because they differ in genus (this was also present in Giacomo), and not just because the *coniunctio* is accidental, but rather because the properties of the sensible in this process are lost.[25] The break shows that bodily perfection is completely different from the perfection of the intellect. In the *coniunctio* a human being does not perform an activity of intellection.

My claim here focuses on evaluating the ambiguity of the text. This is a deliberate ambiguity that Cavalcanti puts forth as a tool for showing the process of *coniunctio* as a break rather than as continuity. What is crucial here is to distinguish the world of physics from that of the intellect. Lines 21–8 deliberately organize an ambiguity that, while indicating the ambiguity of the form itself (as something that belongs to two different spheres), at the same time implies that in the *coniunctio* the sensible has no power. These lines suggest not only that there form is ambiguous, but also that the central ambiguity consists in giving the name love to the process of *coniunctio*. It is this nomination *ad placitum* that reveals Cavalcanti's method of exposing the process of *coniunctio* in order to oppose the opinion that identifies man's intellection with *coniunctio*. This is an opinion that not only Giacomo but also many Schoolmen in that period accepted and emphasized.

According to Aristotle's *Sophistical Refutations*, dialectical reasoning is the reasoning that deduces from premises based on opinion conclusions that are contrary and contradict the premises. This is the method Cavalcanti introduces in the reasoning of *Donna me prega*, which structures the discussion of love as a refutation. By depicting love as the process of form apparently connecting the two genera, he introduces a strategic ambiguity. He seems to accept, in fact, the theory of *coniunctio*. But in reality he transforms it into an examination in order to show that in the conjunction, man does not intellect. This implies that intellectual happiness does not pertain to man.

In the explanation that I have given, Cavalcanti focuses on the process that Giacomo indicates as *continuatio* and gives it a (new) name – love, which he endows with the specific quality of generating the medium between the sphere of the sensitive soul and the intellect. The process that the form undergoes is the process of love itself. The metaphor of the diaphanous contains the concept of its process, its dual being. The process of form is initiated because of love. This is the same process on which Giacomo had focused.

Love, here, appears to be a metaphor, the function of which is to introduce the discussion of the sensitive soul and its relationship with the intellective soul. *Donna me prega* contains a theory of *coniunctio* through the 'veduta forma che s' intende' that Cavalcanti includes in his discussion of love. He establishes a correlation between love and form. Just as form lives as a dual being (both part of the sensitive soul and participating in a passive way in the intellective), so too love participates indirectly (through the form it has generated) in a dual being, of which the highest is active in the moment in which the form, being intellected, becomes an accident of the intellect. Love, for Cavalcanti, involves precisely this same process.

But what Cavalcanti demonstrates is that, although this *coniunctio* (conjunction) takes place, man knows and lives only the sensual part of it. Whatever the extent to which this form is generated by man, it lives on a superior level since it is accidentally connected to the superior order of intellect. The name given to this double being in the process is 'forma,' but Cavalcanti explains that love 'vèn da veduta forma che s' intende' and therefore he relates 'love' to the very process of this 'forma,' which, during the process of abstraction, is an accidental ('in subietto') object of the intellect.

While Giacomo focuses on happiness as an intellectual happiness, Cavalcanti focuses on love. The two different foci are signals of two different attitudes and, as we shall see, of two different beliefs. Cavalcanti is interested in physics, to which man's individuality (sensitive soul) belongs, while Giacomo is interested in ethics and metaphysics.

We may conclude that, in the canzone, Cavalcanti responds to the debate concerning happiness by opposing Giacomo's point of view and/or the point of view of those who affirm the possibility of philosophical happiness. According to Cavalcanti, love offers a great potential in that it can generate the form for the *coniunctio*. Nevertheless, man knows only the sensible being of love. It is evident here that Guido uses love to reveal man's relation to knowledge. Love generates the phantasm through which the *coniunctio* takes place. But Cavalcanti looks at man's condition in the intellective process. He does not follow the illusion that Giacomo embraces.

In addition, by giving the name 'love' to the process, Cavalcanti makes the sensitive soul the protagonist of the process, thus focusing the discussion on its role in cognition. The laws of matter, the accidentality of the conjunction with the intellect, and the phantasm as an *obietto* in the process of intellection – all this is what Cavalcanti's poetry points to. By calling this process 'love,' Cavalcanti celebrates the power of the sensitive soul and, at the same time, its subordinate role in the cognitive process. We may therefore regard Cavalcanti as providing a turning point in the contemporary intellectual debate: he reverses the terms of the discussion by making the sensitive soul central. His accent is on the individual insofar as the sensitive soul belongs to the individual and represents the individual's power.

Relating this process to love, Cavalcanti links love to the ambiguity that is also a property of the form, which partakes of both the sensitive and the superior being of the separate intellect. It is said of the form that, as an abstracted species, it participates in the life of the possible intellect and exhibits identical properties, such as eternity. At the same time, it has as its subject the sensible image and hence is perishable. The second stanza of the canzone states that love is involved in this process, and thus the ambiguities of the phantasm are attributable to it. In this context, the word 'ambiguity' refers to something that exists in two different spheres and possesses different properties. The power of the canzone lies in its creation of a new kind of 'trobar clus,' one that uses obscurity in order to introduce a precise meaning: love (as the process of the phantasm) reveals the double genus of sense and intellect, the accidentality of *coniunctio*, and the subordinate role performed by the sensitive soul. This indirectly suggests an answer to the much-debated question of intellectual happiness.

As we have seen, intellectual happiness is based on a *consideranza* in which the sensitive soul of a human being, according to Cavalcanti, cannot participate. This nonparticipation testifies to the break between the two genera and the break between the two kinds of happiness (the intellectual and the sensual). Love can offer the form for intellection, but it cannot unify the two different genera. Intellectual happiness is not for the individual being. And the name 'love,' attributed to the becoming of form, is a way of asserting that the sensitive soul does not perform an act of intellection, but instead merely offers the form to be intellected. To this break between the two genera there corresponds a break between two different kinds of happiness. But the happiness of 'consideranza' is totally different from the 'diletto' (pleasure) of the senses. To understand Cavalcanti's method here, we must refer to the synchronous debate that, in its radical positions, denied that in the *coniunctio* man intellects. Aquinas's *De unitate intellectus contra Averroistas* is a document of this debate.

Another document, probably conceived (according to scholars) as an answer to Aquinas, is in the anonymous *Quaestiones* on the *De anima*, published by Giele. Gieles's text is extremely useful for understanding the different positions of Cavalcanti and Giacomo da Pistoia. Both Cavalcanti and Giacomo refer to the theory of *coniunctio*. But while Giacomo accepts it, Cavalcanti refers to it in order to criticize it. Guido's radical position appears to be similar to that put forth in the *Quaestiones* on the *De anima*, published by Giele. Here the conjunction is referred to in order to deny that the human being has knowledge through it.[26]

In light of this analysis, the reasoning of *Donna me prega* emerges as a refutation. What Cavalcanti rejects is not the process in itself but rather the role the human being plays in it.

Animal Power

A Theory of Pleasure in Donna me prega

The reading I have offered in the previous section is confirmed in the last stanza of the canzone, where Cavalcanti gives his answer to the last question – whether it is possible for man to see love. I have already discussed the importance of this section in relation to optics in chapter 2. At this point, I will focus on it in relation to the two opposed terms: 'consideranza' and 'diletto.'

In stanza 2, the discussion was centred on love. Here in stanza 5 the subject of discussion is man's relation to love. In this section, Cavalcanti explains, in terms of the metaphor of the diaphanous, that man cannot see love, and that he can only have an experience of love's darkness. Man generates the phantasm but he knows only its sensitive being. Since the form is visible only when illuminated, man can participate in the process only in relation to the form but only insofar as the form lives its sensitive being – not when the form is illuminated by the light of the intellect, that is, when it dwells in its abstract being. The process of intellection requires human participation, but intellection does not belong to human nature.

Related to this point is the final assertion that the pleasure of love resides in this darkness. The last stanza is crucial if we are to understand what *Donna me prega* implies. The break between the genera of intellect and of the sensitive soul implies a different kind of happiness for these genera. Intellectual happiness cannot satisfy the animal power from which love originates. The disjunction between the two genera, as exposed in lines 21–8 of the canzone, is important to our understanding of the last lines of stanza 5, which focus on the 'mercede' that satisfies love. 'Diletto' (line 27) is the pleasure that satisfies man because he is an animal. The theoretical understanding of Cavalcanti's position is therefore reached when stanza 2 is read in relation to stanza 5. In fact, it is here that we find a clear confirmation of Cavalcanti's radical Averroism.

As we have seen, radical Averroism asserts that *coniunctio* takes place between two different genera and through a medium. In other words, the intellective soul is not the act of the body. Giacomo and Cavalcanti both share this belief. But an even more radical position is the assertion that in the conjunction, man does not intellect. We may list Giacomo's position as radical – and Cavalcanti's among the most radical – because, like the anonymous text published by Giele, he asserts that although the process of form takes place, in this process man does not intellect.

In light of this point, the radicalism of Cavalcanti's position also emerges if we understand that he puts forth two kinds of happiness – intellectual and animal. But by assigning to love the animal happiness or 'diletto' (pleasure), he asserts that intellectual happiness does not belong to the individual sensitive soul. Cavalcanti not only emphasizes the impossibility of reconciling intellectual reasons with animal reasons, body's happiness with intellectual happiness; he also denies that the happiness of 'buon perfetto' (line 39) can be happiness for the sensitive soul. That Cavalcanti's position may have emerged from the medical ambiance to which his poetry appears related is strongly suggested if we consider Taddeus Alderotto's work and the attention he devotes to what he calls animal power. The definition of animal power was a topic of discussion for Taddeo. He was critical of Avicenna's definition because it did not include intellectual activity among the functions of 'virtus animalis.' According to Alderotto, 'virtus animalis' is the power of producing voluntary motion, sense perception, and intellection. He considered also 'imaginatio' as part of 'virtus rationalis.' It is difficult to ascertain what he means by asserting that 'virtus intellectiva' is among the powers of 'virtus animalis.' Alderotto seems to point out that in man, animality encloses the power of individual intellection, which is coincident with the activity of the (compositive) human imagination, that is, the formative activity or cogitative.[27] But in relation to Cavalcanti's thesis about pleasure in *Donna me prega*, it would also be useful to recall Taddeus Alderotto's Italian translation of the *Nicomacheian Ethics* from an Arabian-Alexandrian Latin compendium, in which the importance of bodily pleasure is evaluated. Both Taddeo's translation and the Latin version of the Arabic compendium were also sources for Book 6 of Brunetto Latini's *Tresor*, which is devoted to ethics and in which two kinds of virtue are evaluated.[28]

Cavalcanti's *Donna me prega* seems to provide an answer to Giacomo and/or to the theory of intellectual happiness by taking into account the distinction made by Brunetto and Taddeo between physical and intellectual happiness. The importance and value of bodily happiness refers us to the two philosophies that, in *Donna me prega*, are pitted against one other – the moral and the natural.[29]

For Cavalcanti, an ethics related to the body as part of natural philosophy in fact generates the re-evaluation of the importance of bodily happiness. While the 'buon perfetto' is an intellectual happiness, the subject of Cavalcanti's canzone is love. Through love, the canzone puts forth an account of the sensitive soul and animal power.

In stanza 3, Cavalcanti locates the perfection proper to love in sensibility: 'Non è vertute, – ma da quella vène /ch'e perfezione – (ché si pone – tale),/non razionale, – ma che sente, dico.' This is the perfection of the sensitive soul, to which there corresponds a kind of happiness different from the intellectual. This happiness has another name and is pleasure: 'diletto.' This pleasure accepts and takes into account the animality of man. Intellectual happiness does not belong to love 'che da buon perfetto tort'e /per sorte.' And because love is a metaphor for the natural process and the role that the generative and sensitive soul perform in it, it is clear that the 'buon perfetto' is not the goal of Cavalcanti's canzone. Love reveals the break between the two genera of sense and intellect. Because of this, love implies another kind of happiness, which is sensual happiness.

That the pleasure of love is an animal pleasure, therefore, implies a whole series of meanings. It implies first of all that the canzone, centring as it does on love, focuses on a kind of happiness that is common to human beings and animals. It thus opposes one of the theses of Giacomo's *Quaestio* which had asserted that the *summum bonum* is a good that belongs only to human beings. In opposing pleasure to intellectual happiness, Cavalcanti not only denies that the sensitive soul exists for the sake of the intellective soul: he also and crucially asserts that man's happiness is a kind of 'diletto' common to beasts and human beings.

The Method: A Sophistical Refutation

All these sources confirm that *Donna me prega* contains an answer to the debate on intellectual happiness.[30] What is most difficult to follow here is the method that *Donna me prega* utilizes. In stanza 2, the process Giacomo proposes as the way to happiness is apparently accepted; and, while it is described, it is examined and in reality criticized for its conclusion – that man intellects. This denial of intellection entails the denial of intellectual happiness.

Considering the *Quaestio* as a document of the debate, it is possible to see Cavalcanti's own answer when he declares that love and 'buon perfetto' have different destinies, which means that they differ with respect to their very nature. This corresponds to what the poet said in stanza 2: that the sensitive soul and the possible intellect live in two different spheres, and that the sensitive soul and the phantasm it generates do not share any intellectual activity with the possible intellect. Thus, when, in stanza 5, he asserts that man cannot see love in this process, he confirms his own most radical position. What is also radical is the reasoning by which he distinguishes the satisfaction of the body from the happiness of 'consideranza.'

Donna me prega therefore contains a thesis on bodily happiness that parallels the debate on intellectual happiness. If love is an excess, it is this very excess that guarantees the specific pleasure of love. And Cavalcanti's thesis, focusing as it does on the idea that man can be satisfied by bodily happiness, suggests not only an opposition to the theories of intellectual happiness, but also an attempt to reverse the terms of the discussion. Because Cavalcanti's method organizes his reasoning in terms of a refutation, he adopts a thesis in order to oppose it. Lines 21–8, in which the theory of *coniunctio* is taken up in order to argue against man's intellection, thus represent the core of the canzone's theoretical meaning.

What has most contributed to the impenetrability of this text is the way in which Cavalcanti organizes his reasoning. In stanza 2 love is discussed in relation to the process of form, in stanza 5 in relation to man.

He starts by putting forth the view that love is not visible to man and concludes with the assertion that the pleasure 'mercede' of love consists in its darkness. Changing the focus of discussion between stanza 2 and stanza 5, Cavalcanti deduces from his reasoning the theory of pleasure as an answer to the theories of intellectual happiness – an answer that implies the denial of intellection for man.

Before concluding, let me offer a few more words on the central metaphor of the canzone in order to focus on the method Guido utilizes. Cavalcanti structures this metaphor on the theory of the diaphanous, which in Aristotle's *De anima* introduces the theory of vision. In *Donna me prega* this metaphor is used as a kind of syllogistic demonstration divided between two different sections of the canzone (stanzas 2 and 5). Love, vision, and the generation of the image are identified.

In the first section, love is said to be 'formato,' like the diaphanous. This means that love's form is like that of the diaphanous, which enables vision and, from that, the generation of form. The reader therefore follows simultaneously vision and the generation of form. The second section (stanza 5) states 1) that once intellected, the form loses its light ('compriso, – bianco in tale obietto cade'); and 2) because of this, form is not visible ('e, chi ben aude, – forma non si vede'); and 3) from this derives the nonvisibility of love for human beings, since, like the diaphanous, love's visibility depends on the illuminated form ('dunqu' elli meno, che da lei procede'). But since man does not participate in the phase in which the form is illuminated from the light of the intellect, man does not see the form.

The three logical moments make evident that what is 'altero' in love's being is the process of form, in which man participates, but only in the phase related to the sensible and in a subordinate way. A further indication of the being of love is given in terms of its relationship to the theory of vision. In stanza 5, the love that resides in darkness and is divided from its being ('d'essere diviso') because it has no light, is nothing other than the being of the diaphanous, which is actual only when it is illuminated. It is obscure now because the form itself, after being intellected, is dark ('For di colore, d'essere diviso,/assiso – 'n mezzo scuro, luce rade').

The conclusion of the canzone confirms that Cavalcanti, through love, refutes intellectual happiness and relates happiness to physics and to that part of the soul that Aristotle (as emphasized by Averroes) relates to physics. This suggests that the diaphanous refers not just to vision but also to the process of the form itself. We therefore have the following relation: love formed as the diaphanous implies that the generated form is also diaphanous, wherein lives the *coniunctio*, that is, the phantasm in the moment in which it is illuminated by the light of the intellect, which performs the abstraction.

But love that has its seat in the nonilluminated medium suggests something else about the metaphor: the metaphor further implies, in relation to love's pleasure, the negation of the importance of the illuminated phase that is coincident with the moment in which the form is intellected. Here the focus is in fact on love's pleasure, which in itself has nothing to do with the moment in which form is illuminated. It is this obscurity that guarantees the pleasure of love: 'For d'ogni fraude dico, degno in fede,/che solo di costui nasce mercede.'

If we connect these final lines to lines 51–2, where the process that may obstruct the formation of image is related to 'ira' (anger) and the heat it generates ('e vol ch'om miri – 'n non formato loco,/destandos' ira la qual manda foco'), we may understand the meaning of what I call the dark pleasure of love. Because heat is related to spermatic activity, an activity that is influenced by the stars (in this case Mars), we must connect the difficulty of vision (and obscurity) with the spermatic activity to which pleasure is related.[31] Since, as we have seen, heat presides over the cycle of matter in physics and over the generation of animals as well, this confirms that darkness is related to the theory of matter that presides over the theory of love in *Donna me prega*.[32] From matter derives the perfection of the animal, which cannot be satisfied by intellectual happines, which does not belong to man's genus.

Love in Cavalcanti leads to a theory of pleasure. The will of the heart ('di cor volontate') is in fact 'appetitus.' The pleasure of love belongs to it and does not coincide with the phase in which the process of image-formation lives its illuminated phase, which love nevertheless originates. *Donna me prega* therefore contains a philosophical theory of happiness based on physics and matter, which was crucial to the Epicurean theory of happiness. In *Donna me prega*, the central focus is on the sensitive soul, where love has its seat. This part of the soul is perishable according to 'elli è creato' because it is part of the material world ruled by generation and corruption. A theory of happiness emerges that is related to the perishable nature of the individual soul. The fact that logic organizes the reasoning for an earthly happiness as the direct consequence of the theory of matter and the denial of the survival of the individual soul can be considered among the reasons for Cavalcanti's fame as an Epicurean.[33] It is this reputation that Dante introduces and Boccaccio expands upon.

Phantasia and Animal Power

In light of the previous section, we must now rethink the relation between the word 'love' as it is used in the canzone and what in the medical school is termed animal power. As has been said, love is a metaphor that encloses the double being of form. As we read at the beginning of the canzone, love is 'fero' and 'altero.' 'Altero' is not synonymous with 'fero,' as has been suggested by some scholars, but on the contrary includes the process of form that love generates, while 'fero' includes love's animality. 'Fero' (ferox) implies the animal power on which Taddeo Alderotto was working in Cavalcanti's time. According to Alderotto, this power includes the perfection of sense and individual intellection, that is, a power which implies the formative activity of *phantasia*.[34] In light of Taddeus, we may say that love is 'altero' because it is 'fero.' That is, since animal power can generate the form, love participates indirectly, through form, in the intellectual process, a process in which love per se has no intellective role but which love has the power of originating by offering the form to be intellected.

Love is 'fero' because it is rooted in animal power. But this power, through the activity of imagination, generates the phantasm, which makes love 'altero.' The reason is that it offers the form that enters into connection with the intellect when this performs its abstraction.

The most important activity that a human being can reach is related to the activity of *phantasia*. This is clearly said in the third stanza, which states that the power of love can generate death: 'Di sua potenza segue spesso morte, / se forte – la vertù fosse impedita / la quale aita – la contraria via' (Death often follows on [love's] potency if the power should be obstructed that furthers the contrary course).

In order to understand these lines, it is essential to evaluate what the 'virtus' is that, if obstructed, can lead to death. Since it is said that this virtue helps toward the contrary direction, against love's excess that sometimes generates death, we may infer that the direction contrary to love's excess is the way toward intellection. This virtue is therefore either the formative or the cogitative power that paves the way toward the *coniunctio*.

According to the theory of internal senses, the cogitative virtue and the formative power of *phantasia* are coincident. Thus, death in *Donna me prega* is coincident with the death of the form generated from the *vis formativa* or *phantasia*. But whatever this power is, according to the theory of internal senses of which it is part, it belongs to the sensitive soul and is an animal power, which implies the power of generating the phantasm, i.e., of activating individual cognition.[35]

The positive values that *Donna me prega* recognizes for human beings are *phantasia* and *diletto*, both of which belong to the sensitive and generative souls. Both are related to the perishable soul of human beings. *Phantasia* is the core of Cavalcanti's poetry, and it is because of the importance of imagination that Cavalcanti, like Giacomo, accepts the theory of the control of the passions.

The excess of passion in the canzone is, in fact, condemned because balance and love as balance are required in order to reach the formation of the image 'non pò dire om ch'aggia vita, / ché stabilita non ha segnoria' (One cannot say that one is alive, / if one has not established self-mastery'). But also the forgetting of the sensitive life is condemned, because a sensitive life is necessary for reaching the 'vis formativa.' 'A simil pò valer quand' om l'oblia' (a like result can obtain when one forgets [love]). Animal power determines the power of love. The generation of form cannot take place if love imposes itself as an excess – which it often does ('spesso'). Both Cavalcanti and Giacomo focus on the control of passions. However, while Giacomo sees imagination as a step toward intellection, Cavalcanti sees in imagination the highest cognitive level a human being can generate. The life of *phantasia* is the only intellectual life that Cavalcanti recognizes as belonging to the individual human being. The goal of ethics is not only related to the sensitive soul: its aim, apparently, is also determined by an individual sensible happiness. The relation between Cavalcanti's *Donna me prega* and the materialism ascribed to Epicureanism is confirmed. Cavalcanti's canzone affirms its relation with the old philosophy not only when it applies logic to physics, but also when the poet establishes for ethics a good that belongs to the sensible.

In light of all this, it is possible to reread the eight theses that the canzone puts forth in its reasoning in relation to the debate on happiness. Organized as answers to eight questions, the theses throw light on the being of love as something that is in itself opposed to intellectual happiness:

1 Love has its seat in the sensitive soul. It is a potentiality for the creation of form; the process of imagination is led back to the process of generation of form as it starts from vision. Here Cavalcanti introduces the most important metaphor of his poetry. The complexity of this metaphor focuses on the technical meaning of the theory of the

diaphanous. The key to understanding the canzone lies in this metaphor, which will unfold in stanza 5 (lines 63–8).

2 Love is created. This means that love is governed by the laws of generation and corruption that preside over sublunar physics. The influence of Mars on love suggests that Cavalcanti begins his reasoning by putting forth love as part of a natural process (which is also the initial focus for Giacomo). The process of form is examined by showing the opposition between sense and intellect, because they belong to different genera. The theory of *coniunctio* is put forth in order to refute the possibility that intellection is performed by human beings through this *coniunctio*. The word 'diletto' is introduced as the opposite of 'consideranza' in order to show that to every genus there corresponds a diffent kind of happiness. 'Diletto' is the happiness proper to love. We have here a clear opposition to the thesis of intellectual happiness.

3 Love is not a virtue in the ethical sense but a power derived from the perfection of the sensitive soul. This power is based on desire and is in itself opposed to the rational activity of judgment and of free choice. Love is part of the natural process.

4 The power of love is strong enough to bring about the death of the intellectual activity of the sensitive soul as in the 'virtus formativa,' an event which can take place when love places serious obstacles in the process of image-formation. Love, therefore, makes the process of *phantasia* difficult and can thus generate the death of the form. This section contains an important meaning because love appears to be crucially diverted from 'buon perfetto' because of destiny, that is, necessity. The thesis of Giacomo is openly refuted. 'Buon perfetto' echoes the 'summum bonum' of Giacomo and is used in order to oppose love's power to intellectual happiness. Cavalcanti's answer to the thesis of intellectual happiness not only asserts the different being of love and 'buon perfetto' but also shows that, because of love's power, the unfolding of the formative process is difficult. The generation of form cannot take place if love imposes itself as an excess, which it often does ('*spesso*').

5 This thesis shows the essence of love. It gives an ontological description of love in its subjection to the laws of matter. The nature of love, rooted in a desire that is beyond measure, is suggested as being derived from the generative spirit and its spermatic activity. This stanza shows that Cavalcanti regards the unfolding of the generative

process of nature as responsible for the essence of love. In this respect, he is close to Giacomo, who puts forth the generative process of nature as basic for reaching the process of intellection. But Cavalcanti uses the generative process in order to show that, because of its essence, love's being is rooted in desire.

6 Love's rootedness in the theory of matter is repeated by inquiring into the movement of love. The focus is on alteration ('la nova qualità'), which explains that while love can originate the genesis of the image, it at the same time obliges man to look at the world of matter (''n non formato loco'). This is what makes the formative process (imagination as 'vis formativa') difficult. Cavalcanti corroborates this assertion with a precise detail: anger is the alteration that occurs. This is 'accensio cordis,' which may hinder vision and thus 'vis formativa.'

   The laws of matter are opposed to the 'vis formativa.' Not only, therefore, can love cause the death of 'vis formativa' (thesis 4), but it is also asserted (in thesis 6) that, because of the excess of heat that love generates, love makes difficult the perfect vision which is required in order to bring about the process of *phantasia*.

7 Love's pleasure derives from its being determined by a physical attraction, and its 'mercede' (favour) is physical. Cavalcanti here introduces the medical term 'complessione' in order to explain physical attraction as the balance of elements.[36]

8 It is impossible for man to know love through vision. In other words, love for man is not visible. Man lives only the obscurity of love, and in this obscurity lies the pleasure and the satisfaction of love. Intellectual happiness does not belong to love. The pleasure of love is determined by the principles of matter and by the generative process of nature.

In light of these theses, we must now recall Kristeller's introduction to the *Quaestio de felicitate*. As I indicated at the beginning of this chapter, Kristeller suggested that Giacomo's *Quaestio* contained a confirmation of Nardi's reading of *Donna me prega*. As I noted earlier, Nardi was the first scholar to organize the theoretical framework of the canzone. He emphasized not only Guido's Averroism, but also the fact that this Averroism denies intellection to the individual human being. In this respect, therefore, Giacomo's thesis, although Averroistic, does not reflect Cavalcanti's position in *Donna me prega*. In fact, while human beings for Giacomo are able to get intellection and intellectual happiness, *Donna me prega* clearly denies that man performs an intellectual activity and therefore implicitly denies that intellectual happiness belongs to human beings.

Giacomo's belief in an intellectual happiness suggests a point of view that, although it is derived basically from Averroism, is far from the position Cavalcanti assumes in *Donna me prega*. The *Quaestio de felicitate* does not, in this respect, confirm Nardi's reading of the Averroism of Cavalcanti, who focused on the denial of intellection as the central theme of *Donna me prega*. Giacomo and Guido both think that the possible intellect is separated from the body. They are therefore both Averroist. However, their Averroism involves different conclusions about philosophical happiness. Guido states clearly in the canzone that love is diverted from 'buon perfetto' by necessity. Human beings do not participate in the intellectual activity of the possible intellect and therefore cannot have philosophical happiness as a goal. Kristeller was therefore right when he listed Giacomo's *Quaestio* as a text belonging to radical Aristotelianism. But he was clearly wrong in suggesting that Giacomo's *Quaestio* confirms Nardi's reading.

The theory of intellectual happiness is in fact built on the theory that individual beings can reach intellectual knowledge through *continuatio* and *coniunctio*. That is, through a natural process and the control of passions, they are able to get *coniunctio* with the separated genus of the possible intellect. And in this *coniunctio*, they perform an intellectual activity by reaching a philosophical happiness. This theory, however, is clearly in opposition to Nardi's reading. According to Nardi, the individual being does not in fact have intellectual knowledge. Although Nardi does not concern himself with the theme of philosophical happiness, it is evident that no philosophical happiness belongs to human beings since philosophical happiness is the correlative of intellectual knowledge.

In the envoi of *Donna me prega*, Cavalcanti writes:

Tu puoi sicuramente gir, canzone,
là've ti piace, ch'io t'ho sì adornata
ch'assai laudata – sarà tua ragione
da le persone – c'hanno intendimento:
di star con l'altre tu non hai talento.

(You, canzone, can safely go where you like, for I have so adorned you, that your argument will be greatly praised by those persons who have understanding; you have no desire to be with the others.)

Here 'adornata' (adornatus) has the rhetorical meaning of something that is impossible to oppose.[37] Cavalcanti does not utilize the 'ornatus' in terms of beauty, but in terms of that which renders irrefutable the thesis of *Donna me prega*. The reason is that this poetry was, according to Cavalcanti, a reasoning ('*ragione*') that contains a refutation of some of the most credited theories of the time.

However obscure it may. be, the goal of this canzone was not to be deliberately obscure. On the contrary, it sets out to organize itself as a 'theorem' (Contini) with its proper, irrefutable demonstration. In order to achieve this, the laws of rhetoric may deliberately violate grammatical or syntactic structure because the conceptual perspicuity is obtained against the perspicuity of the first level. Referring to his ideal reader as 'conoscente,' as someone who has 'intendimento,' Cavalcanti specifies the type of reader equipped to judge the clarity or obscurity of his text. *Donna me prega*'s syntactic ambiguity is connected to amphibology. Its reasoning is, in fact, ambiguous because of the presence of terms or grammatical structures that can be interpreted in different ways or, more importantly, in opposing ways. As a logician, Cavalcanti subjects language to the logic of the concept he wishes to express. While the grammarian looks to construction, the logician looks to truth and meaning and their expression. We may say that Cavalcanti fashions what is termed in rhetoric a 'sermo congruus' to his own meaning. To fail means, for Cavalcanti, that he has built an incongruous 'sermo' or solecism.

As I noted earlier (see chapter 1), during the thirteenth century, the Arabs brought about a re-evaluation of the role of logic by establishing a distinction between logic and grammar. Logic, in fact, was related to the intellect and the intelligible, while grammar was related to language and expressions.[38] Cavalcanti utilizes logic to connect the field of poetry with physics. For instance, the metaphor of the diaphanous was the result of a new science, optics, which formed part of physics. Cavalcanti uses this metaphor to give a concrete being to love. But he also introduces a kind of syllogistic procedure in order to enclose something like an experimental proof in the text, as I have previously proposed.

If *Donna me prega* has spoken to us at such great length, its attraction lies precisely in its difficulty. The metaphor of the diaphanous has been principally responsible for this difficulty. Misunderstood by Nardi (a misunderstanding variously reiterated), the metaphor cannot be understood without recourse to the new science that was being diffused in the thirteenth century: a theory of optics mediated through Averroes, Alhazen (probably), and through physicians related to Averroism, such as Taddeus Alderotto.

In conclusion, it may be said that Giacomo's text must be considered as crucial to our understanding of the debate in which *Donna me prega* participates. Kristeller's suggestion that medieval studies cannot be done without the intervention of philosophy and science must be taken up today with an even greater emphasis on the latter.[39] Cavalcanti's fame as a natural philosopher and logician in fact tells us that he heralds the connection between logic and physics – a connection from which modern science emerged in Western civilization. The extent to which these themes and relations have given a new role to poetry will be discussed in the next chapter, which is devoted to Ezra Pound as a reader of Cavalcanti's *Donna me prega.*

Chapter Five

Cavalcanti at the Centre of the Western Canon: Ezra Pound as Reader of *Donna me prega*

For Ezra Pound, Cavalcanti's poetry was at the centre of the Western canon that he, Pound, would reshape by introducing a criterion of beauty and alternative values that he judged to be at the centre of Western culture. Pound's Canto 73 (written in Italian) opens with the image of Guido Cavalcanti riding at a gallop as he returns from a 600-year exile. Pound's invention here aims at creating a correspondence between Cavalcanti's name and its literal Italian meaning – Cavalcanti being the equivalent of a rider.[1] But the major contribution is a subtle suggestion that the image of Cavalcanti riding emphasizes, namely, the relationship between name and thing that Cavalcanti's gallop supports. Here Pound applies to Cavalcanti the method that Dante had introduced in the *Vita nuova*, i.e., that of the agreement between name and thing ('nomina sunt consequentia rerum').[2]

   This association between Cavalcanti's name and his galloping generates, for Pound, a third element. This galloping resounds, in fact, in the devastated Italian landscape of World War II to which Cavalcanti returns in order to condemn it and to excite Italy to a revolt. Cavalcanti as the hero of a devastated Italy, as the purest voice of tradition transfigures the chronicle of those days through the hammering rhythm of Pound's Italian verses:

> E poi dormii
> E svegliandomi nell'aere perso
> Vidi e sentii,
> E quel ch'io vidi mi pareva andar a cavallo,
> ...
> Sono quel Guido che amasti

pel mio spirito altiero
E la chiarezza del mio intendimento

...

già cavalcante
(mai postiglione.)

Recalled through quotations from Dante, and through Dante's tone, the meaning of this return is unequivocal. Cavalcanti is associated with Dante. At the centre of Pound's text, however, we find not Dante but Cavalcanti. Cavalcanti's return from exile marks an end to the exile of poetry itself.

The agreement between name and thing, on which Pound structures Cavalcanti's return from exile, indirectly recalls Cavalcanti's method that Pound emphasized in his reading of the *Rime* (1932), i.e., that of utilizing, in *Donna me prega*, a technical vocabulary that implies the literal meaning that certain specific words held in Cavalcanti's time. Cavalcanti's return, in a context of destruction, dramatizes the meaning of the poetry he has written. If, according to Pound, poetry is the value that can stop destruction and death, then Guido's return acquires a meaning that goes well beyond the words he pronounces. His return claims the new role that poetry will play in the Western canon. *Poiesis*, as part of the things that nature produces, opposes, for Pound, at once usury, which is contrary to nature, and the war that was dictated for reasons of usury.[3]

Cavalcanti's metaphor has given a cognitive power to the image. According to the American, 'Cavalcanti's metaphor has created a language of things that are also ideas. What Pound had called the ideogrammic method was an attempt to elevate to a method of knowing the method on which, according to Pound, the metaphor itself is based. Cavalcanti confirms Pound's theory of the Chinese written ideogram, which Pound reads in light of Fenollosa's essay (*The Chinese Written Character as a Medium for Poetry*).[4]

It is from this line of thought that Cavalcanti emerges as the model to which poetry must look. Of extreme importance for Pound specifically is the metaphor that Cavalcanti had introduced in *Donna me prega*: 'sì formato, – come /diaffan da lume, – d'una scuritate – which, as Pound reads it, equates love with the physical theory of the generation of light.[5] Pound's reading and misreading of this metaphor, which he defines as 'precise interpretative,' is valuable for an understanding of what he sees as central to Cavalcanti and of what will shape his own idea of poetry.[6]

According to Pound, poetry is knowledge because it is the production of an image: we know what we make.[7] A metaphor embodies the same process of knowing because it is the generation of an image. Pound regards such knowing as opposed to the knowledge based on abstraction. In the essay *How to Write*, written more or less in the same years in which he was working on Cavalcanti's *Rime*, we may follow the line of thinking he was pursuing in the coincidence he puts forth between gestalt, or form, and thinking. By focusing on the relational as a form-function, which the concept of gestalt implies, Pound looks at Cavalcanti's metaphor as a perfect example of gestalt.[8]

If indeed the canzone reveals its true centre in the 'metaphor on the generation of light,'[9] then Pound regards it as metaphorical of the process of knowing. The lines related to the diaphanous that constitute the gestalt-form of the canzone represent the heart of the relational whole implied in the metaphor. Pound's reading and translations aim precisely at highlighting this connection between the metaphor and the gestalt of the canzone.

According to Pound, Cavalcanti identifies the form-gestalt of the canzone with the metaphor of the generation of light. As Pound reads it, this is a metaphor for the process of knowing. This metaphor, for him, is a perfect example of the interpretative metaphor in the sense that the generation of light is, according to Pound, not an ornament but the very image around which the meaning of the canzone itself is organized.

Pound also looks at Cavalcanti's language in relation to the form-metaphor of the canzone. The modernity of the tone of Cavalcanti's poetry, which for Pound lies in the rupture with the predictable, depends on the coincidence between this central metaphor and the language of the canzone. When in his essay on *Donna me prega* he recalls 'the rose that the magnet makes in iron filings,' he speaks at the same time of energy and form, thereby suggesting that this form-energy is the form itself of the canzone.[10] It is this form, in fact, that can represent that energy which activates at once the process of *phantasia* and the generation of the phantasm-image. Poetry as an activity of production (as *poíesis*) coincides with the process of *phantasia* and its generation of the phantasm-image.

This point is clearly of great importance for Pound, mainly in the late 1920s and early 1930s, insofar as this interpretation of *Donna me prega* corroborates his theories on poetry and language that he includes in works such as *How to Read* and the *ABC of Reading*. But, whatever the importance of this point, for Pound, *Donna me prega* will include much more. In order to understand the complex role that Cavalcanti assumes for him, it is useful to begin with the years around 1910, the years in which Pound puts forth the structure of his own critical theory.

Reading and Misreading

Pound's penchant for Cavalcanti dates from his early poetry. In 1910 he wrote a letter to his parents from Sirmione explaining that he was planning a book on Cavalcanti. It is worth noting that Pound's interest in Guido parallels his interest in Dante's *Paradise*. And probably because *Paradise*, like *Donna me prega*, shapes a metaphorical-philosophical poetry, both poems will be crucial in organizing Pound's late Cantos.

At that time, Pound's interest in Cavalcanti was influenced by the suggestions he received from reading Dante Gabriel Rossetti's translations. Evident traces of Rossetti's influence were present in Pound's translations of *Sonnets and Ballate* (1912) of Cavalcanti. But something different was also active in his introductory essay. Here he introduces a relationship between Cavalcanti's poetry and the concept of energy. Pound underscores, for instance, the relationship in medieval culture between virtue and energy. He connects medieval virtue with modern radium. He provides, in addition, a technical reading of Cavalcanti's words. The 'spirits' that populate Cavalcanti's minor poems and which Pound defines as the intelligence of the senses are read by Pound in the context of medieval philosophy and introduce the theory of the body's intelligence. Anticipating future themes, he refers also to the concept of magnetism in order to explain the relationships among bodies disclosed by Cavalcanti's poetry.[11]

Whatever the importance of his first edition of Cavalcanti, Pound's allocation of a new place for Cavalcanti in the Western tradition derives mainly from the rethinking that this edition inspired in him. This rethinking included a re-evaluation of *Donna me prega*, which Pound did not include in his 1912 edition of Cavalcanti, but on which he concentrates his attention during the late 1920s.

Cavalcanti's future importance for Pound is foreshadowed in Pound's two major manifestos: Imagism, with its emphasis on the image-thing, and Vorticism, with its concept of art as a relational ensemble. But it is likely that Pound began to consider another aspect that makes Cavalcanti important in the same years in which he was reshaping the concept of the historical process (in *Vortex*, 1914).

But even more interesting is the fact that in the manifesto of Vorticism, his emphasis on the now (the present) shows traces of Aristotle's theory of time, which Pound reshapes and articulates through twentieth-century language.[12] By focusing on the present and regarding the future as the awareness of the past that the present can organize, Pound emphasizes time as a relational ensemble in *Vortex*.[13] Crucial to Pound was the idea (which comes from Aristotle, directly or indirectly) that the present is created from the relationship between the past and the future. In opposition to the future conceived as a dimension of progress, Pound focuses on the past as a special memory, which creates the identity of the present.

But this 1914 manifesto brought another aspect into play. Vortex was the spatio-temporal point of 'maximum energy.' To be a Vorticist is to produce an original work of art by using a language never before used. Cavalcanti was therefore a 'Vorticist' above all because his poetry created a present by reshaping an alternative past for the future. At the same time, his 'pigment' was so vital that by comparison Petrarch's poetry shows itself to be a second-hand art.

But the crucial importance Pound will give to Cavalcanti develops from his increasing awareness (as *Vortex* announces) that the identity of the past is something to be invented on the basis of the now of the present. Tradition may be assumed to be an invention in the classical rhetorical meaning of the thing to be found. Temporal dimensions are merely the result of our invention. The present itself is an invention that our awareness of past and future creates. Cavalcanti's poetry is thus a contemporaneous poetry. In his 1914 essay *Renaissance*, Pound gives the following epigraph: 'All criticism is an attempt to define the classic.'[14] Rather than revitalizing the notion of the classic, Pound seeks to change the notion altogether. The 'classical' is not the achieved form – not an Apollinian dimension – but, on the contrary, a perennial potentiality. A classic is a work capable of organizing a process of further creation. What is perennial is not the static concept of an achieved beauty but the enduring latent energy that will bring about reactions.

In this sense, Pound reverses the concept of form. He does so by including in it the concept of a continuous energy. Form, properly understood, is not a result, but rather a continuous potential that generates objections and responses. Cavalcanti thus represents the essence of this process through which the identity of Western culture comes to be revised.

By focusing on the accident, Cavalcanti structures poetry on the process of potentiality. His language is the technical language to this end. *Donna me prega* furnishes the ontology of the process because there love is identified with accident. This word 'accident' is, for Pound, of crucial importance and is understood by him in its technical meaning. Pound translates it as 'affect,' thus connecting 'accident' with the field of sensibility, and with the language of Aristotle's *De anima* and *De sensu et sensatu*.[15] But in *Donna me prega* Pound is aware that 'accident' was more inclusive, and the Cantos will focus on the field of 'accident' with increasing awareness. This is testified to by Pound's rereading in the early 1940s of Aristotle's *Metaphysics* and his reading marks to the sections devoted to discussing the field of accidentality.'[16]

According to Pound, Cavalcanti's work not only makes possible a reversal of the concept of the 'masterpiece,' but also focuses on something that had been marginalized during the Middle Ages. Cavalcanti looked, in fact, at accidentality in a culture that was organized around placing the substance of Aristotle's *Metaphysics* in the highest rank. Cavalcanti concentrates on physics and on movement. He emphasizes that which belongs to time and becoming. For Pound, Cavalcanti's poetry is highly significant because it shapes a method and in that respect represents a new concept of what a classic could be.

Machine Art, an essay of the late 1920s and synchronous with the years in which Pound returned to Cavalcanti, announces a concept of aesthetics that will preside over his rereading of Guido. In this essay, the concept of beauty is rethought in terms of 'function,' and the concept of 'form' in terms of an inner law that presides over the plural ensemble we call motor. The point of maximum energy in the machine is located in the motor, which is also the point of crisis – crisis being the point of latent energy.[17] In this way, Pound goes further to reshape the concept of crisis. He transforms it into a point of latent energy that the future will reveal. Cavalcanti too works as a point of crisis for Western culture, as the latent energy that the future will manifest. To gain a new sense of the historical process, Pound proceeds from the canonized Dante backwards to Cavalcanti, working through what may be termed Cavalcanti's 'function.' For Pound, this 'Cavalcanti function' works to deconstruct what Dante had built as absolute values. It does so essentially in two ways: by opposing Cavalcanti's literal method to Dante's allegory, and by pitting physics and time against metaphysics and theology.

Cavalcanti's poetry functions at first to deconstruct the canonized values of the Western canon. But the new values Pound tends to impose look toward designating a new centre for the canon, in which poetry works as the dynamic point that attracts and reorganizes the various disciplines by means of its language. Pound's axiom of the early 1930s, that 'literature is language charged with meaning,' is thus foreshadowed by his reading of *Donna me prega*.

Guido Cavalcanti, Rime, by E.P., was part of a major edition that Pound initially planned to publish in English for Aquila Press but, because of Aquila Press's failure, he published at his own expense in Genoa in 1932 for Marsano, a small publishing house.[18] The subtitle for the edition, *edizione rappezzata fra le rovine*, eloquently introduces Pound's attempt to save Cavalcanti not only from the ruins of his planned English edition but also from the ruins of tradition.[19] Peculiar to the Marsano edition was Pound's new attention to *Donna me prega*. The book included, along with Pound's old translations, new essays and an Italian text of the canzone with Pound's version. A few reproductions in *Rime* of the Chigiano manuscript containing del Garbo's commentary on the canzone show the importance Pound gives to this historical interpretation of *Donna me prega*.

Mediaevalism, the first of the 1920s essays devoted to Cavalcanti, appears to aim at nailing down the philosophy of the age. The key phrase is 'natural philosopher.' Pound connects Cavalcanti with the philosophy of Aristotle. He points out that the teaching of Aristotle was forbidden in Paris in the early thirteenth century, but that such prejudice had been worn down during the century. Pound observes: 'Guido shows, I think, no regard for anyone's prejudice.'[20]

By stressing Cavalcanti as the authoritative *physicus*, Pound refers in one of his studies to a claim by Tempier: The philosopher has to captivate the intellect in the limit of faith. Because Pound sees in Cavalcanti a transgressor of this dictum, it is evident that his adherence to Cavalcanti originated in what we may call *sumpáthos*. But what is most important is the fact that Pound discovers as the canzone's essence what he indicates as the metaphor of the generation of light. The importance of this discovery is crucial, and it acquires its proper importance only when it is related to Pound's observation in the same essay, which defines Cavalcanti's metaphor as precisely 'interpretive' (*Partial Explanation*, p. 214).

The two nuclei crucial for an understanding of Cavalcanti's importance for Pound are both connected to Cavalcanti's use of the metaphor: natural demonstration, the metaphor of the generation of light.[21]

Of even greater importance is the genealogy he furnishes for Guido's ideas: 'We may trace his ideas to Averroes and Avicenna; he does not definitely proclaim any heresy but he shows leanings towards not only proof by reason, but towards proof by experiment.' Having denied Aquinas's influence on Cavalcanti, he prudently hypothesizes: 'It may be impossible to prove that he had heard of Roger Bacon, but the whole canzone is easier to understand if we suppose ... that he had read Grosseteste on the Generation of light.'[22]

This observation can be linked to what Pound himself underlines: the importance of luminous matter in Cavalcanti's poetry. According to Pound, this matter is absolutely important in the Tuscan's aesthetics and refers to a 'corporeality.' For Pound, this corporeality is 'active matter,' as opposed to 'opaque matter.' In Pound's *Mediaevalism*, after a long preamble on the qualities of Provençal poetry and a lament on the loss of the clear medieval line, Pound defines the Tuscan's aesthetics in this way: 'The term "metaphysical" might be used if it were not so appallingly associated in people's minds with unsupportable conjecture and devastated terms of abstraction' (p. 206). At a later point we read: '[The Tuscan] declines to limit his aesthetics to the impact of light on the eye ... the conception of the body as perfected instrument of the increasing intelligence pervades' (p. 206).

Also important is Pound's attention to a sense of matter as radiating, an idea he sees active in Cavalcanti's canzone, and in which converges a line of observation that Pound introduced since his first edition of Cavalcanti. He makes a comparison with the Renaissance sense of the plasticity of the body and quotes H. Springer to note the difference: On account of Raphael the ideal of the Virgin becomes flesh. 'The metamorphosis into carnal tissue becomes frequent and general somewhere about 1527. The people are corpus, corpuscular, but not in the strict sense "animate"; it is no longer the body of air clothed in the body of fire; it no longer radiates' (*Mediaevalism*, pp. 207–8).

The body as the centre of emotions and intelligence – as the energy of living matter – is part of a new set of values that Pound, through Cavalcanti, seeks to impose. By focusing on technical terminology (against Karl Vossler's assertion that Cavalcanti's vocabulary was imprecise), Pound refers the reader to a series of precise meanings. These meanings, Pound asserts, are understandable because the technical terminology that Cavalcanti introduces furnishes the key for their true comprehension (*The Vocabulary*, pp. 221–2).

Pound also intuits the importance of the 'diaphanous' as a metaphor crucial for the comprehension of the poem itself. He distinguishes Cavalcanti's use of the metaphor from that of Petrarch (which to him seems merely ornamental). He thinks that the being of love is described in *Donna me prega* through the metaphor of the generation of light – a metaphor that Cavalcanti shapes according to the knowledge of the time. Pound reads in this metaphor (which associates love and the diaphanous) a relationship between love and knowing, where 'diaphanous,' according to him, is a metaphor for both the generation of light and knowing. For Pound, Cavalcanti's focus on love implies the notion that the body participates in knowing; that knowing is consequently not an abstraction; and that it is the body that furnishes the manifold data of the senses that generate knowing.

What converges in Pound's reading of Cavalcanti is a line of thought that Pound had explored in his essay on the French symbolist poet, Remy de Gourmont (1922). There the relationship between the activity of the sperm and the activity of the brain correlated the form produced by mind with the formative activity of sperm.[23] For Pound, Cavalcanti's metaphor of love as illuminating, taken in its literal meaning as the generation of light, identifies the generation of light as a metaphor for knowing. The activity of imagination is thus suggested as related to love's activity of production in the double sense of spermatic and phantastic activity. The process of intelligence and the process of poetry are identical. Both are productive activities, and intelligence is originated by the process of *phantasia*, in its literal meaning of producing a phantasm or form.

In proposing Cavalcanti's *Donna me prega* as a historical document that places Western hierarchies in crisis, Pound considers the fame that tradition attributes to Cavalcanti, and the tradition that converges in his poetry. Pound thus focuses on Cavalcanti's Averroism as the philosophy that had celebrated the perfection of the sensible as an alternative to the abstractions of medieval theology.

As mentioned earlier, Pound seeks the reshaping of the canon. This was already evident in Pound's edition-translation of 1912, where he had asserted Cavalcanti's superiority to Petrarch. But later, in his introduction to the 1932 edition of the *Rime*, he makes a more radical assertion when he writes that Cavalcanti did *not* stand in relationship to Dante as the moon to the sun. Here he not only opposes Cristoforo Landino's (1425–98) assertion that Cavalcanti was to Dante as the moon to the sun, but also suggests that Guido shines with his own light – a light that is not dependent on that of Dante. While unable to write a heretical comedy, Cavalcanti, for Pound, nonetheless holds a distinguished place in Tuscan poetry, second only to Dante.[24]

Two points are worthy of mention in his short introduction. The first and crucial one is that the quality of Cavalcanti's work is not inferior to that of Dante. The second is the assertion that both Cavalcanti and Dante have given the world a poetry that did not exist before them. He concludes with a non-obscure affirmation that 600 years after their 'exile,' Italian poetry has yet to reach their level.

But in his edition of *Rime*, Pound starts to dismantle Dante's superiority. According to Pound, Cavalcanti appears to be much more modern than his younger friend Dante. Cavalcanti's relatives (the Uberti family) were opposed to the Tuscan bourgeois and ecclesiastical circles. Pound organizes a tradition in which Cavalcanti represents a position opposed to what he calls 'a form of stupidity not limited to Europe, that is, idiotic asceticism and a belief that the body is evil' (*Mediaevalism*, p. 204). In the poetry of Cavalcanti, Pound sees active the positive elements found in Byzantine and Romanesque architecture. He recalls, as examples, the churches of St Hilaire in Poitiers, San Zeno in Verona, and the Modena Duomo.

Pound emphasizes the relationship in Cavalcanti between rational thought and the virtue of matter, finding a kind of correspondence with the law on which the *section d'or* (golden section) is built. The same mathematical concept of proportion, for Pound, governs Cavalcanti's poetry. The same law that organizes the structure of these cathedrals presides over Cavalcanti. The law of this relation is proportion.

Here in Cavalcanti, proportion becomes harmony, since it is built on the harmony of sensibility, where thought has its demarcation and substance its virtue.[25] Of great importance in Pound's reading is the notion that the body's perfection is a tool of the intellect ('The conception of the body as perfected instrument of the increasing intelligence pervades'). This reading looks at Cavalcanti's Averroism by emphasising the perfection of sensibility, but leaves out the division between senses and intellect, on which Averroism is built.[26]

It is likely that Pound sets out to refute the whole perspective of Aquinas's *De unitate intellectus contra Averroistas*, which Pound apparently reads while working on Cavalcanti.[27] In opposition to Thomism, he tries to understand the Arabic message freed of the conditioning of Catholicism. Pound's polemic tone against Christian asceticism and its hatred of the corporeal culminates in his emphasizing what for him is the crucial message of *Donna me prega*: the perfection of the body as the basis of intellectual perfection, and the body as responsible for organizing the activity of intelligence. Pound's Pisan cantos, which will focus on memory in connection with image-formation, will represent a further stage of Pound's understanding of Cavalcanti's theory of imagination.

In Pound's reading of *Donna me prega*, the focus on energy culminates in the suggestion that the form of the canzone is like a flower-form.[28] Because Pound sees in the metaphor of the 'generation of light' the form of the canzone, he suggests that the form of *Donna me prega* is the very light-energy that creates the form or phantasm.

Looking at the translations he made of *Donna me prega*, we may, in fact, see an important change in Pound's perspective between the first translation as it appears in *Rime* and the second as it appears in Canto 36. The line, 'And [love] wills man look into unforméd space,' as we read in the first translation, is changed in Canto 36. Here 'unforméd space' becomes 'forméd trace.' Love here is identified with the process of image-formation, and this image-form is for Pound the product of energy. The plasmatic activity of love is the activity that produces at once the phantasm and the form itself of the canzone. Although his reading[29] is incorrect in light of the text of the canzone we have today, it nevertheless captures a true sense of Cavalcanti's theory of love, which attributes to human beings the power of *phantasia* and denies abstract knowledge. For Pound, it is this denial that makes Guido's poetry so important. The generation of images as a cognitive process is the foundation on which Pound will base the alternative process of knowing as part of what he calls in the 1930s a biological logic. Such logic will be opposed by Pound to the logic of syllogism and its method of abstraction.[30]

Pound summarizes this line of reflection when he finds that harmony is peculiar to Cavalcanti. But in order to understand what this harmony implies for Pound, we must look at a harmony between intellect and corporeality. A correspondence between the form that the sperm can exteriorize and the form that the *phantasia* creates shows that both are built on the generation of a form. 'The brain' also, according to what Pound has written in his essay on Remy De Gourmont, is 'a maker or presenter of images.' Here we also read that creative thought is an act similar to fecundation. Poetry, based as it is on an organic process of the generation of form, is the only language that can free the West from the evil of abstraction and metaphysics. Poetry and knowing coincide, and this knowing realizes itself through a thinking which, while it is productive, also works in combining and comparing forms.[31]

The years in which Pound was working on Cavalcanti's *Rime* coincide with those during which he was writing *How to Read* (1929) and *How to Write* (1930). He was at that time establishing the flaws of Western culture, blaming the Renaissance for a lacuna – that of not updating language in light of the new science that Francis Bacon had presented through his *Novum Organum*. In order to furnish Western culture with the cornerstone on which to enlarge or revitalize the canon, Cavalcanti's model is crucial. Pound states that the laboratory of the scientist is the model of the new knowledge through which written language has to be renewed. The biological logic he proposes and sets in opposition to the logic of syllogism is a relational logic. The process of knowing as the capacity of establishing relations is constructed, for Pound, through the same process that metaphor presents.

According to Pound, these manifold relations enter Western poetry through Cavalcanti and his use of the metaphor. Because Cavalcanti was a natural philosopher, his poetry registers – according to Pound – the first entrance of scientific topics, through which the poet is able to empower the language of poetry. Pound emphasizes the importance of literal meaning in Cavalcanti, a meaning obtained by simply bringing technical words into poetry as they are taken from the culture of Guido's time.

Partial Explanation, another section of Pound's commentary, focuses again on Cavalcanti and stresses Dante's quality as a *bien-pensant* who lives with certainty in the orthodoxy of Guido Guinizzelli. He emphasizes his own sympathy for Guido's disrespect for Virgil (assuming that in *Inferno* X the passage 'forse cui Guido vostro ebbe a disdegno' introduces a disdain Cavalcanti nourished for Virgil) and makes a few remarks about the tradition conveyed by Cavalcanti. Some of his suggestions are of great value – for instance, his use of Avicenna's name in connection with Cavalcanti's theory of spirits. Others are less relevant or else imprecise, such as his attribution of Albertus Magnus as the source for Cavalcanti's proof by experience. The core of Pound's admiration is expressed in the emphasis he gives to 'non razionale, ma che si sente' (according to Pound's text). For him this shows Cavalcanti's propensity for 'experiment ... against the tyranny of the syllogism, blinding and obscurantist' (p. 211).

Crucial here is Pound's assertion that we find in Guido's poem no implication of a belief in a geocentric or theocentric material universe (*Partial Explanation*, p. 211). Pound reiterates the idea or suggestion that Guido probably read a manuscript by Roger Bacon, 'although that is, perhaps, unlikely' (p. 214). Another important point that Pound makes is that what we need in order to understand the meaning of *Donna me prega* is not so much a commentator as a lexicon: it is the precise sense of certain terms as understood at that particular epoch that one would like to have set before one.

'The other dimension' of the canzone is, according to Pound, its lyricism in the strictest sense of the term (p. 215). He concludes by emphasizing that *Donna me prega* was written to be sung and not for rhetorical declamation. He recalls *De vulgari eloquio* II, 12 because of Dante's mention of *Donna me prega* in connection with his own *Donne ch'avete intelletto d'amore* and in comparison with his *Poscia ch'Amor del tutto m'ha lasciato*. In the section entitled *The Vocabulary* (pp. 221–31), Pound stresses the importance of the literal sense of the poem. He insists on the philosophical sources of *Donna me prega* and suggests that Cavalcanti had probably some acquaintance with Grosseteste.

This section shows Pound looking for the meaning of the expression 'in subject' in Avicenna's *Metaphysics* or for that of the word *ira* in Aristotle.[32] In the section entitled *Further Notes*, we follow Pound's understanding of the core of the canzone. He writes that Cavalcanti is safe confining himself to a discussion of an accident (pp. 234–5). Pound also discusses the meaning of the expression 'possible intellect,' thereby showing his knowledge of Aristotelianism. And his own reading of Renan's book, *Averroès et l'averroïsme*, as well as his reading of Avicenna, furnish him with useful tools for an understanding of the new themes that enter poetry through Cavalcanti.

As a reader of Cavalcanti, therefore, Pound looks to poetry and finds in its language the vortex of the tradition active in architecture, science, and philosophy. The focus is on harmony and function. For Pound, it is because of this harmony that Cavalcanti must occupy the centre of the Western canon. Cavalcanti's poetry achieves this result because it is written through mathematical laws. His role as *mathematicus egregius* may be found as an epigraph at the opening of the *Rime*. It shows Pound's idea of a correspondence between the numerical laws of metrics and the balance of themes.[33]

Cavalcanti makes poetry by constructing harmony: between body and intelligence, and between language and content. To understand Cavalcanti requires that the reader put himself in a harmonic state of mind. Cavalcanti's poetry, like the poetry Pound himself wants to write, makes its own reader.

Pound's translation and interpretation of Cavalcanti's canzone *Donna me prega*, inserted in Pound's semi-anonymous 1932 edition of Cavalcanti's *Rime*, was reviewed by the famous medievalist Etienne Gilson.[34] In an article published in 1932 in *The Criterion* (the literary magazine directed by T.S. Eliot), Gilson, while reiterating the sentence Pound wrote in capital letters in a passage of his commentary, 'The poem is very obscure,' at the same time highly valued the importance Pound gave to Dino del Garbo's commentary (the Florentine doctor who died in 1327). Gilson thus understood that the commentary of del Garbo, a near contemporary of Cavalcanti, would play an important role in searching for the meaning of the canzone. In his review, the illustrious medievalist began by trying to decipher those sections of the commentary that Pound introduced in his edition, in which some plates of the Chigiano manuscript L. V. 176 containing del Garbo's commentary were reproduced. Gilson concluded the article with a proposal that Pound send him the entire set of photographs of del Garbo's commentary so that the text might be transliterated (see Appendix 2). This transliteration was later made by Otto Bird, who was at that time one of Gilson's students, and published as 'The Commentary of Dino del Garbo on Cavalcanti's Canzone d'Amore,' in two issues of *Mediaeval Studies* in 1940.[35]

According to Gilson, Pound's method of making an interpretative translation fails when applied to translating medieval technical terminology. Gilson suspected that in the translation inserted in his edition of *Rime*, Pound was unable to understand the exact meaning of the more common medieval terminology, e.g., 'possibile intelletto,' that Pound translated as 'latent intellect.' The translation was criticized by Gilson as incorrect: 'With all due apologies for my boldness, I must confess that I cannot reconcile the translation with the text. In the first place, it seems obvious that "possibile intelletto" cannot be rendered by 'latent intellect.' This part of the text is not really obscure, for it is a commonplace application of a conception of human knowledge almost universally admitted in the thirteenth century ... Why not, then,' suggests Gilson, 'stick to the technical term in the translation? ...' I feel very strongly inclined to think that he [Cavalcanti] was a poet, using a commonly received terminology and trying to turn it into beautiful verses' (Gilson, p. 109).

Pound, who was convinced that beauty and precision were one and the same thing, evidently took Gilson's advice to heart. A letter written by Pound to Gilson in 1932, now preserved in Etienne Gilson's archive at the Pontifical Institute for Mediaeval Studies (see Appendix 2), is an important document for the transition from the version inserted in the Cavalcanti edition and the one that will be a section of Canto 36. But the letter is also important in that it summarizes the conceptual nucleus of Pound's reading of Cavalcanti. In a passage of the letter, Pound writes: 'I didn't mean to imply that my interpretation of Guido (character, etc.) could be *proved* by the isolated text of *Donna me prega*, [...] but that, taking that poem with the others and with Papa Cavalcanti down in the burning tombs, etc., one had more or less the right to try the line of conjecture indicated.'

Pound continues by focusing on Cavalcanti's 'heresy' and finds a confirmation of it in the scene of the Epicureans of *Inferno* X ('che l'anima col corpo morta fanno'). Pound's insistence on this point contradicts Gilson, who puts into doubt that Guido is a natural philosopher, asserting that 'there is not the slightest evidence that he was an Averroïst, still less an Epicurean.'

Two strategic passages of the canzone are taken up in Gilson's examination. One is referred to 'largir simiglianza' ('laire simiglglianza' in Pound's text), which he explains through the medieval concept of form that generates its own likeness by a process similar to irradiation. The other is 'egli è creato' (Love is created, hath a sensate name, / his modus takes from the soul, from the heart his will.) In taking up this latter passage Gilson offers an explanation of the two lines of the canzone suggesting that 'love is created,' implies that Cavalcanti has taken its name, 'amor,' from 'anima,' for it has its seat in the soul. Pound's opposition to Gilson's etymology shows how much he is aware of the importance of this passage: 'The only place where I am sure is on p. 110 of your review about etymology. NO, that is against the whole grain of Guido, that kind of diddling belongs to the poetasters; of whom he was NOT.'

In the revised translation inserted in Canto 36, there are some technical words that were not used in the previous translation, among them the following: 'formed like a diafan from light on shade,' and 'intellect possible.' The variation in translation, however, shows that Pound has used not only Gilson's suggestion but also some suggestions contained in del Garbo's commentary. The literal translation of 'diafan' is an important example of this, because this word was related to Aristotle's *De anima* and to the theory of light on which Pound focused his interpretation of *Donna me prega*. A crucial change occurs, as mentioned above, when Pound transforms the translation of the following passage: 'E vol ch' om mirj in un formato locho' according to Pound text of the canzone.' What Pound has translated in *Rime* as 'unforméd,' he translates in Canto 36 as 'formed' (willing man look into that formed trace in his mind).

This change is worthy of further attention. 'Unformed' sounds as if it has the opposite meaning of 'formed'. In a note Pound explains that the discrepancy between his Italian text, which reads 'formato locho,' and his translation, which reads 'unformed place,' derives from the reading of different manuscripts. But probably, and despite appearances, Pound was using the term 'unformed' as echoing the Latin *informans*; that is, he was giving an interpretive translation. But whatever the meaning of 'unformed,' the change shows Pound's decision to emphasize what is for him the central meaning of the canzone: the making of the mental image. In *Further Notes* section the following is especially noteworthy: 'To keep all the distinctions the 'formato locho' would have, I should say, to be the fantasia itself, already pervaded by the accident which comes from the seen form.'[36] In the new version (Canto 36), we find 'formed trace' instead of 'unfórmed place.' 'The formed trace' will be central from now on, not just as an interpretation of Cavalcanti, but, since it is a metaphor for the activity of imagination (and for the making of the image itself), as something central to the process of knowing. In Pound's identification of intelligence, imagination, and poetry, the 'formed trace' or 'formato locho' is a process in becoming in which intelligence and imagination coincide.[37]

It is in the transition between the *Rime* edition and the new version (as in Canto 36) that Cavalcanti becomes the 'point of crisis' of the new canon. All this is according to the definition of 'crisis' as latent energy that Pound had given in the late 1920s. In 1940 Pound offers for the 'European Paideuma,' his Notes on 'Medievalism' in Cavalcanti along with the Ethics of Mencius.[38]

At the same time as Gilson's article, another review of Pound's edition of the *Rime* was written by the Italian literary scholar Mario Praz. Much less friendly than Gilson, Praz, in a well-known article ('Corriere della sera,' 1932), attacked Pound's edition with particular emphasis on the philology of the Italian text of *Donna me prega* and Pound's editorial methodology.[39] Praz's article betrayed a good deal of antipathy for the American poet, who at that time was living in Italy. However, it was Praz who was the first to understand the value of Pound's indication of the importance of Cavalcanti's technical terminology. He in fact emphasized that Pound contrasted this viewpoint with the opinion of the medievalist Karl Vossler, who judged Cavalcanti's terminology to be philosophically imprecise.[40] Praz's article inaugurated the Italian attitude, mainly academic, of regarding Pound with suspicion. This tradition, which culminated in Contini's reductive reading of Pound as both poet and scholar, has become easier in more recent years with the great work on Pound and modernism that has been done by the American Academy and has been recognized by Italian scholars.

Some years ago, Maria Corti wrote a note on Dante in which she recalled Pound's Cavalcanti.[41] She appreciated the importance Pound attributed to the precision of vocabulary, evaluating his emphasis on medieval technical terminology as crucial for an understanding of Cavalcanti's poetry. According to Corti, many of Pound's assertions have no scientific value. She noted Pound's confusing Aegidius Romanus with the Pseudo-Aegidius, who wrote a commentary on Cavalcanti's canzone,[42] but her emphasis was mostly on Pound as poet and translator, and on his acoustic power and innate knowledge of the universe of poetic word. In Corti's perspective, Pound's Cavalcanti starts to be considered in a more balanced way. Pound did not have the tools for a correct interpretation of *Donna me prega*. We must not look at the philology of the edition of *Rime*, but rather regard it as the hommage that a poet gives to a great poet. The edition of Pound's Cavalcanti is crucial in order to understand Pound.

Corti's point of view introduces us to a topic of importance: whether and how Pound's reading contributes to our understanding of Cavalcanti as a poet. It is certainly true that Pound wanted to pay hommage to Guido. But Pound's hommage was much more important as an attempt to focus on Cavalcanti as a poet. Pound's discussion of 'form' in *Medievalism* shows how much he was attempting to find the true sense of Cavalcanti's writing.

What Pound writes at the beginning of his edition now should be taken into consideration: '[Cavalcanti] ... Non aveva la pazienza per scrivere una Commedia Eretica. Commedia Eretica' shows that Pound sees in Cavalcanti the confluence of an alternative tradition to that of Dante – a tradition that will be basic for Pound's poem. But the insertion of *Donna me prega* into Pound's *Cantos* suggests something more. It must be related to the crucial question Pound put forth in *Rime*: how is it possible to define the poetry Cavalcanti has written?

The natural philosopher that tradition sees in Cavalcanti does not explain the qualities of Cavalcanti's poetry. The disdain for Guido in *Inferno* X, which the first commentators of the *Commedia* read as a disdain for poetry, shows that tradition recognizes the peculiarities of Guido's writing as unusual in Dante's time. Pound worked and conducted research in many Italian libraries. He found in Ugolino Verino (fifteenth century) what appeared to him to be the essence of Cavalcanti's poetry, which he quotes as an epigraph in *Rime*. Here Guido becomes 'egregius' for mathematics. But it is the tradition Ficino initiates, when he defines Cavalcanti's poetry written 'artificiosissime,' that explains Pound's quotation from Verino. He connects Ficino's 'artificiosissime' with Cavalcanti as 'egregius for numeris.' 'Artificio,' as Pound reads it, implies that the rules for making poetry are rules of construction and calculation – that is, mathematical rules.

The Platonism of humanism allows Pound to reread Cavalcanti's poetry in light of *téchne*. Pound utilizes Verino's excerpt as an epigraph. More than an introduction to the topics Pound focuses on in *Rime*, the epigraph opens up a future rethinking of Cavalcanti. What I have indicated above as a rhetoric of harmony gets its very specific meaning once we connect the epigraph Pound uses with what he will assert a few years later when he apparently returns to and clarifies a thought that was implicit in his Vorticism. For Pound, the rhetoric of harmony implies mathematical rules of construction.[43] This is a method that probes Pound's research of the late 1920s as well as his thinking of the late 1930s as he exposes it in a text (*Estetica pragmatica*) written to George Santayana. Here he connects writing to mathematics and detaches it from what the Middle Ages termed the trivium.[44]

The process for inventing the modern culminates at the very moment in which Pound deliberately returns to his Vorticism and radicalizes his position of the 1910s. Poetry is related to mathematics because its rules are those of construction. The generation of the image, which is the natural process of *phantasia*, needs, in order to be transcribed into language, rules of construction that imply a new logic of relations. Metaphor embodies such construction, which is at once intuitive and calculated.

Cavalcanti's Function in Pound's *Cantos*: Writing and Accidentality

From Pound's reading of *Rime* to the inclusion of *Donna me prega* in Canto 36 until the introduction of Guido speaking his own language in Canto 73, the increasing importance of Cavalcanti becomes evident. In Canto 73, for instance, the hommage paid to Guido (which parallels the one Dante makes in *Purgatorio* XXVI to Arnaut) is eloquent and speaks for itself. Pound wrote in *The Spirit of Romance* about the uniqueness of Dante's relation with Arnaut, to whom alone in the *Commedia* is given the honour of speaking in his own language. Canto 73 makes the same hommage to Cavalcanti. Like Arnaut, Guido speaks his own language.

The title Pound gives to Cantos 72–3, 'Presenza,' sends us back to *The Spirit of Romance*. Here we read that a peculiarity of Provençal poetry was to concentrate its attention on the present. Important too is the fact that Pound, by introducing Cavalcanti's presence through an image, creates a metaphor for Cavalcanti by deliberately recalling to memory and attention the qualities of Guido's art. According to Pound, this was also the method Dante had used when he introduced Arnaut. The image of Guido galloping thus presents the major quality of Guido's art: to create images that are things, to utilize a language of precision that makes things come alive on the page.

For Pound, this unfolding clarity of perspective includes a rethinking of *Donna me prega* that takes place during the 1930s – in *Make It New,* for instance, in the opening section 'Date Line,' Pound writes that he has read *Donna me prega* as psychology. In addition, Pound clarifies that his Cavalcanti represents a 'criticism by translation.' In unpublished notes preserved at Yale, we read that Cavalcanti must be considered as a chapter of *How to Read* – a special chapter, we may say, if Pound devotes an entire book to Cavalcanti after the first edition of 1912.

It is therefore most important, on the one hand, to understand Pound's reading, and on the other to connect it to Pound's work. Canto 73, which follows the canto devoted to Marinetti, indicates a new awareness. Pound's love for the past contrasts with Marinetti's futurism. Both the past and the future create the identity of the present. The way in which Pound introduces Guido apparently continues Dante's and Boccaccio's tradition. But to the 'altezza d'ingegno' that Dante attributes to Guido, and to the 'motto ingegnoso' of Boccaccio, Pound opposes a Guido who has 'chiarezza d'intendimento.' 'Intendimento' is not synonymous with intelligence but encloses the meaning of tending toward something with the intention of making something. 'Intendimento' encloses the magnitude of a project Pound recognizes in Cavalcanti's poetry. This project enters in the third part of the *Cantos* and will be operative through what may be called Cavalcanti's function in Pound's poem. The word 'function,' as I use it here, has a specific meaning. Function is what establishes a relationship among different orders of events or things. To understand Cavalcanti's function in the *Cantos* requires that the reader organize his thinking around a logic of relations.

Usually scholars focus on memory as the essential meaning of Cavalcanti for Pound. Related to this fact is the connection they establish between *The Pisan Cantos* and Cavalcanti. Pound's paradise, interpreted by some scholars as a paradise of memory, brings them to relate Cavalcanti to the Pisan cantos too. Cavalcanti was, of course, one of the sensible centres of *The Pisan Cantos.* Because Pound wrote this section of his Poem during his detention in Pisa – where he did not have books (with the exception of Confucius) – Pound was compelled to use memory as a book. But the central invention there was the role given to his own body. Memory and the power of *phantasia* are crucial in the Pisan cantos, but what is important is that they are presented as the result of the body's power. The great invention in these cantos derives from Pound's use of Cavalcanti. The centrality of the body in Guido's poetry also becomes basic for Pound, who puts forth his own body activity as a text that he reads.

Here the 'formato locho' as the activity of *phantasia* records Pound's experiencing the intelligence of the senses. The generation of the image, because it is a generation, is at the centre of the reconstruction implied by the Pisan cantos. 'Formato locho,' which introduces the formative activity of *phantasia*, resounds in Canto 74 with 'beauty is difficult': 'and that certain images be formed in the mind / to remain there / formato locho.' The Pisan cantos are built on the activity of imagination and its discontinuity that the prisoner experiences.

The body's power and the intelligence of the senses are at the centre here. Poetry records the events that the body activates and generates. But the central idea is that poetry is a generative activity that produces and compares forms. The Pisan cantos include Cavalcanti's poetry as the milestone through which Pound works to reverse and rebuild the values of the West. The notion of paradise as 'spezzato' (Canto 74) is introduced here. In it, layers of thought are active that Pound will unfold in the new section, entitled *Rock-Drill.* It is in this section of the poem that we find another nucleus of what I call Cavalcanti's function.

In order to retrace this function, I will start by returning to what, for Pound, is the central metaphor of the canzone, that is, in his words, 'the metaphor on the generation of light.' This metaphor is incorrect when it refers (as Pound does) to love (in the canzone) as an illumination. I have discussed this metaphor at length in chapters 2 and 4 of this book. To understand the importance Pound gave this metaphor, we must look at the connection he makes between Cavalcanti and Robert Grosseteste – the medieval Schoolman, translator, and commentator on Aristotle. Pound derives this connection (which today appears either ingenuous or as yet another of Pound's errors) from a mistake made by Ernest Renan, who attributed Averroism to the Franciscans of Oxford and to Grosseteste.[45] In his emphasis on light, Pound was therefore convinced that emphasis should be given to topics that were important for Averroism.

Pound's references to light and the quotations from Grosseteste (which appear in *Partial Explanation*) are, as he explains in a footnote, in part based on Gilson's *History of Medieval Philosophy*, and in part on Baur's 1912 pivotal edition of Grosseteste. Using Baur's edition, Pound quotes excerpts from Grosseteste's *De luce* and *De lineis* with a few more texts.[46] What is crucial here is the connection Pound makes between Cavalcanti's Averroism and the theory of light as 'multiplying,' which he finds in Grosseteste.[47] That is, he regards light in terms of the physics of light and specifically in terms of Grosseteste's idea of light as an energy that multiplies itself. This idea was opposed to what Pound in those years was putting forth as the root of evil – monotheism, that is, the belief that God was one and immobile, which he finds in Aristotle's *Metaphysics*. We can only guess how much he may have been influenced by what he read in Renan about Averroes's criticism of Aristotle's *Metaphysics* XII, a book in which Aristotle puts forth his idea of God as one and 'per se stans et immobile,' coinciding with the substance of metaphysics.[48] Averroes's criticism of it as introduced by Renan is probably part of Pound's agreement with Averroes.[49]

In light of this reading, we may evaluate Pound's insistence on seeing light and energy as central to the canzone. It is sufficient to read some passages of Grosseteste's *De luce* to understand what Pound is looking for – namely, a connection between the energies he sees in Cavalcanti's canzone and the theory of light as expounded by Grosseteste.

To summarize, we may say that at the centre of his reading, Pound put the idea of the coincidence between body and energy, and he sees in the formative power of imagination the result of that coincidence. He did not take into account the theory of the possible intellect as separate – a theory to which Renan dedicates more than a chapter. Pound does not take into account Cavalcanti's division in man between the senses and the intellect. He understands the theory of love as the perfection of the sensible, and he emphasizes the values of the perfection of the body. In other words, Pound sees in Cavalcanti's theory of love the coincidence between the theory of light as energy (which he finds in Grosseteste), and the theory of love as energy as he reads it in Cavalcanti's metaphor of the generation of light. Pound no doubt identifies this metaphor with the power of image-formation as a theory of intelligence.

In light of the studies we have today, we may say that however inaccurate Pound may have been as a philologist, there is great power in his idea of the body as central to Cavalcanti. Pound's idea of the body as the centre of energy was the result of deep reflection on the traditional meaning of Cavalcanti as 'physicus' ('philosophus naturalis'). The opposition of natural philosophy to metaphysics sums up the pivotal role that Cavalcanti plays in the *Cantos*, which, we recall, seek to oppose Dante by seeking their basis in an alternative tradition. The break between the two poets becomes central for Pound and also paradigmatic of a break within Western culture itself.

The return of Cavalcanti, which Pound puts forth in Canto 73, heralds a new awareness. What Pound opposes derives its basis from metaphysics, from which the logic of syllogism and the method of abstraction are (according to Pound) in turn derived. He finds in Cavalcanti the alternative basis on which to build his poem. That basis is twofold: from one side, it is the generation of the image (as we have already seen), and from the other, accident. The whole poem will be shaped by this notion, and its historical importance permeates both the poem and Pound's awareness.

Initial evidence of this fact is shown by Pound's insertion of a revised translation of *Donna me prega* in Canto 36 of the Cantos. The first stage of Pound's relationship with Cavalcanti culminates in this insertion, while a new stage is opening. Pound's use of Cavalcanti's text as his own in this canto speaks for itself, but the place Cavalcanti occupies has a specific meaning. *Donna me prega* deliberately gives the poem a new direction. According to a prevailing practice in the *Cantos*, Pound inserts the canzone as a long quotation. Here the poem seeks to make explicit a coincidence of method, and hence Pound's own method.

Pound's attempt to introduce an ideogrammic language, the meaning of which lies in the correspondence between thing and word, first appeared in the Western literary tradition in Cavalcanti's technical vocabulary. The 'nomina sunt consequentia rerum' in Dante's *Vita nuova* shows, as Pound no doubt thinks, Dante's debt to Cavalcanti. Literal meaning is the essence of Cavalcanti's poetic method, which Pound sees as the alternative on which to fashion poetry's new role.

Pound's Cavalcanti works as the deconstructor of the tradition of Western culture. He is the model on which this culture can be rethought and reshaped. Documentary evidence of this attempt may be found in the chart Pound includes in the new edition of *The Spirit of Romance* (1929). Here, against the 'fat-headed Aquinas,' are counterposed the names of Arabic philosophers and of Roger Bacon and Robert Grosseteste.[50] Cavalcanti's name does not appear here, but in his reading of *Donna me prega*, Pound's connection of Cavalcanti's work with Roger Bacon and Grosseteste on the one hand and Avicenna and Averroes on the other, reveals that he was already examining the tradition that converges in Cavalcanti.

Cavalcanti is a milestone in an alternative mode of thought that was obliterated by metaphysics, which had been triumphant in the Western tradition. Pound therefore associates Cavalcanti with a thirteenth-century renewal that occurred with the introduction of Arabic culture and philosophy to the West. The Arabic reading of Aristotle, as opposed to Aquinas's reading, is at the centre of Pound's reflection.[51] Dante's 'swallowing' Aquinas[52] is tacitly opposed to Cavalcanti, who did not swallow him.

Because Cavalcanti's poetry is rooted in a nonmetaphysical tradition, Pound begins to compare Cavalcanti's tradition with Chinese culture, which, for Pound, has no abstract implications. Pound's essay, *How to Write*, which looks at an updating of written language in light of the new science of matter, and which Pound projects in order to fill the gaps that Renaissance culture failed to fill, regards Cavalcanti as responsible for a new method. The establishing of this new method becomes much clearer when Pound works on *Donna me prega* in the late 1920s.

A confirmation that Pound read Cavalcanti in this way is offered in the final section of Canto 36, where *Donna me prega* is connected with the medieval philosopher Scotus Erigena (ninth century). As we saw earlier, Pound, in his 1929 edition of *The Spirit of Romance*, had indicated what he saw as a conspiracy of intellects against medieval abstraction. Among these intellects he included Scotus Erigena. Canto 36 thus introduces us to what we may call Cavalcanti's function in Pound's *Cantos*.

Let us briefly focus on the generally inexplicable connection that Pound suggests in Canto 36 between Cavalcanti and Scotus Erigena. The sources of this connection can be partly found in Renan, who connects Arabic peripatetism to the heresies of Amaury of Bene and his disciple David of Dinant. But Pound used other sources to link them with Scotus Erigena's *De divisione natura*. He probably read Gilson for the relation between the heresies of Amaury, David Dinant, and Scotus Erigena. Another source could have been the *Manuale* of Francesco Fiorentino. We know that this association between Scotus, Amaury of Bene, and David of Dinant was already circulating among scholars from the beginning of the nineteenth century.[53] According to scholars, Amaury of Bene and David of Dinant, in order to understand Aristotle's works on physics, used Scotus Erigena's *De divisione naturae*: they 'went so far as to identify God with Aristotle's pure potentiality, called first matter.' This was the reason for the 1210 ban on Aristotle, repeated in 1215, which prohibited the teaching of Aristotle's works on natural philosophy.[54]

The banning of Scotus Erigena's works corroborates Pound's idea that in the thirteenth century an opposition existed to the Aristotle of the *Physics*. In a 1940 letter to Otto Bird, a student of Gilson who was then engaged in transcribing del Garbo's manuscript, Pound informs him that he is reading Scotus Erigena (vol. 122 of Migne, *Patrologia Latina*) and afterwards will turn again to *Donna me prega*.[55] Two sets of Pound's notes on Scotus Erigena preserved in the Beinecke Library show that here Pound's interest is concentrated on the philosophy of light.[56] Pound probably sees in Scotus Erigena the philosopher who introduced light and physics simultaneously into the West. Pound's interest in Scotus Erigena is thus related to Cavalcanti because Pound had focused on the metaphor of the generation of light as the form of *Donna me prega*. But evidently Pound is seeing a medieval line of thought that had focused on physics and light. What I would like to emphasize, by way of conclusion, is that the connection between Cavalcanti and Scotus Erigena, while based on a misunderstanding, confirms once more Pound's attempt to organize a line of opposition to metaphysics and its abstractions.

In this opposition, we have, as I have previously indicated, Cavalcanti's function in the *Cantos*. His function works in a specific way. Function, as I am using it, has the technical meaning that Pound suggested in *Machine Art* (1927–30).[57] It is, as previously suggested, that which creates a relationship among different classes of things or events.[58] Our discussion of Cavalcanti's function therefore goes beyond what we read in Pound's edition of the *Rime* to an inclusion of documents belonging to Pound's work of the late 1930s and early 1940s.

The first document to be considered is a scheme for the poem that Pound wrote in Italian during the early 1940s.[59] This scheme, however, needs to be read in light of some letters Pound wrote during the same period to George Santayana, who, at that time was living in Italy. These documents have to be related to his *Guide to Kulchur* (1938) and to Pound's attempt here to reshape the Western tradition, opening with Confucius and concluding with his criticism of Aristotle's *Nicomachean Ethics*. Within these documents we must also include Pound's reading, or rather rereading in the early 1940s, of Aristotle's *Metaphysics* as documented by his library.[60] Here we see that Pound, following Aristotle, characterizes the 'accident' as a notion that is in itelf opposed to that of the substance of metaphysics. Here in the margins the capital C written by Pound links C[avalcanti] and accident. To this corresponds the attempt Pound put forth in the 1930s to oppose contemplation as the highest activity according to what he reads in the (*Nichomachean Ethics*,

Book X).[61] In a letter to Santayana in 1940, Pound says that the poem is ideally divided into three sections. The third, not yet written, will contain the 'notion' of the topics Pound had put forth in the two preceding sections. These topics, as he explains, are 'being' and essence.[62]

In order to establish this notion, Pound takes Aristotle's *Metaphysics* as his own point of reference and opposition. Here he evaluates the connection between accident, movement, time, and matter. These themes go along with those he focuses on in the scheme of the 1940s.[63] We find here the word 'fortuitous,' described as crucial in the poem.[64] Pound's marginalia show that, in his reading of Aristotle's *Metaphysics* V, XXX, 1025a14–30, he was focusing on the theory of accident in relation to the fortuitous. We may thus conclude that accident was a notion crucial for Pound while he was preparing the structure of what he indicates as the third section of the poem. The letter to Santayana, mentioned above, if read in light of the scheme drawn up in the 1940s, suggests that time and matter are at the centre of the poem and that both are governed by the notion of accident. Cavalcanti's accident thus enters Pound's work charged with all the complexity that tradition has given it.

Pound builds his poem on accident, but he connects his notion of it with Galileo's new method and new science. With the condemnation of Galileo ('Galileo indexed 1616'), Pound opens the *Rock-Drill* section (Canto 85). Galileo's name suggests a historical awareness with which the new section begins: thanks to Galileo, science centred on laws of matter and motion, in short, on accidentality. The fact that, as he writes in *Rime*, accident was at the centre of Cavalcanti's poetry is therefore the core of Cavalcanti's importance for Pound's late cantos. The twentieth-century poem seeks to organize its own language around accident. This new language – made of relationships shaped by the notion of accident – implies that change and mutability, in one word the *discontinuous*, shapes the writing and the structure of the poem. Pound introduces the word 'accidens' (accident) in the *Cantos* (74 and 83). But the word 'sensibility,'[65] which is connected to the Chinese ideogram 'Ling,' Pound introduces in the opening of Canto 85, is among the elements to be evaluated if we are to recognize the further importance of Cavalcanti and his function. Because he considers Cavalcanti as a representative of a culture free from metaphysical implications, Pound sees in the evaluation of that tradition the possibility of a connection with Chinese culture, which he sees as free from the abstractions that Pound judges to be dependent on metaphysics. Accident as the being of potentiality, as what can either be or not be, is the notion that shapes the poem. A poem based on accident and matter implies a reversal of the tradition that culminates in Dante.

By focusing on Cavalcanti, Pound seeks to locate the foundation on which modern tradition is based. What Pound sees as the line of the Renaissance is continuous with the natural philosophy on which Cavalcanti focused in the thirteenth century. According to Pound, the Renaissance constructs its identity through an opposition to metaphysics. Bacon, Galileo, Leibniz, and Vico are the structures for the Western 'New Organum' that Pound seeks to establish. Moreover, his 'Organum' attempts to establish a new written language for this tradition in which words and things must be in agreement. The Chinese ideogram is the model for a new kind of writing that must enter into Western culture, which has no ideogrammic language. Here the continuity between Guido's use of the metaphor and Pound's 'New Organum' becomes crucial. The emphasis is on the metaphor as something able to organize a language at once concrete and relational. Cavalcanti's interpretive metaphor allows Pound to establish a kind of Western ideogrammic language based as it is on nature. In the same way, the Chinese ideogrammic language is the result of a culture which does not have abstract implications.

Pound's new canon implies the acknowledgement of 'the other' as something alien to Western culture and crucial as a model for reversing the hierarchy. Physics against metaphysics, knowledge conceived as generation and production of an image instead of as an abstraction, poetry as true thinking – all these are parts of Pound's reversal. The idea that poetry does not coincide with the genre but that all knowledge is poietic (i.e., from *poiesis*: productive) is Pound's claim. The *Cantos* move step by step through this process of reversing the established hierarchy. What Pound indicates as paradise encloses the fact of this reversal as well as its meaning. Cavalcanti's function presides over the third part of the *Cantos* (from *Rock-Drill* onward), if we consider, as Pound announced in the previously mentioned scheme, that the third section will contain as a subject a 'philosophical heaven.' Here heaven means science, that is, the knowledge that Pound will introduce in Canto 93 through a quotation from Dante's *Convivio*.[66] The notion of paradise is given in Canto 92: Paradise ... 'is jagged.' In this word Pound concentrates layers of thought, referring to Dante's *Convivio* as his source. In Canto 93, 'jagged' is reiterated and related to Dante's 'non sempre,' which, as Pound writes, is a quotation from Dante's *Convivio* III. This connection between 'non sempre' and 'jagged' compels us to look at the context of

Dante in the *Convivio*. Here the 'non sempre,' as Dante explains it, contains the idea that happiness for human beings is in part conditioned by the principles of matter, whereas for Dante, the angels, as pure intelligence or separate substances, are free from such conditioning. According to the *Convivio*, contemplation for human beings is 'discontinous' because human beings are different from angels.[67] A new meaning thus enters into the relationship that Pound introduces between 'jagged' and 'non sempre.' What for Dante represents the limit of human nature is at the centre of Pound's poem – around which a modern concept of paradise is shaped. This is an earthly paradise, which Pound builds utilizing Dante's vocabulary but reversing Dante's theory.

However, Pound's word 'jagged' encompasses a further meaning that has to be seen by returning again to Pound's reading of Cavalcanti. In *Rime*, Pound wrote that Cavalcanti introduced the metaphor of the generation of light. *Phantasia* (from *phos*) was itself associated with light.

In Canto 92, 'jagged' is used with a specific technical meaning. It is related to movement and light as intermittent or discontinuous. This is suggested by Pound's connection of 'jagged' to light as flashing:

> Le paradis n'est pas artificiel
>   but is jagged,
> For a flash,
>   for an hour
> Then agony,

But this connection of 'jagged' with light is even more relevant if we consider that *Rock-Drill* (Canto 85) opens with an ideogram ('Ling') that visualizes the process of light.[68]

Of relevance too is the fact that Pound connects this light-process with the word 'sensibility,' a word Pound had emphasized in relation to love in *Donna me prega*.[69] This detail is of great importance. Pound indicates the principle governing this section by means of the Chinese language. He does so because he wishes to escape from the metaphysical implications that Western tradition has given to light.[70] A connection can be established between light, sensibility, and 'jagged' in the *Cantos*. Discontinuity appears to be the rule presiding over light and 'sensibility.' 'Jagged,' which includes the notion of something changing in time, links time, light, and 'sensibility.'

What is suggested here is that the word 'jagged,' as it appears in Cantos 92–3, contains the notion of the poem Pound was looking for according to what he wrote in his letter to Santayana previously mentioned. If we accept that the notion of paradise is the notion of accident, insofar as accident is the fortuitousness of what can either be or not be, then accident becomes the basis for Pound's organization of the poem – its structure and language.

The third section brings to the surface a method that Pound had sought from the very beginning of the *Cantos*. Poetry is the tool for a new kind of awareness. If accident is the notion of Pound's paradise, it is important to underline Pound's translation of the word accident as 'affect' in *Donna me prega*. Important too is the ideogram 'Ling' and the word 'sensibility,' which Pound associates with the ideogram. Affect, sensibility, and emotions were at the centre of Cavalcanti's poetry, which had focused on the perfection of the corporeal, on imagination and memory as the intelligence of the human being. Because this intelligence works in generating images (phantasms), poetry for Pound is the natural language that this intelligence produces and understands. *Phantasia* as the production of images coincides with the process of poetry and with the process of intelligence itself. Sensibility and light become interpretative metaphors, as they were in Cavalcanti – metaphors that include the process of productive imagination, the intelligence of the body, and the happiness derived from the emotions. Pound had utilized the process of imagination as redemptive in the Pisan cantos, and there the body as part of the process of nature was central. Against the destruction brought about by a war dictated by reasons of usury, the poet in that destroyed Europe made the activity of the generation of imagination paradigmatic of both poetry and salvation. In doing so, Pound utilizes Cavalcanti's method. Through Cavalcanti he seeks to oppose the cognitive process of the Western tradition and its basis on abstractions with a new kind of knowledge that poetry makes active.

In an interview later in his life, Pound will say that the difficulty in *Rock-Drill* was that of hammering the dominant thesis.[71] 'Sensibility,' as the intelligence of senses central in the cognitive process, can introduce the dominant thesis of the section. In order to understand this thesis, 'sensibility' must be related to 'jagged' on the one side and to the process of light (as in the ideogram 'Ling') on the other. An intermittency shapes 'sensibility,' and it is here that Pound locates the limit and power of human beings. A historical awareness shapes the poem: the dominant thesis of *Rock-Drill* is the correspondence between 'Ling' – 'sensibility' – and 'jagged.' This thesis grows on the strata of meanings of a notion (accident) that Cavalcanti made central to his poem.

Light is accidental ('jagged'), and it is related to the human activity of creating forms. 'Ling,' while rendering visual the process of light descending, makes it coincident with our activity of forming an image, which the ideogram itself, because ideogram, represents and which the word 'sensibility' suggests. The generative process of imagination is coincident with the process of intelligence and knowledge. Knowledge, emotions, are all shaped by accidentality, so that imagination and happiness are discontinuous.

But Pound's emphasis is on language – written language. What he describes as a process of light may be related to the process of writing itself. 'Jagged' as something marked by sharply broken or varying movement is also a technical word. It can be associated with a diagram that is written by a machine that records a movement and can also show a time-relation and chronological fluctuation. Cavalcanti was a *physicus*, as Pound pointed out, because he utilized a technical language. Pound updates Cavalcanti's method in light of the new tools that mediate the relationship between human beings and nature. According to what Pound wrote in the 1930s, language must be on a par with knowledge. It is the machine that, in modernism, can mediate between human beings and nature. In the section *Rock-Drill*, which is governed by an 'aesthetics' of the machine, paradise as 'jagged' (*Cantos* 92–3) updates the paradiso 'spezzato' of the Pisan cantos, if we associate it with the writing of a machine that furnishes us with a recording of a motion and its fluctuation in time. Poetry here becomes a writing that similarly attempts to record. Pound updates Cavalcanti's method. The new precision that machines have introduced demands a new *dictatus*. The rules for writing that Pound put forth in the early 1940s, which were mathematical rules,[72] suggest a twentieth-century rethinking of Cavalcanti's method. The notion of discontinuity (which in Pound implies the discontinuous nature of light and thus the discontinuity of knowledge and imagination) regulates the *form* of the poem. 'Jagged' includes the idea of a writing determined by discontinuity. Light and its discontinuous nature presides over the poem and its structure and language as well as over knowledge, happiness, and sensibility.

Pound's interpretation opens a new chapter in the history of Cavalcanti's reception that needs to be better recognized. T.S. Eliot, who quotes Cavalcanti in his *Ash-Wednesday* and in *Four Quartets* (*The Dry Salvages* V), includes Pound's studies on Cavalcanti in *Literary Essays* (1954) because he understands the invention at work in Pound's reading.

The perception of body as a kind of matter-light that is not material, which Pound regards as peculiar to Guido, goes on to generate the interest of a few subtle readers. And these readers in turn will bring Cavalcanti into Italian contemporary poetry. In the early 1940s, Mario Luzi will associate Cavalcanti with Giotto, describing them as 'uomini assorti,' who were able to create a sense of human body as a being secret and pure.[73] Many years later, Italo Calvino will return to this sense of living and animated body as central to Cavalcanti. Thanks to Calvino, when we reread Boccaccio's novella (VI, 9), the image of Guido leaping over the graves suggests 'lightness' as the essential and enduring quality of Cavalcanti's poetry. With Calvino's 'lightness,' Cavalcanti's poetry becomes a 'memo for the next millennium.'

Donna me prega: The Italian Text and an English Translation

In this Appendix, I offer the Italian text of *Donna me prega* as given by de Robertis (Cavalcanti, *Rime*, 1986) and an English translation of the canzone. The English text mainly reproduces the version of *Donna me prega* by Lowry Nelson (*The Poetry of Guido Cavalcanti*, 1986). The changes, where they occur, reflect my own interpretation of the canzone.

Donna me prega, – per ch'eo voglio dire
d'un accidente – che sovente – è fero
ed è sì altero – ch'è chiamato amore:
  sì chi lo nega – possa 'l ver sentire!
Ed a presente-conoscente-chero,
perch'io no spero – ch'om di basso core
  a tal ragione porti canoscenza:
ché senza – natural dimostramento
non ho talento – di voler provare
là dove posa, e chi lo fa creare,
  e qual sia sua virtute e sua potenza,
l'essenza – poi e ciascun suo movimento,
e 'l piacimento – che 'l fa dire amare,
e s'omo per veder lo pò mostrare

  In quella parte – dove sta memora
prende suo stato, – sì formato, – come
diaffan da lume, – d'una scuritate,
  la qual da Marte – vène, e fa demora;
elli è creato – (ed ha, sénsato, – nome),
d'alma costume – e di cor volontate.

Vèn da veduta forma che s'intende,
che prende – nel possibile intelletto,
come in subietto, – loco e dimoranza.
In quella parte mai non ha possanza
   perché da qualitate non descende:
resplende – in sé perpetüal effetto;
non ha diletto – ma consideranza;
sì che non pote largir simiglianza.

Non è vertute, – ma da quella vène
ch'è perfezione – (ché si pone – tale),
non razionale, – ma che sente, dico;
   for di salute – giudicar mantene,
ché la 'ntenzione – per ragione – vale:
discerne male – in cui è vizio amico.
Di sua potenza segue spesso morte,
se forte – la vertù fosse impedita
la quale aita – la contraria via:
non perché oppost'a naturale sia;
   ma quanto che da buon perfetto tort'è
per sorte, – non pò dire om ch'aggia vita,
ché stabilita non ha segnoria.
A simil pò valer quand'om l'oblia

L'essere è quando – lo voler è tanto
ch'oltra misura – di natura – torna,
poi non s'adorna – di riposo mai.
   Move, cangiando – color, riso in pianto,
e la figura – con paura – storna;
poco soggiorna; – ancor di lui vedrai
   che 'n gente di valor lo più si trova.
La nova – qualità move sospiri,
e vol ch'om miri – 'n non formato loco,
destandos' ira la qual manda foco
   (imaginar nol pote om che nol prova),
ne mova – già però ch'a lui si tiri,
e non si giri, – per trovarvi gioco,
né certamente gran saver né poco

De simil tragge – complessione sguardo

che fa parere – lo piacere – certo:
non pò coverto – star, quando'è sì giunto.

Non già selvagge – le bieltà son dardo,
ché tal volere – per temere – è sperto
consiegue merto – spirito che'è punto.

E non si pò conoscer per lo viso:
compriso, – bianco in tale obietto cade;
e, chi ben aude, – forma non si vede:
dunqu' elli meno, che da lei procede.

For di colore, d'essere diviso,
assiso – 'n mezzo scuro, luce rade.
For d'ogni fraude – dico, degno in fede,
che solo di costui nasce mercede

Tu puoi sicuramente gir, canzone,
là've ti piace, ch'io t'ho sì adornata
ch'assai laudata – sarà tua ragione
da le persone – c'hanno intendimento:
di star con l'altre tu non hai talento.

('A lady bids me, and so I would speak of an accident that is often fierce and
is so haughty that is called love. Would that he who denies that were able to
feel its truth! And for the present purpose I want someone who is an expert,
as I do not expect that anyone base-hearted could bring knowledge to such
reasoning: for without natural demonstration I have no intention of wishing
to bring proof where it resides, what creates love, and what its virtue and
potency may be, its essence and each of its movements, and the pleasure that
makes it called love, or whether one can show it to be visible.

In that part where memory resides, [love] takes its state, formed like diaphanous from light on a shade, that comes from Mars, and dwells there; it is created and its name is the sensate. It is a habit of the soul and an intention of
the heart. [Love] derives from a seen form that is intellected, that takes place
and dwelling in the possible intellect as in a substance. In that part [love]
never has any power. Since it does not derive from quality; it shines in itself as
perpetual effect; it does not have pleasure but rather contemplation; and thus
it cannot create likeness.

[Love] is not a virtue, but comes from that [power] which is a perfection
(for so it is posited); not the rational do I mean, but the sensory. [Love] keeps
its judgment independent of well being, since intention is operative in place
of reason, discerns poorly who is a friend to vice.

Death often follows on [love's] potency if the power should be obstructed that furthers the contrary course: It is not because love is against natural process; but so far as by chance it is diverted from the perfect good, one cannot say that one is alive, if one has not established self-mastery. A like result can obtain when one forgets [love].

Love's mode of being is when desire is so strong that it goes beyond nature's measure, because [love] it is never at rest. It moves making the colour change, turning laughter into tears, and through fear it puts the image to flight; it stays a brief while; moreover, you will see that it is to be found mostly in people of worth. The new quality [love induces] provokes sighs and it obliges man to gaze at an unformed place, arousing one's anger that gives off fire (who has not felt it cannot imagine it), and that one cannot turn elsewhere for relief: of course, one's mind has neither much nor little learning.

From a like temperament [love] draws a glance that makes pleasure seem certain: it cannot stay hidden once it is thus conjoined. Beauties, but not uncouth ones, are an arrow, for such longing is dispelled by fearing: the spirit that is pierced gets its reward. And [love] cannot be known by sight: once understood white falls down from this object, and – who listens well – form cannot be seen: even less, thereby, [love] that from form proceeds. Lacking in colour, separate from being, set in a dark medium, light is erased. Without any deception, I say, as one worthy of trust, that only from [such love] is favour born.

You, canzone, can safely go where you like, for I have so adorned you, that your argument will be greatly praised by those persons who have understanding; you have no desire to be with the others.'

The Letters of Ezra Pound
and Etienne Gilson

Ezra Pound to Etienne Gilson

via Marsala 12–5
Rapallo, Italy

6 Nov. 1932

Dear Professor Gilson

Your review of Cavalcanti has just reached me, hence the delay in answering; and what may have seemed indifference to your offer.

I will be only to [sic] glad to send you the complete photos of the Garbo commentary if you will send me your address. Also a somewhat distressing publication of Fr. Pasquaglio's, not perhaps calculated to attract lovers of the muses.

I did, by the way, try to get your help before publishing my edition, I can't remember whether it was simply a general wail for assistance or a queery [sic] on some definite point. I don't know whether the letter ever reached you.

The translation //// I suppose, as usual, I left too much to be implied. I meant the translation to attract, and to convey the general impression that the Canzone was IN THE FIRST PLACE a poem. I knew, and thought I had made clear, that it was inexact, as translation. Have since made what I hope is a better one, both as poem and as sense.

I didn't mean to imply that my interpretation of Guido (character etc.) cd. be *proved* by the isolated text of Donna mi prega but that, taking that poem with the others and with Papa Cavalcanti down in the burning tombs, etc. one had more or less the right to try the line of conjecture indicated.

The only place where I am 'sure' or where I wd. bet ten to one, you are wrong is on p. 110 of yr. review. about etymology. NO, that is against the whole grain of Guido, that kind of diddling belongs to the poetasters; of whom he was NOT.

I have since set a good deal of the text to music, having, let us hope, more chance of convincing by that argument than philologically.

The 'perfection' passage differs so in the various mss/ that despairing of any satisfactory reading of the original I was not in the least sanguine of any satisfactory translation.

re/ the Garbo. Cicciaporci published the Italian translation found in Mm., but that merely leaves one with the still more 'roreful job' of deciding how far Mangiatroia understood Dino del G. quindi the Garbo original is the only satisfactory place to start.

M. Barbi suggested in conversation (I don't know that he has ventured it in print) that the Roman ms/ was in Boccac[c]io's hand writing, copied late in his life when his hand had begun to shake a little.

P. 108 of yr/ review. If you have ever come up against Luigi's Valli's enormous what-which about Linguaggio Segreto etc. you might wonder whether not only in 1290 but in 1920 there weren't plenty of people who did or do not know that the emotions are a means to understanding.

Where I have failed was probably in not insisting that every line of my comment, be considered in relation to the shorter poems (ballate and the Una Figura)

I suppose I had Valli as phantom disputant, at same time did not want to drag THAT red herring across the perception of the text.

    / this is

    / explanation not excuse /

the 'latent' is matter of style, not wishing to let the reader lie down on a set phrase, but make him at least wonder a little as to what his bleating intellect IS.

The fair comparison (as literature) is probably with passages in the Commedia where Dante is attempting similar philosophic definition or exposition.

I can't pass 'knowledge' as adequate for *consideranza*. I don't believe *consideranza* can be taken apart from mediaeval contemplation, e.g. as in Richard St. Victor.

I believe I have got hold of something at least in 'ardour of thought' which is mediaeval and religious as distinct from (cliche) 'cold scientific etc ...'

On the other hand you are very convincing about the next line, and I must admit that etc. etc.

At any rate, I am content if the edition prevent 'the reader' from thinking that the subject can be sealed up in a can labled [sic] 'answered.'

The testimony of the time is that G.C. *was* a philosopher, open question if he didn't spend more time at that than in writing peosia [sic].

Lorenzo Medici wasn't a philos. and it shows very clearly in his poem about a conversation with Ficino.

How far Guido was being a philosopher WHILE writing the Donna mi prega, is another kettle of fish.

///

Footnote. I did by the way try to smoke up a Brit. Pubr. into printing a translation of yr. Hist. of Mediaeval Philos. but by the time he was ready you were rewriting the book. This is as good a place as any to say that I enjoyed reading the first edition.

Old Garbo's comment don't in the least sustain all my beautiful argument about 'chel prende,' he has *chel* in the text and *che* in comment. I forget whether he does anything to palleate [sic] that.

Sincerely yours,
/s/ Ezra Pound

excuse the length of this

Etienne Gilson to Ezra Pound

The Institute of Mediaeval Studies
St. Michael's College
University of Toronto
Toronto 5

7th December 1932

Dear Mr. Pound:

I feel very grateful to you for your interesting and friendly letter. It is not often that authors are able to understand in what spirit of cooperation a discussion of their work has been written. You felt it and I thank you for your understanding. I am not at all sure that you were always wrong and I was always right on the points under discussion. I am rather sure the contrary is true. But where are you right and I wrong, we cannot say until the commentary enables us to establish the meaning of at least that version of the text whose commentary it is. I am exceedingly glad to think that, owing to your generosity, we shall be able to procure an edition of Garbo's interpretation. It will be very useful in any case and cannot but clear up a number of real difficulties. You might send the photographs to the following address:

The Librarian of the Mediaeval Institute
St. Michael's College
Toronto (Ont.)
Canada

Somebody has already been put in charge of the work and will undertake it under my supervision as soon as the photographs are here.

With best thanks, believe me,

Yours very sincerely
/s/ Et. Gilson

I am leaving Canada next week for Paris, where my adress [sic] is: 2 avenue Emile Acollas (VII). I would gladly receive *there* Pasquaglio's publication, but the transcription of Garbo's commentary will be done here and I shall correct it and study it, when the work is completed.

Ezra Pound to Librarian of Mediaeval Institute

19 Dec. 1932
Via Marsala 12–5
E. Pound /Rapallo

Librarian
Mediaeval Institute
St Michaels College
Univ. Toronto, TORONTO, Canada

Dear Sir:

In accordance with instructions recd. from Prf. Etienne GILSON, I am sending you registered by the post the photos. of the mss/ of Dino del Garbo's commentary on Cavalcanti's 'Donna mi prega.'

Dr. Gilson says someone has been 'put in charge of the work' to be done on these reproductions.

Very truly yours,
/s/ Ezra Pound

Etienne Gilson to Ezra Pound

2, Avenue Emile Acollas (VII)
15th January 1933

Dear Mr. Pound:

Many thanks both for the photos and for Pasquaglio. The first thing for us to do, is to establish a correct Latin text of the commentary and to have it printed; but there will be no difficulty at all in doing that, it is only a question of time. You will, of course, be informed of any results that might have been achieved, though I do not see any progress to be hoped for, just now, except getting the Latin text itself. *Then* there will be a version, and an attempt to apply it to the text of Cavalcanti, and God alone knows what the result will be.

I wish I could go to Rapallo and avail myself of your kind invitation; I thank you for it, but I have now to stay here and teach where I am a professor.

Yours very sincerely,
/s/ Et. Gilson

NOTE
Pound's letter to Professor Gilson and to the Librarian of the Mediaeval Institute are now preserved in the Gilson Archive of the Pontifical Institute of Mediaeval Studies at the University of Toronto. Professor Gilson's letters to Ezra Pound are preserved in the Beinecke Rare Book and Manuscript Library at Yale University.

Notes

Introduction

1 Ezra Pound's notion of 'vortex' is given in his two 1914 manifestos of Vorticism, now contained in *Ezra Pound and the Visual Arts*, pp. 151 and 199.

2 Leaman, *Averroes and His Philosophy*, pp. 140–3.

3 Thillet, 'Reflexions,' p. 106.

4 Black, 'The Imaginative Syllogism,' p. 259 et seq.

5 Ibid., p. 243.

6 Cavalcanti, *Rime* (ed. De Robertis) pp. 185–6, and p. 212.

7 D.L. Black, 'Logic and Linguistics Arts,' in *Aristotle and His Medieval Interpreting*, ed. Bosley and Tweedale, p. 35.

8 Panvini, *Le Rime della Scuola Siciliana*, vol. 1, pp. 645–6.

9 Ibid., p. 643.

10 Ibid., p. 647.

11 Ibid., p. 369 and p. 582. See also Guido delle Colonne, 'Ancor che l'aigua per lo foco lassi,' where 'amore' is defined as 'uno spirito d'ardore, che non si pò vediri.' Ibid., p. 80.

12 'Ancor che l'aigua per lo foco lassi /la sua grande freddura/ non cangeria natura /s'alcun vasello in mezzo non vi stassi ... /ma per lo mezzo l'uno e l'autra dura ...' The word *mezzo* is reiterated in the last stanza 'se no che l'aire in mezzo lu consenti.' See Panvini, *Le Rime della Scuola Siciliana*, pp. 79–82.

13 Contini, *Poeti del duecento*, vol. 2, pp. 481–3. For Guinizelli's canzone, see pp. 460–4.

14 See Pound's *Cavalcanti*, ed. Anderson, Introduction, p. xix.

15 For culture at the court of Frederick II, see Haskins, *Studies* and Kantorowicz, *Federico II*. For the curriculum in Naples, see De Vaux, 'La première entrée,

and Weisheipl, *Tommaso d'Aquino*, pp. 17–23. For Giacomo da Lentini, I must refer the reader to my work in progress, *Multiculturalism and Sicilian Poetry*, a section of which is dedicated to Giacomo da Lentini.

For Guinizzelli, see my article 'Guido Guinizzelli's "Al cor gentil," and its revised version: 'Love and Natural Law in the Manifesto of Dolce Stil Novo.' For Bologna University and the Faculty of Arts and Medicine, see Siraisi, *Taddeo Alderotti*. For the discussion on logic, in addition to the already recalled studies: Black, 'The Imaginative Syllogism,' and 'Logic and Linguistics,' Leaman, *Averroes and His Philosophy*, and Thillet, 'Reflexions'; see also Buzzetti, Ferriani, and Tabarroni, *L'insegnamento della logica a Bologna*. On logic and the influence of the Arabic model, see Maieru, 'Influenze arabe.'

Chapter One: Love as a Metaphor

1 'And let the birds sing of it, each one in its own tongue.' These two lines are quoted from Cavalcanti's ballad, *Fresca rosa novella*. As is well known, Cavalcanti quotes these lines from a poem written by Guilhem IX, *Ab la dolchor del temps novel*. We find a similar passage in a poem by Bonagiunta Orbicciani. All quotations from Cavalcanti's poems are taken from De Robertis's edition of *Rime*. The roman numeral, where it appears, indicates the number of the poem in De Robertis's edition. All translations of Cavalcanti's poems are from *The Poetry of Guido Cavalcanti*, ed. Nelson. Changes, where they occur, reflect my own interpretation of the text.

2 Bacon, *Opus Maius*, vol. 2, p. 120 et seq. (chapter 7 on *De scintillatione*).

3 This aspect of Aristotle's philosophy was emphasized by the Arabs. Avicenna's *De anima*, conceived as 'Sextus de naturalibus,' explicitly connects the soul to the philosophy of nature. What was discussed from Greek culture onward was to establish whether the study of man belonged in its entirety to the field of physics or not. See Verbeke, Introduction to *Avicenna Latinus, Liber de anima*, vol. 1, pp. 10–12. I will focus on this topic in chapter 3.

4 De Robertis, *Rime*, pp. 9–11

5 Ibn Al-Haytham (Alhazen), *Optics*, vol. 1, Book II, 3, pp. 200. See propositions n. 202–3: 'therefore light by itself produces beauty. Colour also produces beauty. For every bright colour, such as purple, purpure, vegetable green, rose ... please the eye ... Therefore colour by itself produces beauty.'

6 *Fresca rosa novella*, in De Robertis, *Rime*, p. 7.

7 For Taddeo Alderotto see Siraisi, *Taddeo Alderotti*.

8 For the discussion on love defined as an 'accident' in *Donna me prega*, see chapters 2 and especially 3 of this book. For Cavalcanti's rhetoric, see Calenda, *Per altezza d'ingegno*, especially pp. 11–98.

9 In Aristotle's *De anima* II, V, VII, vision enters as part of the discussion of sen-

sation. For Alhazen's theory of vision as a passion, see Sabra edition of Ibn Al-Haytham [Alhazen] *Optics*, vol. 1, chapter I,4. For 'passion,' see chapters 2 and 3 below.

10 Cavalcanti's introduction of the visual *pneuma* or spirit seems to follow Avicenna and Averroes in their development of the Stoic-Galenic tradition. Avicenna's *De anima* accorded great importance to the visual *pneuma*, attributing to it the activity of vision. See *De anima* I, III, 8, and Verbeke's introduction to it, specifically vol. 1, pp. 83–90. Averroes speaks of the pneuma 'through which vision is brought in the effect' in *Epitome of Parva naturalia*, I, p. 18. For medieval theories of vision, see Lindberg's discussions on Avicenna's and Averroes's theories, in *Theories of Vision*, pp. 45–57. The importance Cavalcanti accords to vision and to the visual spirit must be seen in the context of the debate on these themes that took place in the ambience of the University of Bologna's Faculty of Arts, which included doctors as well as philosophers. See Delhaye, 'La Place des arts liberaux,' p. 170; and especially Siraisi, *Taddeo Alderotti*.

11 Brunetto Latini, *La Rettorica*, in Segre and Marti, eds., *La prosa del duecento*, p. 148. Translation is mine.

12 Ibid., p. 149.

13 Cavalcanti's utilization of the term 'spirit' derives from the medical tradition which was active also in Avicenna and Averroes. Generally in this tradition the *pneuma* is conceived as an element indispensable for the functions of physiological life. The term 'spirit' derives from the Greek *pneuma*. The term was utilized in antiquity with a material sense. See Verbeke, *L'Evolution de la doctrine du pneuma*. For Avicenna's notion of 'spirit,' see *De anima*, in particular, II, V, 8, *De ostensione instrumentorum animae*. See also Verbeke's important introduction to Avicenna's *De anima*, in particular vol. 2, pp. 52–5: 'Aux yeux d'Avicenne, toute connaissance sensible, y compris celle des sens internes se fait a l'aide d'un instrument corporel ... Si les réalités corporelles sont perçues aussi longtemps qu'elles restent présentes à la faculté sensitive, c'est que celle-ci opère à l'aide d'un instrument corporel.' On medical spirits, see Bono, 'Medical Spirits,' which includes an important section on Alfred of Sareshel's *De motu cordis*, a book that was greatly influential in the 13th century as a textbook. See Van Steenberghen *La Philosophie*, p. 115.

14 Avicenna, *De anima* II, V, 8, 176: 'Unde si anima una est, oportet esse membrum unum propter quod principaliter pendeat ex corpore et ex quo regat corpus et augmentet, et hoc fiat mediante hoc *spiritu*; et ut prima actio quam facit anima sit *ipsum membrum* quo mediante diffunduntur eius virtutes in alia membra; et ut ipsum membrum sit generatum ante omnia membra, et sit *primus locus ubi generatur spiritus: hoc autem est cor* ... Oportet Ego ut *anima*

principaliter pendeat ex corde, impossibile est autem prius eam pendere a corde et postea a cerebro: cum enim pendet a primo membro fit corpus animal; in secundo autem non operatur nisi mediante primo' (emphasis mine).

15 Avicenna, *Liber Canonis*, f. 258: 'Anhelitus: Sermo universalis de anhelitu.'

16 Siraisi, *Taddeo Alderotti*, pp. 413–15.

17 Alessio introduces the debate on interjection as part of the discussion on the *modi significandi*. See 'Il commento di Gentile da Cingoli a Martino di Dacia.' However there is no evidence that Cavalcanti makes use of this theory in utilizing the interjection; what emerges from this debate is that importance was given traditionally to interjection as a way to signify an affection of mind (*affectus mentis*).

18 See Alessio, 'Il commento di Gentile da Cingoli a Martino di Dacia,' and in particular, Alessio's introduction, pp. 3–16. The date of this commentary is attributed to the 1290s. The *deh*,' because it is an interjection or exclamation, can be associated with the debate on interjection; see pp. 16–18.

19 The relationship between spirit and respiration is implied in the term spirit itself. *Pneuma* in fact derives from the verb *pnéo* – to blow. See Verbeke, *L'Évolution de la doctrine du pneuma*, p. 1 et seq. *Pneuma* as a vital breath circulating through the arteries and veins was at the basis of physiological functions from antiquity.

20 See Avicenna, *De anima*, IV, 2, pp. 18–19 and Averroes, *Epitome*. Both texts speak of the possibility of seeing things that are not present due to the effect of debility or excessive imagination or sickness. *Epitome*, p. 41, states: 'Thus it occurs that a person is able to apprehend sense-objects even though they are not present externally, because the objects of these senses have already taken form in the sense-organs, and it makes no difference whether these objects come from without (as during waking), or whether they come from within (as during sleep). Sometimes, a similar condition will occur during waking, to one who is frightened or sick, and this as a result of the excessive activity of the imaginative faculty on such occasions ...'

21 The activity of imagination is the first step toward the process of knowing, of which memory represents the highest degree for the individual. For Averroes (*Epitome*, p. 24) this faculty functions in man through reason and deliberation. The difficulty in the process of memory is due to the influence of the senses in that they are related to the separation of man's faculties, while the process of recollection is the joining of the same faculties (*Epitome*, p. 28 and p. 94 nn 42–4).

22 *Vita nova*, ed. Gorni, 15, p. 142. Gorni attributes to Cavalcanti the role of the '*impositore*' of name. Cassata's edition of Cavalcanti's *Rime* (1993) considers *che parli* to be hortatory, which confirms this reading.

23 'Videtur autem quod sapientes et sequaces eorum consenserint in hoc quod gaudium et timor et dolor et ira sunt ex passionibus propriis spiritus qui est in corde.' From 'De medicinis cordialibus,' a text appended to Avicenna's *De anima*, in Van Riet's edition, II, 190. For domicilium vitae, see Baeumker, pp. 12–14.

24 Avicenna, *De anima* II, 193–4.

25 'Sed in quanto, hoc est, ut spiritus delectans sit multae quantitas: propter hoc roboratur virtus eius; ex augmento enim substantiae in quantitate provenit augmentum virtutis in robore suo, sicut declaratum est in principiis naturalium ... Cum autem fuerit parvae quantitatis et materia fuerit pauca, sicut in convalescentibus qui sunt graciles ex infirmitatibus et in senibus, et non fuerit temperatae complexionis, sicut est in aegris, sed fuerit nimis grossis et spissus, sicut est in melancholicis et senibus, non dilatabitur eo quod est grossus, aut fuerit tenuissimus, sicut in macilentis, non erit in eo tantum quod possit dilatari, aut fuerit obscurus, sicut in melancholicis, erit aptissimus tristitiae (*De anima* II, 193–4).

26 See Agrimi and Crisciani, 'Medicina e logica,' in particular pp. 190–1.

27 'Causa autem huius hoc est quod virtutes animales quae sunt in cerebro, quae egent temperamento humoris ad hoc ut ipsae oboediant motui cogitationis et imperio intellectus, sunt multi humoris et non subduntur intellectui. Praeter hoc etiam habent motum multum propter vapores ascendentes commotos qui admiscentur ei, et propter humorem suum non obtemperant motui, nisi motui violento corporali, et tunc fit difficile cogitationi oboedire eis. Virtuti autem intelligibili accidunt ex eis accidentia secundum hoc quod exigit eorum dispositio, ita quod temperatur eorum complexio, et quiescit commotio' (*De anima* II, 195–6).

28 Anger (*ira*) – which he will introduce in *Donna me prega* – generates heat and vapour and disorder in the movement of humours, making extremely difficult the activity of vision and – as we shall see – of imagination, which depends on vision. See chapters 3 and 4.

29 'Qui vero est ex lassitudine, est propter hoc quia id quod vocatur spiritus, de quo postea scies suo loco, dissolutus et debilitatus est, et refugit ad interiora et sequuntur eum virtutes animales. Et haec lassitudo aliquando contingit ex motibus corporalibus, aliquando ex curis, aliquando ex pavore; ex pavore etenim aliquando accidit somnus et etiam mors' (*De anima* II, IV, 33).

30 'Dolor ... non est nisi contrariae rei contrarietatem sentire.' *Canon*, f. 41 D 4. At f. 561 E 6, we read that 'dolor virtutem membri debilitat.'

31 See Wolfson, 'The Internal Senses.' For a discussion on these themes in Bologna's medical ambience during the second half of the thirteenth century, see Siraisi, *Taddeo Alderotti*, and in particular, chapter 7.

32 See for instance, Avicenna, *De anima* II, 207–8, and Averroes, *Epitome*, p. 6.

33 For my discussion of internal senses, I am utilizing the classic article of Wolfson, 'The Internal Senses,' which traces this tradition to Latin, Arabic, and Hebrew philosophical texts and emphasizes the importance of internal senses in Arabic culture.

34 Verbecke, Introduction to Avicenna, *De anima* II, IV, p. 47.

35 Ibid.

36 The first to introduce *wahm*[arabic for aestimatio] into the classification of internal senses ... is Alfarabi.' In addition, Wolfson explains that 'estimatio produced changes in the meaning of the word imagination which in Alfarabi appears to be divided into retentive imagination, compositive human imagination, compositive animal imagination ... he counted human and animal imagination as one ... sometimes [he] uses the general term imagination to include both retentive and compositive imagination as well as estimation' (Wolfson, 'The Internal Senses,' pp. 93–5). For 'aestimatio,' see also pp. 86–90. For the distinction between animal (sensitive) and human (rational or deliberative) imagination and the discussion about it, see pp. 89 et seq.

'Avicenna was the first to introduce Aristotelian common sense among the internal senses ... the description of common sense which recurs in his writings is analogous to Aristotle's characterization of it as faculty, which distinguishes and compares the data of sense-perception' (p. 95).

37 Verbecke, Introduction to Avicenna, *De anima* I, 89.

38 See *De anima*, I, III, 8, p. 269–71 et seq. See also Verbecke, Introduction, vol. 1, p. 86 et seq.

39 'Averroes openly rejects the introduction of estimation as a special faculty ... He further mantains that according to the ancients the unspecified faculty of imagination ... contains also the function of the estimative faculty ... the fact that both compositive animal imagination and estimation are omitted indicates that he considered them, together with retention, as subfunctions of imagination' (Wolfson, 'The Internal Senses,' pp. 107–10).

40 See Averroes, *Commentarium magnum*, Book III, which contains Averroes's theory of intellection.

41 The connection betwwen the process of imagination and the activity of intellection may be read in Averroes, *Epitome*, mainly in the chapters on 'Memory and Recollection' and 'Dreams.' The central discussion is contained in Averroes, *Commentarium magnum* in *De anima*, Book, III.

42 See Van Steenberghen, *La philosophie au XIIIe siècle*, pp. 112–13, which contains an useful scheme-summary of Gundissalinus's classification of sciences in *De divisione philosophiae*. Gundissalinus conceives logic as being 'pars et istrumentum [philosophiae].' *De divisione philosophiae* proposes logic as a sci-

ence which 'media' acts as an intermediary between the sciences of *elocutio* (speech) and those listed as philosophic. See Baur, *De Divisione philosophiae*, pp. 18–19 and 43 et seq.

43 See Maierù, 'Influenze arabe,' pp. 251 et seq.

44 See Black, 'The Imaginative Syllogism.'

45 See Agrimi and Crisciani, 'Medicina e logica,' p. 191. See in this article the reference to Maierù 'logiche speciali,' pp. 187–8.

46 See Maieru, 'Influenze arabe.'

47 Dante, *Vita nova*, ed. Gorni, X; *Vita nuova*, ed. De Robertis, XIX.

48 Potentiality and act are basic in *Amor e 'l cor gentil sono una cosa*, in which Dante repeats notions which were crucial in Guinizzelli, *Al cor gentil rempaira sempre amore* (sì come il saggio in suo dictare pone'). In the prose which follows, Dante utilizes, in fact, an Aristotelian terminology in order to explain his meaning: 'Questo sonetto si divide in due parti. Nella prima dico di lui quanto è *in potenzia*; nella seconda dico di lui in quanto di *potentia* si riduce *in acto* ... Nella prima dico in che suggetto sia questa *potentia*; nella seconda dico come questo suggetto e questa *potentia* siano producti in essere, e come l'uno guarda l'altro come *forma materia* ... dico come questa *potentia* si riduce *in acto*' (emphasis added; *Vita nova*, ed. Gorni, pp. 109–10). For Guinizzelli, see Ardizzone, 'Love and Natural Law.'

49 'Negli occhi porta la mia donna Amore, / per che si fa gentil ciò ch'ella mira, / ... fugge dinanzi a llei Superbia e Ira.' In the prose Dante explains: 'dico sì come virtuosamente fa gentile tutto cio' che vede, e questo è tanto a dire quanto inducere Amore in potentia là ove non é' (*Vita nova*, pp. 111–14). This passage shows Dante's attempt to detach love from the principles of natural philosophy. Although his language is still involved in the Aristotelian terminology (*in potentia*), Dante uses it in a metaphorical way.

50 *Donna me prega* also appears recalled and opposed. In Cavalcanti's canzone we read that love 'oltra misura-di natura-torna' and in *Donne ch' avete* instead we read: 'non for misura: / ella è quanto di ben pò far Natura.'

51 'A me convenne ripigliare materia nuova.' *Vita nova*, ed. Gorni, p. 86.

52 'Apparuit iam beatitudo vestra.' *Vita nova*, ed. Gorni, p. 10. Beatrice-beatitudo is connected to the theory of 'nomina sunt consequentia rerum' in the opening of *Vita nova*: 'La quale fu chiamata da molti Beatrice, li quali non sapeano che si chiamare.' For 'nomina' as 'consequentia rerum,' see *Vita nuova*, ed. De Robertis, XIII, 4; and *Vita nova*, ed. Gorni, p. 66.

53 *Vita nova*, ed. Gorni, pp. 85–93.

54 *Rime*, ed. De Robertis, p. 159–60.

55 Quentin, *Études sur le vocabulaire*, pp. 107–9.

Chapter Two: Vision and Logic

1 The entry of the Aristotelian theory of vision into Europe is related to the entry of the new Aristotle, and in particular to that of *De anima* and the commentaries on it. Avicenna focuses upon vision in his *De anima*, Book III. Averroes devoted much space to a discussion of the theory of vision in his commentary on *De anima*. However, it was with the translation of the work of Alhazen that optics in the West began to be organized on a scientific basis. See Lindberg, *Studies in the History of Medieval Optics*. For an introduction to the entry of Aristotle, see Van Steenberghen, *Aristotle in the West*, and *La philosophie au XIIIe siècle*; see also Grabmann, *I divieti*.

2 In connecting Love to light, Dante refers to an essential light that is a self-illuminated being like the sun. See, for instance, *Convivio* III, II, 5–6, and III, VII, 1–7. Dante, *Opera Minori*, ed. Vasoli and De Robertis. In his studies on light, Alhazen distinguished the essential light as derived from self-illuminated bodies like the sun from the accidental light of non-self-illuminated elements; he also explained that the behaviours of the accidental and substantial lights is the same. See Alhazen, 'Le Discours de la lumiere,' and Ibn al-Haytham (Alhazen), *Optics*, I, 3 and Sabra's introduction, II, pp. lii.

3 Van Steenberghen, *La philosophie a XIIIe siècle*, pp. 321–425.

4 For an introduction to the Averroism in Bologna, see Grabmann, 'L'Aristotelismo italiano al tempo di Dante,' and Corti, *Dante a un nuovo crocevia*, pp. 17–31. Corti also furnishes an excellent bibliography. See also Nardi, 'L'Averroismo del primo amico Dante' and Alessio, 'La grammatica speculativa e Dante.'

5 Bruno Nardi, 'L'Averroismo del primo amico di Dante.' *Studi danteschi* 25 (1940), 43–79, anthologized in *Dante e la cultura medievale*, 93–129.

6 Kristeller, 'A Philosophical Treatise from Bologna Dedicated to Guido Cavalcanti.'

7 Corti, *La felicità mentale*, pp. 3–37; see also her *Dante a un nuovo crocevia*, pp. 9–31.

8 Giele et al., *Trois commentaries anonymes*, pp. 17–20.

9 Ibid. See also Corti, *Dante a un nuovo crocevia*, p. 27.

10 For an introduction to Cavalcanti's 'fortuna,' see De Robertis's introductory essay to his edition of Cavalcanti's *Rime*, pp. xi–xxiv.

11 Boccaccio, *Decameron*, ed. Bianchi et al., pp. 448–51.

12 The text of the 'sonetto' written by Guido Orlandi is reproduced in De Robertis's edition of Cavalcanti's *Rime*, pp. 90–2.

13 Favati, *Inchiesta sul dolce stil novo*, pp. 101–4 is generally suspicious about the

fact that *Donna me prega* originated as an answer to Guido Orlandi and hypothesizes that the 'sonetto' was fabricated a posteriori.

14 Aristotle, *Metaphysics* V, VII, 1017a explains that 'the senses of essential being are those which are indicated by the figures of predication for "being" has as many senses as there are ways of predication. Now since some predicates indicate (a) what a thing is, and others its (b) quality, (c) quantity, (d) relation, (e) activity or passivity, (f) place, (g) time, to each of these corresponds a sense of "being."' Translated by Hugh Tredennick, pp. 237.

15 See how Bonitz, in his *Index Aristotelicus*, indicates at first for *páskein* its derivation from the category of passive.

16 Van Steenberghen, *Maître Sigier de Brabant*, p. 84.

17 Van Steenberghen, *La philosophie au XIIIᵉ siècle*, pp. 112–13, and Gundissalinus, *De Divisione Philosophae*, pp. 81–2.

18 See Weisheipl, 'Classification of the Sciences in Medieval Thought,' pp. 68–71.

19 'Un commentaire semi-averroiste du "Traite de l'ame,"' in Giele et al., *Trois commentaires anonymes*, p. 190.

20 Bird, 'The Canzone d'Amore of Cavalcanti,' pp. 150–203. See also Favati's revised editions of del Garbo's commentary in *La glossa latina* and *Guido Cavalcanti's Le rime*. The latter text is now reprinted in Fenzi, *La canzone d'amore*, pp. 86–133.

21 Bird, 'The Canzone d'Amore of Cavalcanti,' p. 162. The English text is from Bird's translation, p. 182.

22 Aristotle, *De anima*, transl. by W.S. Hett, pp. 105–6. Aristotle speaks of the theory of vision and transparency also in *De sensu et sensato* (II, 439a, 20–5): 'in that treatise [*De anima*] we have already said of light, that it is indirectly, the colour of the transparent; for whenever there is a fiery element in the transparent, its presence is light, its absence is darkness. What we call "transparent" is not peculiar to air or water or any other body so described, but a common nature or potency which is not separable but resides in these bodies and in all others, to a greater or less extent.'

23 Averroes, *Commentarium magnum*, pp. 235–6.

24 '*Complexio* was a term applied to the controlling balance of elemental qualities in any body or its part' (Siraisi, *Taddeo Alderotti and His Pupils*, p. 159). For the heavens as acting on natural mixtures as in human complexio, see ibid., p. 158. According to Alderotto, the efficient causes for mixtures are the heavenly bodies because they are the cause of all terrestrial motion, while the final cause of mixtures is the perpetuation of the universe by generation (because mixture produces generation), p. 158. This could suggest a relationship between the excess of heat and the heat of spermatic activity. For

spermatic activity as an activity which is generative because hot (see Aristotle *De generatione animalium* II, 3 736 b). For the relationship between spermatic activity and the influence of the heavens on this activity, see Touati: 'Le probleme de la generation.'

25 See Corti, *La felicità mentale*, p. 22: '*Sensatum* sostantivo neutro indica nella filosofia aristotelica la qualita' sensibile in atto, cioè percepita dal *sensus*.'

26 Averroes, *Epitome of Parva naturalia*, ed. Blumberg, p. 6.

27 According to Grant, *Planets, Stars, and Orbs*, p. 195, in medieval Aristotelian cosmology celestial matter was assumed to be incorruptible and therefore lacked the contraries which are responsible for changes here below. Change occurred only in the sublunar region where things were always in the process of generation and corruption. Therefore when astrologers or natural philosophers described Saturn as cold and dry, and Mars as hot and dry, they intended that the heavenly region possesses this quality only virtually, not formally. 'That is, the heavens can cause changes involving hotness and coldness in bodies below the Moon, but they do not possess any of those qualities formally or *per se*.'

28 'Marte influisce a "conturbare ... è riscaldativo e incensivo del corpo"' (Cittadini, *L'Esposizione*, f. 17). See also Pseudo-Aegidius text as in Fenzi, *La canzone d'amore*, pp. 187–219, p. 195.

29 Averroes, *Epitome of Parva naturalia*, ed. Blumberg, pp. 6–7.

30 Ibid., p. 27.

31 Corti, *La felicità mentale*, p. 35.

32 Ibid., pp. 23–6.

33 Ibid., p. 21: 'Allora, come il diafano riceve la sua forma ... ad opera del *lumen*, così l'amore riceve la sua forma da una *scuritate*; sarà quindi di necessità *obscurum*, torbido.'

34 Ibid., p. 35.

35 Boehner, *Medieval Logic*, p. 8. For the sophism as enigma, see also Weisheipl, 'Curriculum of the Faculty of Arts at Oxford,' pp. 177–8. Kretzmann describes it this way: '[A sophisma is] a sentence puzzling in its own right or on the basis of a certain assumption, designed to bring some abstract issue into sharper focus ... Because sophismata are sentences rather than arguments and intended to be illuminating and instructive rather than specious and misleading' ('Syncategoremata, exponibilia, sophismata,' in *The Cambridge History of Later Medieval Philosophy*, ed. Kretzmann, Kenny, and Pinborg, p. 217).

36 'Sophisma sentence: it is ambiguous, being true in one of its senses and false in the other' (Kretzmann, 'Syncategoremata,' p. 219).

37 See Alain De Libera, 'La problematique de "L'instant du changement,"' in

Studies in Medieval Natural Philosophy, ed. Caroti, pp. 43–81. In this volume, see also, John E. Murdoch, 'The involvement of Logic in Late Medieval Natural Philosophy,' pp. 3–28.

38 See Lindberg, *A Catalogue of Medieval and Renaissance Optical Manuscripts*, pp. 17–19, and also his 'Alhazen's Theory of Vision and its Reception in the West,' in Lindberg, *Studies in the History of Medieval Optics*.

39 White in Alhazen seems to correspond to transparency in act. '*Albus* = white. Like the Greek *leukos* can be said ... of clear untinted transparent bodies' (Sabra, commentary to his edition of Ibn al-Haytham (Alhazen), *Optics* (vol. 2, pp. 41 and 43. In Averroes, 'white is inferior to the color of light' (*Epitome of Parva naturalia*, p. 11).

40 See Ibn-Al Haytham (Alhazen), *Optics*, vol. 1, chapter 8, 'On the Reasons for the Conditions without the Combination of Which Vision Is Not Effected,' pp. 104–9.

41 See Vescovini, 'Biagio Pelacani a Padova e l'Averroismo,' pp. 147–8. See also Lindberg, *Studies in the History of Medieval Optics*, pp. 357–8.

42 I will return to it in chapter 3, in which I discuss the medieval theory of matter in *Donna me prega*.

43 *Vita Nuova*, ed. De Robertis, in Dante, *Opere minori*, vol. 1, part 1, ed. De Robertis and Contini, pp. 171–2. For the meaning of this passage of *Vita Nuova*, see also chapter 4, note 39.

44 'Primo queritur utrum anima sit accidens. Videtur quod sic nam est actus entis in actu, ergo accidens est. Antecedens patet, nam corpus unde est corpus, ens actu, cuius actus est anima. Oppositum vult Aristotles hic dicens quod sit substantiam secundum formam' (Giele, *Quaestiones De anima*, in *Trois commentaires anonymes*, pp. 64–5). I will return to this topic in chapter 3.

45 Freccero, 'Ironia e mimesi.'

46 What these implications include will be focused on in the next chapter, which discusses the medieval theory of matter. On this basis the final section of chapter 3 will return to Canto X to look for a relation between Dante's theory of time and Cavalcanti's theory of matter as it emerges in *Donna me prega*.

47 'From the very beginning of the tradition as it is known, the sophism was a short disputation centering on propositions that presented logico-linguistic difficulties (largely due to the fact that they contained a syncategoric word)' (Maierù, *University Training in Medieval Europe*, ed. Pryds, p. 134).

48 On the adverb as *syncategorema* Boethius writes in *Quaestio* 122: 'Cum adverbium sit dictio *syncategorematica*, quaeritur, utrum dictio syncategorematica trahat suum significatum ab adjunctis.' Boethius writes that *syncategoremata*

words have a proper meaning, but they exercise their functions when placed in a propositional context. What Boethius stresses is therefore the importance of the *syncategorema* in the oration: 'exercet suum officium quando in oratione ponitur ... extra orationem idem semper habet significatum, sed non habet officium suum, nisi cum in oratione ponitur' (*Modi significandi*, pp. 282 and 284). In *quaestio* 108 Boethius introduces the *syncategoremata* referring them to the indeclinable parts of speech, and indicates that this word is utilized by the logician in order to define them. He writes that he will speak of them as a grammarian and not as a logician (*Modi significandi*, p. 246).

49 Murdoch analyses the positional difference of a syncategorematic term like *semper* in two different propositions in order to show that a proposition could be false or true according to the place the term *semper* occupies (Murdoch, 'The Involvement of Logic,' pp. 16–17). See also Norman Kretzmann, 'Syncategoremata, exponibilia, sophismata,' in *The Cambridge History of Later Medieval Philosophy*, ed. Kretzmann, Kenny, and Pinborg, pp. 211–15.

50 The importance of 'forse' has been pointed out by Pagliaro, *Saggi di critica semantica*, pp. 357–80. Pagliaro however did not discuss 'forse' in relation to logic.

51 'This, then, is the general nature of syncategorematics terms: They are determinations of other terms or propositions, having no signification when taken alone, but exercising their signification only as co-predicates, which is the literal translation of syncategorema ... Since they depend in their signification upon another term which has signification or signifies by itself ...' (Boehner, *Medieval Logic*, p. 22).

52 See Corti: 'Molto si è scritto su quel *cui*, se vada riferito a Virgilio o a Beatrice; personalmente incliniamo per Beatrice, ma la cosa non conta molto perchè sia Virgilio sia Beatrice qui sono simbolo di un' operazione mentale ortodossa, teologicamente in regola: ragione al servizio della teologia e pronta a cedere il ruolo ad essa. Due modi di concepire il sapere qui si contrappongono' (*Dante a un nuovo crocevia*, pp. 84–5).

53 For the long exegesis on this canto, and in particular on this line, see Barolini, *Dante's Poets*, pp. 145–7, and Malato, *Dante e Guido Cavalcanti*, pp. 75–94.

54 Boethius, *Modi significandi*, p. 199.

55 Ibid.

56 Bursill-Hall, *Speculative Grammars of the Middle Ages*, p. 175.

57 See Freccero, 'Ironia e mimesi,' p. 50.

58 According to Boethius and grammarians in general, a pronoun signifies substance: 'omnis enim pars orationis, quae significat rem suam per modum habitus et permanentiae, substantiam significat, sicut loquitur grammaticus de substantia' (*Modi significandi*, p. 238).

59 Concerning Dante's knowledge of Boethius's *Modi significandi*, see Corti, *Dante a un nuovo crocevia*, *La felicità mentale*, and *Percorsi dell'invenzione*. See also Alessio, 'La grammatica speculativa e Dante.' For a criticism of Corti's position, see Pagani, *La teoria linguistica di Dante*, and Maierù, 'Dante al crocevia?' For Dante and logic, see Mazzotta, *Dante's Vision and the Circle of Knowledge*, pp. 96–115.

60 'Medieval grammarians, i.e., the Modistae, in context with their philosophical theories, now established the *partes orationis* as the correlates of reality; the metaphysician had established within the world of things two primary elements, that of permanence and that of becoming (*habitus* and *fieri*), the expression of which became the province of grammarians ... the metaphysical device of the contrast of matter and form is introduced to distinguish the *nomen* and *pronomen*, and the *verbum* and *participium*' (Bursill-Hall, *Speculative Grammars of the Middle Ages*, p. 39). Of Bursill-Hall, see also 'Some Notes on the Grammatical Theory of Boethius of Dacia,' in *History of Linguistic Thought and Contemporary Linguistics*, ed. Parret, pp. 164–88.

Chapter Three: Love as Passion

1 'Ista cantilena quae tractat de amoris passione dividitur in tre partes ... Volens igitur auctor determinare de passione amoris' (Bird, 'The Commentary,' p. 160). The word 'passion' is reiterated throughout the commentary. Dino's commentary was republished by Favati (*La glossa latina di Dino del Garbo*) in 1952. Favati makes a few corrections on Bird's transcription (see *La glossa*, pp. 70–4 et passim). For the importance of the del Garbo commentary, see Favati, pp. 74 et seq., and Quaglio, 'Prima fortuna della glossa Garbiana.' In 1957 Favati produced a new revised text of del Garbo in his edition of Cavalcanti, *Rime*. This text, with a few more corrections, is now reprinted in Fenzi, *La canzone d'amore*. In quoting del Garbo I will use Bird's transcription, and where Favati offers a version strongly different I will also quote Favati, 1957, as now in Fenzi, pp. 86–132.

2 'Dicitur autem haec passio accidens primo, quia non est substantia per se stans, sed est alteri adherens sicut subiecto ut appetitus animae ... Secundo, dicitur accidens quia potest advenire et etiam recedere sicut accidentia alia. Tertio, dicitur accidens quia advenit ab extrinseco ... tamen accidens ipsum principaliter est res extrinseca' (Bird, p. 161); 'tamen causans ipsum principaliter est res extrinseca' (Favati, p. 90).

3 'De causa autem quare haec passio vocatur amor ponere non curamus quoniam de nominibus nulla debet esse cura, cum rei essentiam cognoscamus. Nam secundum Philosophum, nomina rebus ad placitum imponuntur' (Bird, p. 161).

4 'Deinde subdit: "che senza natural dimostramento," etc., id est, sine naturali demonstratione quasi velit dicere quod ea quae dicet extrahet ex principiis scientiae naturalis ...' (Bird, p. 161).

5 In Boccaccio's *Decameron*, VI, 9, p. 449, we read that Cavalcanti was 'ottimo filosofo naturale'; in his *Esposizioni*, p. 516, Cavalcanti is called 'buon filosofo.'

6 'Un de' migliori loici che avesse il mondo,' in *Decameron*, p. 449; 'ottimo loico,' *Esposizioni*, p. 516.

7 'E per ciò che egli alquanto tenea della opinione degli epicurei si diceva tra la gente volgare che queste sue speculazioni eran solo in cercare se trovar si potesse che Iddio non fosse' (*Decameron*, VI, 9, p. 449).

8 See Grabman, *I divieti*, Van Steenberghen, *La philosophie au XIIIe siècle*, pp. 75–81 and 112–20.

9 The meaning of natural philosophy in the Middle Ages largely coincided with the word 'physics,' which by the thirteenth century was equivalent to its peripatetic definition, namely, the study of the material world, insofar as it is carried in the stream of change, *motus*. See Clagett, 'Some General Aspects' p. 29.

10 'The cause of accidental is matter, which admits of variation from the usual.' Aristotle, *Metaphysics* VI, 2 1027a14–15. See also Reale, Introduction to Trendelenburg, *La dottrina delle categorie in Aristotele*, p. 46.

11 See Grabmann, *I divieti*, and Weisheipl, *The Development of Physical Theory*, pp. 26–7.

12 'Aristotle utilises categories just for the being which is sensible and because it is sensible. The transcendent substance is not comprised among Aristotle's categories' (Reale, Introduction to Trendelenburg, *La dottrina delle categorie in Aristotele*, 1994, pp. 49–50).

13 This discussion has been identified by scholars either with chapter I, 7 of *De generatione et corruptione*, or with a book listed by Diogenes Laertius, V, 22, and entitled, *perì toū páskein kaì peponthénai*, a book mentioned also in *De generatione animalium*, as 'perì toū poieīn kaì páskein.' See Aristotele, *Opere*, vol. 4, p. 141, note 56.

14 Ross, *Aristotele*, p. 100 et seq.

15 See J. Owen, 'Matter and Predication,' in *The Concept of Matter*, ed. McMullin, p. 79 et seq. At pages 91–2 we read: 'The presence of matter is proven stringently from the requirements for change, while the nature of matter is established through analogy with the subject of accidental change ... what lacked actuality, or in technical language the potential, could therefore be positive. By establishing the concept of the potential as positive, even though not actual or indeterminate, Aristotle has been able to set up matter as positive ... Because the potential is positive without being determinate, this concept

of matter is possible to the human mind ... its [matter] predicates are notions like purely potential, unknowable of itself, incorruptible.'

16 See *Physics* I, 9, 192a12-20: matter here is defined as 'matrix or womb in the genesis of things ... matter as something the very nature of which is to *desire* and yearn towards actually existent.'

17 Del Garbo's commentary introduces aspects of the theory of matter as the general framework in which love is located when he writes: 'vult auctor ostendere quod amor est res generata vel creata, et ideo dicit, *Egli è creato* ... Similiter etiam vult hic ostendere quae est res generans vel creans istam passionem, et quia ad generationem alicuius passionis in anima concurrunt duae res. Una est dispositio naturalis alicuius corporis; videmus enim quod secundum diversas dispositiones naturales corporum homines sunt apti incurrere diversas passiones ... Alia res concurrit ad causandum aliquam passionem quae est res extrinseca quae suam ymaginem vel speciem causat in virtute sensitiva ...' A few lines after del Garbo mentions Aristotle's physics and relates it to *De generatione animalium* in order to explain what is concurrent in generation he writes: 'nam ut dicit Philosophus in *Physicis, homo hominem generat et sol.* Et in *De generatione animalium* dicit quod in spiritu genitivo est natura existens proportio naturalis ordinationi astrorum' ('Natura existens proportionalis ordinationi astrorum,' Favati). That is, following Aristotle, del Garbo connects the influence of the stars in the sublunar sphere with the theory of the generations of animals, of which human generation is part. See Bird, pp. 162–3, and Favati, pp. 94–6. However different the text of the canzone del Garbo used is from our text, the general framework he provides here is crucial in order to understand what Cavalcanti proposes as the theory of love.

It is evident that 'egli è creato,' which speaks of the generation of form or phantasm at the same time, wants also to insert this generation into the principles of natural philosophy and into the biological process. I will discuss this topic further in the next chapter and in particular in the section titled 'Animal Power.'

18 The ambiguity of the expression 'egli è creato' may be related to the debate that took place in Paris on these topics. According to Siger of Brabant, for instance, matter is created: 'La matière est crée, mais pas directement par la Cause première; elle est crée par l'intermédiaire du ciel ... selon les philosophes ... et elle est donc éternelle comme la sphère céleste dont elle procède ... la matière n'est pas engendrée quant à sa substance ... On peut dire qu'elle est engendrée quant à ce qui lui advient, car, au term de la génération d'un composé, elle possède une certain manière d'être qu'elle n'avait pas précédemment' (Van Steenberghen, *Maître Siger de Brabant*, pp. 327–8).

19 'According to Averroes the world as a whole, together with the outer sphere, are both eternal and temporally originated. They are eternal because their being and activity have no first beginning and no final end, yet they are temporally originated because they undergo constant and continous change' (Leaman, *Averroes*, pp. 44–5). In this context the word 'creation' is utilized with the meaning of 'generation.'

20 The phrase 'egli è creato' (it is created) means that love is subjected to the laws of generation and corruption. Del Garbo explains: 'Idem vult auctor ostendere quod amor est res generata vel creata' (Bird, p. 162). The identification between generation and the eternity of matter derives from Aristotle's *De generatione et corruptione*; here, the theory of genesis does not imply creation but merely coming into being as the result of laws of transformation. In *De caelo*, Aristotle states that what has no beginning cannot come to an end, and therefore the world is eternal. For an introduction, see Grant, *Planets, Stars, and Orbs*, p. 63 et seq. For the medieval debate on the eternity of the world see Dales, *Medieval Discussions of the Eternity of the World*. For the prohibition of 1277 see Hissette, *Enquête sur les 219 articles*, esp. pp. 117–60.

21 Denifle, *Chartularium Universitatis Parisiensis*, pp. 486–7.

22 Weisheipl, *Tommaso d'Aquino*, p. 276 et seq.

23 Van Steenberghen, *Maître Siger de Brabant*, p. 77.

24 'Quant aux *sources lontaines* des erreurs condamnées, seul le monopschisme vient d'Averroès. Les autres doctrines visées remontent toutes, en quelque mesure, à Aristote: l'éternité du monde ... le determinisme (en faisant de la volonté une puissance passive, Aristote ouvrait la voie au déterminisme psycologique; ses conceptions relatives à l'influence universelle des sphères célestes sur les événements nouveaux qui se produisent ici – bas pouvaient conduire à un déterminisme astrologique) ... [Cette philosophie] elle empruntait aux philosophes arabes son exégèse des doctrines obscures ou incomplètes du péripatétisme originel: la théorie averroïste de l'intellect (prop. 1, 2, 7) ... et le déterminisme (prop. 3, 4, 9)' (*Maître Siger de Brabant*, pp. 78–9).

25 Van Steenberghen, *Maître Siger de Brabant*, p. 79 n. 8. See also *La philosophie au XIIIe siècle*, pp. 412–13.

26 Van Steenberghen, *La philosophie au XIIIe siècle*, p. 412.

27 Ibid., *La philosophie*, p. 412 refers to D. Salman ('Sur la lutte "contra Gentiles" de Saint Thomas'), who has counteracted Gorce's connections between the articles condemned in 1270 and Aquinas's *Summa contra Gentiles*.

28 Van Steenberghen does not accept Gorce's theory that Aquinas wrote the *Summa contra Gentiles* in order to oppose pagan ideas which were circulating in Europe. On the evidence of documents, he insists that the *Summa* was writ-

ten for the Dominican missionaries charged with the task of converting the Moslems. That is, he denies that these ideas were circulating at the end of the 1250s when the *Summa* – he assumes – was written. However, he accepts that these ideas were circulating in 1270. See his *Aristotle in the West*, pp. 193–7; and *Maître Siger de Brabant*, pp. 78–9. About dating *Summa contra Gentiles*, see Weisheipl, *Tommaso d'Aquino*, pp. 136–7 and 366–7.

29 Van Steenberghen, *Maitre Siger de Brabant*, pp. 78–9.
30 Gorce, 'La lutte "contra Gentiles,"' p. 224.
31 Ibid., p. 230.
32 Ibid., p 232; Aquinas, *Summa contra Gentiles*, Book III, chapter 69.
33 'Ex hoc autem ulterius apparet quod corpora caelestia non sunt causa voluntatum nostrarum neque nostrarum electionum. Voluntas enim in parte intellectiva animae est ... corpora caelestia non possunt imprimere directe in intellectum nostrum ... neque etiam in voluntatem nostram directe imprimere poterunt ... Item. Quaecumque ex impressione corporum caelestium in istis inferioribus eveniunt, naturaliter contingunt: cum haec inferiora sint naturaliter sub illis ordinata. Si ergo electiones nostrae eveniunt ex impressione corporum caelestium, oportet quod naturaliter eveniant: ut scilicet sic naturaliter homo eligat operari suas operationes, sicut naturali instinctu bruta operantur, et naturaliter corpora inanimata moventur. Non ergo erunt propositum et natura duo principia agentia, sed unum tantum, quod est natura.' *Summa contra Gentiles*, Book III, chapter 85. See Gorce, p. 232.
34 Kretzmann, Kenny, and Pinborg, eds, *The Cambridge History of Later Medieval Philosophy*, pp. 630–1. See also O. Lottin, *Psycologie et moral*, vol. 2, p. 207 et seq. See also the chapter 'Les fondements de la liberté humaine,' p. 225 et seq.
35 Van Steenberghen, *Maître Sigier de Brabant*, p. 330.
36 Albertus Magnus, *Opera Omnia*, vol. XVII, part I, p. 41.
37 Hissette, *Enquete*, pp. 261–2.
38 Giles of Rome, *Errores philosophorum*, p. 2 et seq.
39 'Erravit volens a deo non posse procedere immediate aliquid novum ut patet ex II De generatione ubi ait quod "idem manens idem semper facit idem"' (*Errores philosophorum*, p. 6).
40 'Cum crediderit nihil novi posse immediate a deo procedere, sed omne novum contingere per viam motus et operationem naturae' (*Errores philosophorum*, p. 9).
41 Ibid., pp. 14–15.
42 Ibid.
43 Ibid. p. 22.
44 That 'sensato' ('ha sensato, – nome') is a substantive and not an adjective as

traditionally read has been pointed out by Corti, *La felicità mentale*, p. 22: '*Sensatum*, sostantivo neutro, indica nella filosofia aristotelica la qualità sensibile in atto ... vocabolo usato a indicare i cinque sensi (cfr. il *De sensu et sensato* di Aristotele e i commenti ad esso ...).'

45 'Subtracta enim ab hominibus diversitate intellectus, qui solus inter anime partes incorruptibilis et immortalis apparet, sequitur post mortem nihil de animabus hominum remanere nisi unicam intellectus substantiam; et sic tollitur retributio premiorum et penarum et diversitas eorundem' (Aquinas, *De unitate intellectus contra Averroistas*, in *Opera Omnia*, vol. 43, p. 291).

46 Giles of Rome, *Errores philosophorum*, pp. 22–3. See also his summary of Averroes's errors at p. 24.

47 Cavalcanti here seems to echo in particular a distinction emphasized by Brunetto Latini in his *Ethics*, chapter XXX, *De vertu moral et intellectuele*, 'Li Livres dou Tresor,' p. 200: 'Vertu est en ii manieres; l'une est apelee moral, ki s'apertient a l'ame sensible, en qui n'est veraie raison; l'autre vertu est intellectuelle, ki s'apertient a l'ame raisonable, en qui est intellec et discretion et raison ... donques les commencement de l'election est intellec ... Autresi elections n'a pas leu *es choses ki sont par nécessité* ou ki ne sont possibles' (italics mine).

48 Averroes, *De substantia orbis*, p. 47.

49 For 'Kategoría,' see Bonitz, *Index*, p. 378.

50 See Renan, *Averroes*, p. 110. Nardi in 'Sull'origine dell'anima umana,' discussing the nature of male seed, refers to a passage of *De generatione animalium*, III, 11, in which Aristotle writes that the animal 'calor' is in every part and all things are full of soul. I quote from Nardi: 'Egli dice che 'gli animali e le piante sono generati dalla terra e dall'umore, perché nella terra è l'umore, nell'umore lo spirito, e il calore animale è da per tutto, di guisa che in certo modo tutte le cose son piene d'anima.' Riferendosi appunto a questo concetto, egli afferma (II, c. 3) che quello che rende fecondi i semi è "il così detto calore" che non è fuoco ma spirito e natura analoga dell'elemento degli astri.' Nardi quotes also Avicenna's *De animalibus*: 'Illa virtus est que dat vitam et est proportionale virtuti supercelestium ... Et in spermate est substantia prima potens recipere hanc virtutem, et est spiritus primus deferens hunc calorem ...' *Dante e la cultura medievale*, pp. 208–9.

51 *Ira*, which in the Canzone is connected with Love, is commonly associated with heat. In Avicenna's *Canon*: 'ira est de numero calefacientum' (f.40.B.7); 'Ira calefacit' (f.59.F.3).

52 'Unde natura huius subiecti recipientis substantiales formas, videlicet primae materiae, necesse est ut sit *natura potentiae* ... Et ideo nullam habet formam propriam, & naturam existentem in actu: sed eius substantia est in

posse: & ex hoc materia recipit omnes formas' (Averroes, *Sermo de substantia orbis*, fol. 4 [italics mine]).

53 Del Garbo refers the movement to the genitive spirit: 'Et secundum hoc accidit quod in ipso diversimodo movetur calor naturalis et spiritus ...' (Bird, p. 170). The association between heat and genitive spirit is in Aristotle and also in Averroes's *De generatione animalium* II, 3. Here we read: 'Inest nam in semine ... quod facit ut foecunda sint semina, videlicet quod calor vocatur, idque no ignis non talis facultas aliqua est, sed spiritus, qui in semine spumoso corpore continet, et natura quae in eo spiritu est, proportione respondens elemento stellarum' (Averroes, *Aristotelis De generatione animalium*, fol. 75).

54 'Intendimua inquirere quid fit id ... quod gignit membra, eaque procreat ... vel est quid in semine *infinitum*' (Averroes, *De generatione animalium*, fol. 71). (What is infinite is beyond the measure of nature) (emphasis added).

55 'In prima ergo parte, cum dicit *l'essere* intendit dicere quasi dicat quod essentia amoris in hoc consistat, quod est passio quedam in qua appetitus est cum vehementi desiderio circa rem quam amat, ut scilicet coniungatur rei amatae ... quod est ultra mensuram, id est terminum naturalem; nam istud desiderium in amore adeo est magnum, quod quasi videtur esse *infinitum*, unde non habet terminum, sicut naturalia sunt mensurata et terminata' (Bird, 'The Canzone d'Amore,' pp. 168–9, emphasis added).

56 Averroes in his commentary on Aristotle's *Metaphysics* writes: 'Virtutes igitur, quae sunt in seminibus, que faciunt animata, non sunt animate in actu, sed in potentia ... Et ideo Aristoteles fecit assimilationem de istis virtutibus ad virtutes artificiales, & dicit in libro de Animalibus, que *iste virtutes divinae sunt, cum habeant potentia dandi vita, & sunt similes virtutibus, que dicuntur intelligentie*, quia adduncunt ad fine. Et, quia ista semina non faciunt hoc, nisi per calorem, qui est in eis ... dicit Aristoteles in libro de Animalibus, que iste calor no est ignis, neque igneus. Ignis nam corrupit animalia, non generat, iste autem calor generat. & Ideo videtur similis calori artificiali ... et iste calor habet forma ... et iste forma non est anima in actu sed *in potentia*: & est quam Aristoteles assimilat arti & intellectui ... & iste calor est in seminibus, & fit ab habente seme et a Sole. Unde Aristoteles dicit homo generatur ex homine et Sole: & factus est ille calor ex terra, & aqua ex calore Solis admixto cum calore aliarum stellarum. Et ideo Sol & alie stellae sunt principium vitae cuiuslibet vivi in natura ... ergo calores generati ex caloribus stellarum ... habet *mensuras proprias* illius caloris ex quantitabus motuum stellarum (Averroes, *Aristotelis Metaphysicorum* in *Opera*, vol. 8, fol. 305, emphasis added).

57 'Aristotle believes that change is of two kinds: change of substance, which is called generation and corruption, and change of quality, which is called alteration. The reason for this is the nature of the prime matter and the nature of the distinction between forms and accidents, since the substratum

for this change in both its aspects is the prime matter' (Averroes, *On Aristotle's De generatione et corruptione*, p. 114, and also pp. 24–5).

58 Wolfson, 'The Internal Senses,' pp. 100 and 130.

59 Averroes, *Sermo de substantia orbis*, fol. 4; see note 52.

60 According to Aristotle the affections of the soul are connected with a body: anger, courage, sweetness, fear, love, joy when they are produced the body is subjected to an alteration ... it is evident that passions are forms induced in matter ... anger is a movement of that body or of a part or faculty of the body. It is therefore peculiar to physics to investigate the soul' (*De anima* I, 403a–b). The summary is mine.

61 For fire as an excess of heat, see Ross, *Aristotele*, p. 106.

62 See, for instance, Averroes's commentary on Avicenna's *Cantica*, in Averroes, *Aristotelis Opera* 10, fol. 235.

63 Averroes, *Epitome of Parva naturalia*, p. 6.

64 For heat as responsible for generation and corruption, see Renan, *Averroes*, p. 110.

65 I will examine this stanza in chapter 4.

66 For 'natural dimostramento,' see also chapter 2.

67 Because 'quality' is here described as an affective quality ('la nova – qualità move sospiri'), this quality confirms that we are in the field of passion as alteration because, according to natural philosophy, it is just this kind of quality which allows the occurring of passion. In Averroes, *On Aristotle's De generatione et corruptione*, pp. 215–16, we read: 'From this is evident that passion can occur in none of the types of qualities except the third, as is explained in book VII of *Physics*.' The third type of quality is what Aristotle indicates as affective qualities.

68 Cavalcanti's theory of love shows a relationship with Taddeo's method of conceiving medicine (which deals with human body) as subaltern to natural philosophy and therefore subjected to its principles: [According to Taddeo] medicine could not be regarded as part of moral philosophy, and despite the use of logic in medical argumentation, its subject matter was not the same as that of rational philosophy ... Instead, he maintained strongly that it should be placed entirely under natural philosophy ... medicine was subalternated to natural philosophy and therefore subjected to its principles' (Siraisi, *Taddeo Alderotti*, p. 122).

69 'Ad evidentiam questionis oportet scire quid significatur nomine (terminorum) istius questionis, cum quid nominis sit principium omnis scientie que habetur per doctrinam, ut Aristotle vult primo *Posteriorum* et Galenus satis innuit in primo *De interioribus*' (Agrimi and Crisciani, 'Medicina e logica in maestri bolognesi tra due e trecento,' p. 191, note 12).

70 Ibid., pp. 190–1.

71 I follow the interpretation given by Gorni: '*lo imponitore del nome* qui designa Guido, inconsapevole del significato vero del nome che egli stesso aveva imposto' (Dante, *Vita nova*, ed. Gorni, p. 142).

72 Dante introduces Beatrice's name at the beginning of *Vita nuova* II, 1: 'donna de la mia mente, la quale fu chiamata da molti Beatrice, li quali non sapeano che si chiamare.' At II, 6, Beatrice is identified with beatitude: 'apparuit iam beatitudo vestra.' Beatrice's name, in light of Dante's theory that names are a consequence of the things themselves ('nomina sunt consequentia rerum'), seems to enclose on the part of Dante an awareness and opposition to the theory of happiness which was at the centre of debate in Paris and which was also a topic discussed in Bologna during the 1290s, as emerges from the *Quaestio de felicitate*, written by Giacomo da Pistoia, which I will consider in the next chapter. According to my analysis Dante names his woman Beatrice because through this name he proposes an idea of 'beatitude' that would oppose both Giacomo's theory and Cavalcanti's theory of happiness.

73 'Nam ex eo quod intellectus intelligit rem mediante sua proprietate et movetur ad imponendum vocem, ad significandum talem rem sub tali proprietate ... ipse modus significandi movet intellectum et ex hoc intellectus attribuit quandam proprietatem ipsi voci ad significandum rem ipsam et talis proprietas dicitur modus significandi activus,' G.C. Alessio, 'Il commento di gentile da Cingoli a Martino di Dacia,' in *Logica a Bologna*, ed. Buzzetti et al., p. 27.

74 Alessio, 'Il commento di Gentile da Cingoli,' p. 13: 'Modus significandi passivus est proprietes rei, intellecta et consignificata per vocem.'

75 Rosier, *Mathieu De Bologne*, pp. 75–83.

76 Dante's 'selva' has been suggested by scholars as related to Plato's *Timaeus*. 'Silva' is the Latin translation of *hyle* (matter) as we find in the commentary on the *Timaeus* made by Chalcidius (largely diffused during the Middle Ages), a large section of which is devoted to a discussion of 'silva.' According to Gilson, medieval authors used the term 'silva' following Chalcidius. In Isidorus of Sevilla (*Etymologie* XIII, 3, I) we read: 'Hanc *ulen* latini materiam appellant, ideo quia omne informe ... et eam poetae silvam nominaverunt' (Van Winden, *Calcidius on Matter*, pp. 29–31).

77 Freccero has reiterated this connection. He also connects the 'demora' of *Donna me prega* ('La qual da Marte – vène, – e fa demora') with Dante's 'quando s'accorse d'alcuna dimora,' X, 70. See 'Ironia e mimesi,' p. 53, and 'Ancora sul "disdegno" di Guido', p. 91.

78 Leaman, *Averroes and His Philosophy*, pp. 36–7.

79 Ibid, p. 26. See also Dales, *Medieval Discussion*, p. 40.

80 'Lo tempo, secondo che dice Aristotile nel quarto de la Fisica, è 'numero di movimento, secondo prima e poi,' *Convivio*, IV, II, 6. Dante, *Opere Minori*, vol. 1, 2.

81 It is evident that Dante opposes here also the theory that the world is eternal in its duration (as in Aristotle and his followers) when he explains that the damned's condition of foreseeing the future will stop once the door of the future is closed: 'Però comprender puoi che tutta morta / fia nostra conoscenza da quel punto / che del futuro fia chiusa la porta' (Dante, *Inferno X*).

82 This is reiterated by Aristotle in *Physics* VIII, 1 250b–2b) as quoted by Dales, *Medieval Discussions*, pp. 40–1.

83 'How can there be any before and after without the existence of time' Or how can there be any time without the existence of motion? If then time is the number of motion, or itself a kind of motion, it follows that if there is always time, motion must also be eternal ... Now, since time cannot exist and is unthinkable apart from the 'now,' and the 'now' is a kind of middle point, uniting as it does in itself both a beginning and an end, a beginning of future time and an end of past time, it follows that there must always be time ... Therefore, since the 'now' is both a beginning and an end, there must always be time on both sides of it. But if this is true of time, it is evident that it must also be true of motion' (Aristotle, *Physics*, 8, 1, 250b–2b, as quoted by Dales, *Medieval Discussions*, p. 41).

84 See Hintikka, *Time & Necessity*, esp. pp. 93–113.

85 In article 102 as condemned in 1277: 'Quod nihil fit a casu, sed omnia de necessitate eveniunt, et quod omnia futura, quae erunt, de necessitate erunt, et quae non erunt, impossibile est esse, et quod nihil fit contingenter considerando omnes causas. Error quia concursus causarum est de definitione casualis, ut dicit Boethius libro *De consolatione ...*' As Hissette explains, this article denies that something could be contingent and asserts therefore that necessity is universal. According to Hissette, if this theory is limited to the order of nature, the thesis is not heterodox, but it becomes heterodox if applied to human beings. See Hissette, *Enquête*, p. 172.

86 Omnia futura quae fient, necessarium est fore, antequam sint; similiter etiam de preasentibus et praeteritis ...' (Hissette, *Enquête*, p. 172). As Hissette explains, Siger discusses this *quaestio* in *De necessitate* opposing the teaching of those who betray the authenticity of the thought of the Stagirite when they say that for them everything is necessary. His opposition shows that other magistri were discussing this theory of necessity and of determinism of the future. On this topic, see also Van Steenberghen, *Maître Siger de Brabant*, pp. 94–5, who inserts Siger's *quaestio* in the debate on the 'future contingent.'

87 See *The Cambridge History of Later Medieval Philosophy*, the chapter on 'Modal Logic' by Simo Knuuttila, p. 362 et seq, and the chapter on 'Future Contingents,' by C. Normore, p. 358 et seq. According to what we read in Normore at p. 358: 'Medieval discussions of this problem often rely on our intuitions that the past and the present are 'fixed' in some way in which the future is not, and so these discussion often illuminate medieval views on tense and modality. A second problem has to do with the possibility of foreknowledge ... A third problem is specifically theological. Can complete knowledge of the future by an immutable, infallible, impassible God be reconciled with the contingency of some aspects of the future?' The theological problem was discussed by Thomas Aquinas and Siger too.

88 Calvin Normore, *Future Contingents*, in *The Cambridge History of Later Medieval Philosophy*, pp. 359–60.

89 Ibid., p. 358, and note 1.

90 *Metaphysics* VI, 3, 1027b9–15.

91 Aquinas, *Commentary on the Metaphysics of Aristotle*, vol. 2, pp. 471–8.

92 Aquinas accepts that celestial bodies influence the sublunar region but makes the rational soul free from such influence: 'It is that in the sphere of lower bodies there are some efficient causes which can act of themselves without the influence of a celestial body. These causes are rational souls, to which the power of a celestial body does not extend (since they are not forms subjected to bodies) except in an accidental way, i.e., inasmuch as the influence of a celestial body produces some change in the [human] body, and accidentally in the powers of the soul which are actualities of certain parts of the body, by which the rational soul is disposed to act. However, no necessity is involved, since the soul's dominion over the passions is free inasmuch as it may not assent to them' (Aquinas, *Commentary on the Metaphysics of Aristotle*, vol. 2, p. 477). This quotation is useful in so far as it explains how much instead this notion of necessity is related to the theory of love Cavalcanti exposes in *Donna me prega*.

93 In addition Aquinas writes: 'It must be noted that the doctrine of the Philosopher set forth here seems to do away with certain things which some thinkers hold in philosophy, mamely fate and providence. For here the force of the Philosopher's argument is that not all that occurs may be traced back to some proper cause from which it follows of necessity and nothing by accident.' See Aquinas, *Commentary on the Metaphysics of Aristotle*, vol. 2, p. 475. About a distorted utilization of the thinking of Aristotle, we have traces in Siger's *De necessitate et contingentia causarum*. It appears that here he opposes the thought of certain *magistri* who were betraying the authentic thought of the Stagirite. See Hissette, *Enquête* p. 172, where he comments on article 102.

94 See Hintikka, *Time & Necessity*, and in particular p. 94 et seq., and the chapter on the future contingent, pp. 147–78. Principle of plenitude – according to Hintikka – means: 'each possibility is realized at some moment of time' (*Time & Necessity*, p. 95); see also Knuuttila, 'Modal Logic,' p. 344.

95 Freccero, in 'Ironia e mimesi,' focuses on irony: 'una lettura interpretativa non può evitare di affrontare l'ironia ... le note più strazianti nello scambio di batture con Cavalcante sono in realtà frammenti messi insieme con crudele ironia' (pp. 43–4). In 'Ancora sul "disdegno" di Guido,' p. 81, he focuses again on irony which gives to *Inferno* its 'colore retorico dominante' and which he opposes to allegory. In addition he writes, 'la figura di Cavalcante è un esempio del gioco ironico nell'Inferno' and a few pages later (p. 88) he suggests: 'Potrebbe esserci una tagliente ironia nascosta nel dialogo del pellegrino con il padre dell'amico.'

96 It is worth considering that the commentary of Ottimo (*L'Ottimo commento della Divina Commedia*) connects the Epicureans with notions which seem to echo Cavalcanti's *Donna me prega*. See esp. vol. 1, p. 174, where he discusses and opposes the intellective soul to accidentality: 'impossibile è che quella cosa che è per sè si possa corrompere per accidente; perocchè quello che è per sè, non è sottoposto a generazione, o corruzione ... e così l'anima intellettiva in sè non ha contrarietade.' Ottimo seems to identify the Epicureans with theories that echo those of Averroism. He seems also to take into account some of the topics I have introduced in this chapter on passion and matter.

97 Freccero has insisted in locating in 'ebbe,' in this past tense, the centre of the meaning of this canto. 'Gramsci aveva pienamente ragione nel suggerire che il passato remoto, 'ebbe,' si trova proprio al centro del significato di questo canto' ('Ancora sul "disdegno" di Guido,' p. 82, reiterated at p. 88). Freccero has also emphasized that: 'sia il tema che la problematica del canto X sono la temporalità ... Auerbach sembra essere inconsapevole dello sconcertante effetto di questo urto di temporalità' (Ironia e mimesi,' pp. 43 and 45.

Chapter Four: Pleasure and Intellectual Happiness

1 Kristeller, *A Philosophical Treatise*, pp. 425–63. About the link between Giacomo and Cavalcanti, Kristeller writes: 'Of course we cannot prove that Jacobus was Cavalcanti's teacher, that he exercised a formative influence upon the philosophical ideas of the poet, or even that the treatise on happiness was composed before Cavalcanti's famous canzone ... It would be much more important if we could establish a link between the philosophical ideas

of the two friends ... Moreover, the topic of Jacobus treatise is not the same as that of Cavalcanti's poem. Yet ... the treatise seems to share some doctrinal elements with the Canzone, and they would appear to lend support to Nardi's interpretation of the Canzone' (pp. 439–40).

2 Corti, *La felicità mentale*, pp. 5–7.

3 Ibid., pp. 4–7 and 17–19.

4 Ibid., pp. 28–9. Corti mentions here Boethius of Dacia, *De summo bono*.

5 Ibid., p. 17.

6 Cavalcanti, *Rime*, ed. De Robertis, p. 94.

7 See Nardi, 'L'Averroismo del primo amico di Dante,' reprinted in *Dante e la cultura medievale*, p. 90.

8 However (according to Kristeller), the work can be characterized as a treatise because it seems to have undergone some further elaboration since it contains an introduction as well as explicit transitions and a conclusion and, at least in one manuscript, a dedication (Kristeller, *A Philosophical Treatise*, pp. 434–5).

9 Ibid., pp. 435–6.

10 Ibid., pp. 443–4.

11 Ibid., pp. 453–4.

12 Aquinas, *Summa contra Gentiles* II, 59, p. 187.

13 Ibid., p. 187.

14 Averroes, *Commentarium magnum in Aristotelis De anima*, p. 219.

15 Freccero, *Dante: The Poetics of Conversion*, p. 226 and pp. 310–11, n. 9.

16 For the theory that the possible intellect is a separate substance, see Averroes's *Commentarium magnum in Aristotelis De anima*, Book 3. For an opposition to this theory, see Aquinas, *Summa contra Gentiles*, II, 59: 'That Man Possible Intellect is not a Separate Substance,' and also *De unitate intellectus contra Averroistas*. For 'consideranza' as related to an act of understanding abstract beings, Siger of Brabante writes: 'Unde nota quod anima res considerat et abstracte considerat et universaliter per intellectum possibilem, et per agentem etiam eas considerat abstracte et per ipsum facit abstractionem universalem' (*Questiones in tertium De anima*, p. 60). Aquinas opposes this theory in *Summa contra Gentiles* III, 43: 'Quod non possumus in hac vita intelligere substantias separatas sicut ponit Averroes: Averroes ... adinvenisse ad ostendendum quod quandoque intelligamus substantias separatas ex hoc quod *ponit* intellectum possibilem incorruptibilem, et a nobis secundum esse separatum, sicut et intellectum agentem.'

17 Averroes, *Commentarium magnum in Aristotelis De anima*, pp. 437–9.

18 Giele, in *Trois commentaires anonymes*, pp. 72–3: 'Dictum est nunc animam esse non actum et formam corporis scilicet intellectivam ... tunc sequitur

quod nos non intelligimus; ita quod sequitur ex hoc quod homo non intellegit. Nec valet via COMMENTATORIS: dicit quod quia intellecta nobis sunt
copulata, ideo et intellectus nobis copulatus est ... si igitur homo non est ens
per intellectum non intellegit.'

19 According to what we read in Giele's Introduction, the anonymous *quaestiones* were generated as an answer to Aquinas's *De unitate intellectus*. This text
has promoted two different positions among the Averroists. Some assert that
'homo proprie sumptus non intellegit'; some have given as an answer to
Aquinas: 'concedendo tamen quod homo intellegit.' Giacomo seems to follow the second direction. See *Trois commentaires anonymes*, pp. 17–18.

20 G. Verbeke, *D'Aristote a Thomas d'Aquin*, p. 549.

21 Aquinas indicates that this is a point of debate; for him, this ambiguity has a
precise meaning. In many ways, he opposes Averroes on this point, quoting
and recalling the passages of Averroes's *De anima* that set forth the theory of
continuity. In chapter 3 of *De unitate intellectus contra Averroistas*, Aquinas
denounces Averroes's assertion that the possible intellect does not form part
of the soul: 'Averroes said that the possible intellect is neither the soul nor a
part of the soul and said that the act of intellection of this separate substance
takes place because the possible intellect is linked ('copulatur') to me or to
someone else through phantoms which are in myself or in others.' Aquinas
also considers the role played by form, which is seen and intellected. Its role
is that of connecting two separate beings. In order to connect them, writes
Aquinas, Averroes puts forth the theory of *copulatio* or *continuatio*. The possible intellect makes connections through phantasms, which are produced by
individuals. How this takes place is explained in the following (p. 303):

> Quod sic fieri dicebat: species enim intellegibilis que fit unum cum intel-
> lectu possibili, cum sit forma et actus eius, habet duo subiecta, unum ipsa
> fantasmata, aliud intellectum possibilem. Sic ergo intellectus possibilis
> continuatur nobiscum per formam suam mediantibus fantasmatibus; et sic
> dum intellectus possibilis intellegit, hic homo intellegit.

> ('He said that this happened in this way: intelligible form, which is one
> and the same as the possible intellect, and because it is its form and act,
> has two subjects. One is the phantom itself; the other is the possible intel-
> lect. In the same way in which the possible intellect continues with us
> through phantoms, likewise, while the possible intellect performs an act of
> intellection, so also does man.')

In this passage, Aquinas summarizes Averroes's *De anima*, III, in which

Averroes elucidates the structure of the act of intellection (*Commentarium magnum in Aristotelis*, p. 400).

22 Averroes, *Commentarium magnum in Aristotelis De anima*, p. 400.

23 See Corti, *La felicità mentale*, pp. 23–4, who retraces this expression in Giele.

24 See Aristotle's *Categories*, 2, and Averroes, *Middle Commentary*, p. 34: 'Accident in general, irrespective of whether it is universal or individual, is that which is in a subject.'

25 What we read in Aquinas, *De unitate intellectus*, pp. 309–10 helps us in reconstructing the contest for 'non puote largir simiglianza': 'Deinde si non fiat vis de verbis Aristotelis, ponamus, ut dicunt, quod intellectus possibilis ab eterno habuerit species intelligibiles, per quas continuetur nobiscum secundum fantasmata que sunt in nobis. Oportet enim quod species intellegibilis que sunt in intellectu possibili, et fantasmata que sunt in nobis, aliquo horum trium modorum se habeant: quorum unus est, quod species intelligibiles que sunt in intellectu possibili, sint accepte a fantasmatibus que sunt in nobis, ut sonant verba Aristotelis; quod non potest esse secundum predictam positionem, ut ostensum est. Secundum autem modus est ut ille species non sint accepte a fantasmatibus, sed sint irradiantes supra fantasma nostra.' Aquinas opposes the idea that through this way an act of intellection is performed. This passage from Aquinas seems useful in explaining Cavalcanti's position. Because the phantasm does not accept the species, they (the species) would just shine on the phantasm. In this case, whatever the subject of 'non pote largir simiglianza' might be, it is evident that the focus is on the fact that two different beings enter into a connection which does not allow a unity, insofar as they are different substances. This passage from Aquinas also appears to confirm my reading of the metaphor of the diaphanous in *Donna me prega*. In fact, if love (and the diaphanous) is in act once illuminated, love in act is the equivalent of the phantasm illuminated from the species; however, the phantasm (love) does not accept them.

26 'Phantasmata secundum quod nobis insunt materialia sunt, non abstracta; sed secundum quod sunt intellecta in actu, sunt a materia omnino abstracta; quare non est idem quod est unitum intellectui et nobis; quare non per illa intellecta intellectus erit nobis unitus; nos ergo non intelligimus ... Praeterea, ex modo COMMENTATORIS, scilicet ex hoc quod intellecta sunt nobis copulata, non intellectus secundum sui substantiam, magis videtur quod nos intelligimur et non intelligimus, ita quod phantasmata hominis intelliguntur, sed ipse non intelliget ... Si igitur homo non est ens per intellectum, ergo homo per intellectum non intelligit' (Giele, in *Trois commentaires anonymes*, p. 73).

27 'Dico quod hoc vocabulum, scilicet virtus animalis, accipitur in 4 modis, nam

uno modo comprehendit in se omnes virtutes que sunt in anima, est enim dicere virtus animalis idest virtus anime secundum quod anima accipitur apud philosophos et non prout accipitur apud medicos ... dico quod ista virtus diffinitur ab Avicenna tamen illa diffinitio non comprehendit virtutem intellectivam ... virtus animalis est perfectio prima corporis naturalis instrumentalis ... virtus animali perfectio est animalis activa vel passiva, et dicitur haec virtus perfectio animalis, nam ipsa complet animal, et separat ipsum a plantis. Item dicitur potentia activa: quia motiva semper agit et non patitur, et passiva dicitur pro anima apprehensiva sensibili, nam dicit Galenus et Aristotle quod sentire est pati. Item intellectus dicitur agere et pati agit quidem intellectus agens et patitur materialis ergo dicitur bene virtus passiva et activa. Hec quidem diffinitio non est posita ab aliquo auctore quem ego sciam, se colligi eam ex dictis eorum' (Alderotto, *Isagoge,* as quoted by Siraisi, *Taddeo Alderotti,* pp. 210–11).

According to Siraisi, 'Taddeo adopted a triple division ... of virtus apprehensiva interior into *phantasia, virtus rationalis,* and memory. *Phantasia* he located in the anterior ventricle of the brain, and he stated it to comprise both the *sensus communis* (which organizes the impressions received from the five senses and conveys them to the other mental faculties) and a power that retains those impressions (which he termed *virtus formans or formativa*). He denied that the latter power should be termed *imaginativa,* apparently because he identified *imaginatio* with the faculty termed *intellectus passivus* by Averroes and thus included it under *virtus rationalis*' (Siraisi, p. 211).

Taddeus departs from Avicenna when he speaks of 'virtus intellectiva,' but what he intends by 'virtus intellectiva' is difficult to understand. What Alderotto probably includes in the intellectual faculty of the animal can be related to the cogitative faculty, which in Averroes was a power only of man and did not belong to beasts. According to Wolfson, this faculty corresponds to the formative activity: '*formalis,* which is used in the sense of imagination. Compositive human imagination ... is invariably translated by *cogitativa,* and so is the same term translated also in Averroes' works, where it means ... human thought or reason' (Wolfson, 'The Internal Senses,' p. 116). Siraisi underlines Alderotto's claim that his discussion of animal power is not derived from any single author and that he, Taddeus, had put it together from many sources (p. 210).

28 For Brunetto's *Tresor,* Book 6 in its relation to the Arabian-Alexandrian compendium of *Nicomachean Ethics,* and Taddeo's vulgarization of it, see Marchesi, 'Il compendio.' For the two kinds of virtue, see also p. 192, n. 47, in which I quote Brunetto's *Tresor.*

29 This is a topic that the two historical commentaries by del Garbo and

Pseudo-Aegidius have pointed out. See Cittadini, *L'Expositione del Mro. Egidio Colonna Romano* (f. 12).

30 This theory was so widely diffused in Paris in the late thirteenth century that it was conceived rather as a sort of professional art than just as a topic of philosophical debate. For the importance of the theme of intellectual happiness during Cavalcanti's time, see Bianchi, 'La felicità intellettuale come professione nella Parigi del Duecento.'

31 See Touati, 'Le probleme de la génération et le rôle de l'intellect agent chez Averroes.'

32 For heat in its relation to the generation of animals see Aristotle, *De generatione animalium*, II, 3 736b–737a. The fact that this heat is a kind of spirit which is contained in the sperm and its foam, connects the heat of 'ira' to the heat of the generative process of animals. Del Garbo comments, in fact, in his commentary on Aristotle's *De generatione animalium* and 'spiritu genitivo': 'Et in *De generatione animalium* dicit quod *in spiritu genitivo est natura existens proportio naturalis ordinationi astrorum.* Ideo merito iste auctor vult ostendere a quo corpore caelesti concurrente in generatione alicuius, datur haec dispositio naturalis, per quam aliquis faciliter inclinatur ad incurrendam hanc passionem quae dicitur amor' (Bird, p. 163). The excess of love (which is beyond nature's measure) seems to derive therefore from the influence of Mars on the 'genitive spiritus' or sperm.

33 In the philosophy of Epicurus, logic was applied to physics in the same way that medical school at the time of Cavalcanti applied logic to physics (from Taddeo Alderotto onward). According to Temkin, *Galenism* (p. 170). 'In the Middle Ages, Galen's name was sometimes coupled with Epicurus, notorious for his denial of the survival of the soul.' That Cavalcanti's fame as an Epicurean could be related to his connection with the medical ambience of Bologna is here just a hypothesis which requires further investigation.

34 Siraisi, *Taddeo Alderotti*, pp. 210–11, and this volume, p. 202, n. 27.

35 Wolfson ('The Internal Senses') indicates that Averroes discusses the internal senses in *Parva naturalia* and in *De sensu et sensato.* Internal senses are spiritual but they are part of the sensitive soul. I have introduced internal senses above in the first chapter.

36 Siraisi, *Taddeo Alderotti*, p. 159.

37 For this meaning of the word 'ornato,' see Garavelli, *Manuale di retorica*, p. 139.

38 See Deborah Black, 'Logic and The Linguistics Arts,' in Bosley and Tweedale, *Aristotle and His Medieval Interpreters*, pp. 48 et seq.

39 During the last thirty years many studies have been devoted to Guido Cavalcanti. In this note I mention those few which are sympathetic with the

method I have utilized. I will thus focus on those studies which help to reconstruct the philosophical-scientific culture of which Cavalcanti is an authoritative exponent.

A book I have previously mentioned is that written by Corrado Calenda, *Per altezza d'ingegno*, which offers a subtle reading of Guido's minor poems focusing on Guido's rhetoric. Another book is that written by Giorgio Agamben, *Stanze*. Although it is not a book devoted to Cavalcanti, nor is it written by a scholar of the Middle Ages, Agamben's book nevertheless reconstructs a very useful framework for a rereading of the culture to which Cavalcanti has to be referred, in particular in the chapters 'I fantasmi di eros,' and 'La parola et il fantasma' ('Eros allo specchio,' 'Spiritus phantasticus,' and 'Spiriti d'amore'). For instance, the relation he emphasizes between the phantasm and its role in language ('il carattere semantico del linguaggio ... è associato alla presenza di un fantasma,' p. 89) can be assumed as a corollary to what I have written in chapter 1 about the connection between image and logic. Important as well are the pages he devotes to the theory of *pneuma*. In the chapter 'Spiriti d'amore,' we read that 'Tutta la lirica stilnovistica va posta sotto il segno di questa costellazione pneumatica e solo nel suo ambito diventa pienamente intelligibile ... Non si tratta, com'è stato creduto, di una dottrina medica a cui, più o meno seriamente e non senza eccentricità, si fa riferimento da parte di un poeta, ma di un sistema unitario di pensiero' (p. 122). Most appropriate here is his recalling Cavalcanti's sonnet *Pegli occhi fere un spirito sottile* in order to show that the sonnet seeks to expose the pneumatic mechanism. Appropriate too in this context is his refutation of reading this sonnet as a parody or autoparody – as has been proposed by Contini (pp. 122–3). Unfortunately, the few lines he devotes to discussing the theory of the separated intellect in *Donna me prega* are vague and inappropriate (pp. 125–6).

Less useful for my perspective is the commentary on *Donna me prega* by Savona. Savona's method for a rereading of Cavalcanti's major canzone utilizes both del Garbo's commentary and the text of *De anima* of Aquinas. The limit of his commentary is represented not only by the fact that Aristotle's *De anima* is given in the text of Aquinas but also because he uses Contini, Nardi, and del Garbo but does not enlarge their analysis. For instance, when he speaks of 'memory,' he refers to Nardi or to the entry 'memoria' in the *Dante encyclopedia*. However, some of his suggestions are useful. His work thus confirms that it is precisely through the direct reading of the texts that were part of Cavalcanti's culture that we get a correct and meaningful interpretation not only of *Donna me prega* but in general of Cavalcanti's work.

The book published by Massimo Ciavolella in 1976 (*La malattia d'amore. Dall'antichità al medioevo*) is a useful contribution to the cultural territory of

Cavalcanti in its relation to the medical ambience which Ciavolella traces back to antiquity. It is one of the first studies on such a topic. Ciavolella's book is not focused on Guido Cavalcanti; however, a few pages in the final section are dedicated to him. As an inquiry into the medical theory of love as a sickness, the book helps us to enter into Cavalcanti's culture. It is not, in fact, just the radical Aristotelianism and the debate on the separate intellect that help us to understand Cavalcanti but it is, on the contrary, the insertion of Averroism into the culture of doctors and natural philosophers. The theory of separate intellect was one of their topics of discussion. What I have designated 'the other Middle Ages' is, in fact, the result of the new translations that introduced Greek and Arabic learning into Western culture. This learning was already active at the court of Frederick II and was in part dependent on the Salerno medical school. At the time of Cavalcanti this culture was also active (as mentioned above) in Bologna at the school of Taddeus Alderotto. In Paris this learning was mostly devoted to discussing philosophical themes, but Cavalcanti's culture draws also on the culture of medicine.

Attention to these aspects of Cavalcanti emerges from French scholars. I mention the book written by I.P. Couliano (*Eros et magie à la renaissance 1484*). His chapter, 'Histoire du fantastique' (pp. 21–43), places Guido in a line of Western culture which, through the theory of 'internal sense' and *pneuma*, he defines as unitarian. The theory of 'spirit' and the medical tradition as crucial to the culture of Cavalcanti (and Dante) have been underlined by Robert Klein. See the chapter 'Spirito peregrino' in *Form and Meaning*.

Cavalcanti returns in an essay written by M.M. Fontaine, 'La lignée des commentaires à la chanson de Guido Cavalcanti,' and collected in *La folie et le corps* (ed. Jean Ceard), published in 1985. The essay connects Cavalcanti with the medical tradition of love and retraces the connection between love as it is treated in the medical tradition with the commentaries on *Donna me prega*. By taking up the historical commentaries Fontaine shows how, from Ficino onward, Cavalcanti's culture is lost.

In the last few years in Italy a new discussion concerning Cavalcanti has arisen in relation to a rereading of Dante's *Vita nuova*. Enrico Malato (*Dante e Guido Cavalcanti*) has proposed that *Donna me prega* was written in order to counteract Dante's *Vita nuova*. In other words, Malato counteracts the widely accepted theory that Dante's *Vita nuova* contains an answer to *Donna me prega*. Malato's thesis has opened a large discussion. For a summary of this discussion see Malato, Fenzi (*La canzone d'amore*), who accepts Malato's thesis, and Barolini (*Dante and Cavalcanti*), who does not accept it.

However, I do not want to enter into this discussion since my book is constructed around the thesis that *Vita nuova* answers Cavalcanti. I have to say that the way Malato builds his thesis is not strong. He is weak when he writes about chapter 25 of *Vita nuova*. He fails to understand the core of this chapter and precisely the passage in which Dante writes: 'Amore non è per sé sì come sustanzia, ma è uno accidente in sustanzia.' As I have indicated above, Dante in this chapter introduces the word 'accident' in order to oppose Cavalcanti's theory of love. It is my opinion that it is just because *Donna me prega* has focused on the theory of accident in the way I have proposed in chapters 2, 3, and 4 that Dante writes in chapter 25 of *Vita nuova* that love 'is an accident in substance.' Substance here is precisely that unity of body and soul (of which the intellectual soul is also a part) that represents the core of the theoretical debate between him and Cavalcanti as is confirmed by *Inferno* X. But let me be more precise about this issue and quote Aquinas's *De unitate intellectus contra Averroistas*. The crucial assertion made by Averroes that Aquinas counteracts is evident in the opening of the famous treatise: 'Averroys ... qui asserere ... intellectum quem Aristoteles possibilem vocat, ipse autem inconvenienti nomine materialem, esse quandam substantiam secundum esse a corpore separatam, nec aliquo modo uniri ei ut forma.' In order to oppose this theory, Aquinas recalls the definition of the soul given by Aristotle in *De anima* II: 'ponit dicens quod anima est actus primus corporis phisici organici' and continues: 'Universaliter quidem igitur dictum est quid sit anima: substantia enim est quae est secundum rationem; hoc autem est quod quid erat esse huiusmodi corpori, id est forma substantialis corporis phisici organici' (*De unitate intellectus*, p. 291). If we compare this reasoning with what Dante writes in chapter 25 of *Vita nuova*, i.e., that love is not 'per se sì come sustanza' but is an accident in substance, we may understand that the expression 'in sostanza' (in substance) in Dante encloses precisely the meaning that Aquinas puts forth and opposes to Averroes. Love as an accident in substance means, in fact, that love (which in *Donna me prega* is a metaphor for the activity of the sensitive soul) cannot be detached from the activity of the intellect, i.e., from the intellectual soul. As we have shown, this detachment was precisely the thesis propounded in *Donna me prega*. In conclusion I want to mention the recent book published by Fenzi, *La canzone d'amore di Guido Cavalcanti e i suoi antichi commenti*, which contains a very useful edition of the historical commentaries on *Donna me prega*, such as that of Dino del Garbo (for which he uses Favati's text), and that of the Pseudo-Egidio, plus in addition those of Marsilio Ficino, Pico della Mirandola, Iacopo Mini, and Francesco de Vieri. The book also contains a long introductory essay. Every commentary is introduced by a chapter containing historical-philological information.

Chapter Five: Cavalcanti at the Centre of the Western Canon

1 Pound, *I Cantos*, pp. 832–5.
2 Dante, *Vita nuova*, XIII, 4–7.
3 Pound's categories of *melo-*, *phano-*, and *logopoeia*, which he structures in the 1920s in opposition to the concept of art as imitation, are evidence of his attempt to go beyond the cliché of the genre in order to reconquer the original meaning of the word 'poetry' itself. See Pound, *How to Read* (1929), in *Literary Essays*, pp. 25–7. See also Pound, *Machine Art* (ed. Ardizzone), pp. 23–5.
4 Pound's interest in the Chinese written language is well known. See *Instigations* (1920), to which he appended E. Fenollosa, *The Chinese Written Character as a Medium for Poetry*. This text (which he found among Fenollosa's manuscripts) is the rock on which Pound builds his important theory of the Chinese written ideogram.
5 For a correct interpretation of this metaphor, see chapter 2 above where I quote the section of Aristotle's *De anima* and del Garbo's commentary related to the 'diaphanous.' In Pound's text of *Donna me prega*, which was far from the critical edition we have today, the lines related to the 'diaphanous' read as follows: 'sì formato / chome / Diafan dal lume / d'una schuritade.' In including in his Cavalcanti *Rime* an Italian text of *Donna me prega*, Pound declares that he transcribes the text of the canzone 'as it appears in the manuscript "Ld" Laurenziana 46–60 folio 32 verso with a few errors corrected. Accents added from the Giuntine edition.' This text of *Donna me prega* ('Donna mi priegha,' according to Pound) is now in Pound's *Cavalcanti*, ed. Anderson, pp. 170–3. In this chapter, in order to avoid confusion, I will mostly use Pound's English translation, and will occasionally refer to De Robertis's text of *Donna me prega*. Quotations from Pound's Italian text will always be indicated.
6 I quote from *Pound's Cavalcanti*, ed. Anderson, 1983, p. 214.
7 See Pound, *Machine Art*, my Introduction, pp. 7–10, and pp. 33–5.
8 Pound, *Machine Art*, pp. 102–3. See also my Introduction, pp. 27–9 and pp. 51–2.
9 See Pound, *Partial Explanation*, in *Pound's Cavalcanti*, ed. Anderson, p. 214.
10 See *Mediaevalism*, ibid., p. 209.
11 See *Guido Cavalcanti: Rime*, ed. Pound, pp. 39–44, which reproduces the Introduction to Cavalcanti, *Sonnets and Ballate*, edition of 1912, and *Pound's Cavalcanti*, ed. Anderson, pp. 11–20
12 See Aristotle, *Physica* IV, 11–12 (219b–221a) and VIII, 1 (250b–252b). There is no evidence that Pound is indebted to Aristotle for his theory.

13 Pound, *Ezra Pound and the Visual Arts*, ed. Zinnes, pp. 151–2.

14 See Pound, *Literary Essays*, p. 214.

15 'I am aware that I have distorted *accidente* into 'affect' but I have done so in order not to lose the tone of my opening line by introducing an English word of *double entente* ... His definition of *l'accidente*, i.e., the whole poem, is a scholastic definition in form, it is as clear and definite as the prose treatises of the period, it shows an equal acuteness of thought' (*Partial Explanation*, in *Pound's Cavalcanti*, ed. Anderson, pp. 211–14).

16 See Pound's reading marks to Aristotele, *La metafisica*, V (1025 a) and VI. The copy of Aristotele, *La metafisica*, edited by Armando Carlini (Bari: Laterza, 1928) that Pound purchased in the early 1940s is preserved in Austin, Texas, at the Harry Ransom Humanities Research Center, University of Texas (HRHR). See my Introduction in *Machine Art*, p. 4 and in particular note 15, pp. 37–9.

17 Pound, *Machine Art*, pp. 57–83. For the concept of energy related to the point of crisis, see Pound's text on machines (1927) as collected in *Ezra Pound and the Visual Arts*, pp. 302–3.

18 For the history of this edition, see *Pound's Cavalcanti*, ed. Anderson, esp. his Introduction. See also Gallup, *Ezra Pound: A Bibliography*, pp. 152–4.

19 A note written in Italian preserved in the Beinecke Rare Book Library manuscript is useful in explaining Pound's goal for the edition of *Rime*: 'Diversi furono i miei scopi, ossia: di charire i limiti tra ciò che si sa di Guido, ciò che non si sa, e ciò che forse non si saprà mai; di turbare un' accettazione troppo sonnambolesca della tradizione stampata; di rendere giustizia ad altri studiosi; di mostrare, a differenza del comune testo stampato, un testo medioevale qual' è, con l'ortografia dell'epoca e il significato di certe parole al tempo quando furono scritte; e infine di dare una degna veste tipografica a questo poeta d'Italia il quale, dalla critica intelligente, non fu considerato secondo neppure a Dante. Giacchè la quantità, non è criterio del valore poetico, e nemmeno il "mondano rumore."

'Volevo indicare un metodo, possibile ora ma non ai tempi di Lorenzo Il Magnifico, nè dell'edizione Giuntina. Il risultato fu in linea di massima di rendere onore a Bernardo Giunta per il testo dell'editio princeps e al Cicciaporci per la sua edizione del 1813 ...'

20 *Mediaevalism*, in *Pound's Cavalcanti*, ed. Anderson, p. 203.

21 The importance Pound gives to this metaphor suggests that he had been influenced by the commentaries he had read. Pound's library shows that he read also the historical commentary on *Donna me prega* erroneously attributed to Aegidius Romanus (the so-called Pseudo-Egidio). Both del Garbo

and Pseudo-Egidio focus on the importance of this metaphor. Pound's interpretation seems to be influenced by del Garbo. Pound's library in Brunnenburg (Italy) has the following editions: Celso Cittadini, *L'Expositione del Mro. Egidio Colonna Romano degli Eremitani sopra la 'Canzone d'Amore di Guido Cavalcanti,'* Siena, 1602; and *Rime di Guido Cavalcanti edite ed inedite aggiuntovi un volgarizzamento antico non mai pubblicato del Commento di Dino del Garbo sulla canzone 'Donna mi prega' per opera di Antonio Cicciaporci,* Firenze, 1813.

22 Pound, *Mediaevalism,* in *Pound's Cavalcanti,* ed. Anderson, p. 203

23 Pound's Postscript to Remy de Gourmont. This text was written by Pound in 1921 and was appended to his translation of de Gourmont's *Physique de l'amour, essai sur l'instinct sexuel* (1903), published in 1922 with the title *The Natural Philosophy of Love.* See also Pound, *Machine Art,* pp. 27–9, and 51.

24 'Ad Lectorem E.P.' Pound wrote this introduction in Italian. Anderson translates the original Italian into English; see *Pound's Cavalcanti,* pp. 7–9.

25 *Mediaevalism,* in *Pound's Cavalcanti,* ed. Anderson, p. 209.

26 *Partial Explanation,* in *Pound's Cavalcanti,* ed. Anderson, p. 210, recalls 'Ibn Rachd, *che il gran comento feo,* for the demand for intelligence on the part of the recipient.'

27 The book, Thomas Aquinas, *Saggio contro la dottrina averroistica dell'unità dell'intelletto* (Lanciano: Carabba, 1930), was part of Pound's personal library and is preserved in Brunnenburg (Italy). On the first page, in Pound's hand, we read: 'Possibile intelletto, p. 99. G[uido] C[avalcanti].'

28 'For the modern scientist energy has no borders, it is a shapeless "mass" of force; even his capacity to differentiate it to a degree never dreamed by the ancients has not led him to think of its shape or even its loci. The rose that his magnet makes in the iron filings does not lead him to think of the force in botanic terms, or wish to visualize that force as floral and extant (*ex stare*). A medieval "natural philosopher" would find this modern world full of enchantments ... would probably have been unable to think of the electric world, and *not* think of it as a world of forms' (*Mediaevalism,* in *Pound's Cavalcanti,* ed. Anderson, p. 209).

29 The Italian text of *Donna me prega* that Pound included in his *Rime* has the following *lezione*: 'E vol ch'om mirj / in un formato locho.' Pound, however, because of his attempt to give an interpretative translation, translated in *Rime* 'formato' as 'unformèd.' However, in Canto 36 he prefers to respect 'formato' as a technical word and translates 'formato locho' with 'formed trace.' Here the word 'trace' embraces the meaning of the process toward the generation of the image (p. 170 et seq.).

30 Pound, *Machine Art,* pp. 27–9; and the section *How to Write,* pp. 87–129.

31 Pound, 'Postscript to *The Natural Philosophy of Love* by Remy de Gourmont.' I have included the Postcript in *Ezra Pound e la scienza*, from which I quote (pp. 74 and 82).

32 In Pound's text in *Rime*, we read 'Chome in subgetto': 'Che 'l prende / nel possibile intelletto / Chome in subgetto / locho e dimoranza' (Taketh in latent intellect – as in a subject ready – place and abode). Pound's copy of Avicenna, *Metaphysicae compendium* (Rome: Pontificium Institutum Orientalium Studiorum, 1926) is preserved in Brunnenburg (Italy).

33 Pound recopies here a fragment from Ugolino Verino, *De illustratione urbis Florentiae*. I transcribe here the text as given by Pound in his Marsano edition: 'Ipse Cavalcantum Guido de stirpe vetusta – doctrina egregius numeris digessit hetruscis – pindaricos versus tenerosque cupidinis arcus.'

34 Gilson, 'Guido Cavalcanti: Rime,' *The Criterion* (1932), pp. 106–12.

35 Pound received a copy of *Mediaeval Studies* during his years in Washington, according to what we read in Marshall McLuhan's correspondence (*Letters of Marshall McLuhan*, pp. 195–6). In a letter of 3 July 1948, McLuhan writes to Dorothy Pound: 'The *Mediaeval Studies* printed here at the Mediaeval Institute ... has the Otto Bird thesis in vols 2 and 3 ... It is disappointing that you haven't heard from Otto B. himself ... I think that Kenner, when next in Toronto, will photostat it for you.' In a letter of 7 July to Pound, McLuhan announces: 'Kenner was in town Tuesday and took the Otto Bird material to Peterborough where he will photograph it and send it to you soon.' It is likely that Bird's transliteration brought Pound to a better understanding of del Garbo's commentary, and of the canzone itself.

36 Pound, *The Canzone: Further Notes*, in *Pound's Cavalcanti*, ed. Anderson, p. 238. I quote also another fragment (p. 237): 'In my translation I followed the reading of "non formato." I do not think it can be held as the correct one ... "Non formato" is useful for immediate effect, i.e., of the single line, but does not cohere in the general exposition. The "formato loco" is the tract or locus marked out in the "possibile intelletto."' A few lines later Pound notes that he does not share Egidio's view of the 'formato locho' as a single image. Rather, Pound suggests that the 'formato locho' has to be identified with the *phantasia*, which is made up of many images.

37 Pound reads 'formato locho' (according to his Italian text of *Donna me prega*) more or less as being the equivalent of the Latin *informans*, as something which takes form, that is, the the activity of *phantasia* as what generates form. Both translations enclose therefore the same meaning. When he changes 'unformed place' into 'formed trace' he does not change his interpretation, but rather he makes more explicit just the becoming of the process of form through the word 'trace.'

38 Pound, *Machine Art,* p. 134.

39 The article is now collected in Praz, *Cronache letterarie anglosassoni,* vol. 1, pp. 175–80.

40 'Siccome ... Pound ha speso gran parte della sua vita ad arrovellarsi intorno al testo di Cavalcanti, specialmente attorno a quello della canzone "Donna mi prega", cerchiamo ... di vedere in che consista il suo contributo. A priori il Pound ragiona come un libro stampato e stampato bene: mentre il Vossler ritiene che il Cavalcanti si servisse di una terminologia filosofica vacillante, il Pound sostiene doversi trattare di terminologia precisa, e che prima di tutto occorrerebbe fare un lessico dell'uso di quei termini filosofici negli anni in cui il Cavalcanti scriveva. Benissimo. Purtroppo mancano al Pound gli elementi per risolvere il problema che si pone' ('Due Note su Ezra Pound,' p. 179).

41 Corti, 'Quattro poeti leggono Dante.' What I write derives also from illuminating conversations with Prof. Maria Corti.

42 'Il commento dello pseudo-Egidio, edito nel 1602 da Celso Cittadini e nel 1896 da Nicola Mattioli, è citato già da Filippo Villani come opera di Egidio Romano, attribuzione passata non solo al Cittadini, ma al Crescimbeni, a Carducci, Gaspary, Bartoli ecc. (Corti, *La felicità mentale,* p. 14).

43 Ardizzone, 'Per una estetica della téchne,' contains an introduction to the importance that Pound gives to mathematics.

44 *Estetica pragmatica* is a Pound text inserted in *Machine Art.* See Pound, *Machine Art,* p. 157. For Pound's 'téchne,' see my Introduction to *Machine Art.*

45 See Ardizzone, 'Ezra Pound as a Reader of Aristotle,' p. 215' Renan, *Averroès et l'Averroïsme,* p. 225.

46 *Pound's Cavalcanti,* ed. Anderson, pp. 212–13.

47 Pound makes a connection between 'largir' as he finds it in *Donna me prega* ('perchè non pote laire [largir] simiglianza') and Grosseteste's theory of light as multiplying (*Partial Explanation,* in *Pound's Cavalcanti,* ed. Anderson, p. 212–13).

48 See Ardizzone, 'Ezra Pound as a Reader of Aristotle,' pp. 214–17.

49 Renan, *Averroès et l'Averroïsm,* p. 116 et seq. See Ardizzone, 'Ezra Pound as a Reader of Aristotle,' pp. 215–16.

50 Pound, *The Spirit of Romance,* p. 100.

51 A copy of Aquinas, *De unitate intellectus,* marked by Pound, is preserved in Pound's library in Brunnenburg; see note 27, above, for the edition Pound owned.

52 Pound, *Guide to Kulchur,* p. 343.

53 Grabmann, *I divieti,* pp. 16–19.

54 Ibid., p. 16 et seq.; Weisheipl, *The Development of Physical Theory*, pp. 26–7.
55 Pound, *The Letters of Ezra Pound*, p. 332. See also a letter to Otto Bird dated
    9 January: 'I suggest you gather any available information re Scotus Erigena,
    trial of Scotus Erig., and his condemnation. Was it merely for some fuss
    about the trinity? Does Gilson know aught abaht [sic] it??' (p. 304).
56 The notes are mainly quotations from Scotus Erigena as found in vol. 122 of
    Patrologia Latina. See Ardizzone, 'The Genesis and Structure,' p. 15 n. 8 and
    pp. 32–5.
57 See Pound, *Machine Art*, pp. 57–83.
58 See Ardizzone, 'Per una estetica della 'téchne,' p. 28.
59 The scheme is published in *I Cantos*, pp. 1565–6.
60 See Pound, *Machine Art*. In the Introduction where I speak of the impor-
    tance of Pound's reading of Aristotle's *Metaphysics*, pp. 4–6 and 37–40.
61 Pound, *Guide to Kulchur,* pp. 338–9. See also Ardizzone, 'Ezra Pound as a
    Reader of Aristotle,' pp. 212–13.
62 This letter is now published in Ardizzone, 'Ezra Pound as a Reader of Aristo-
    tle,' pp. 230–1.
63 For the scheme in my English translation, see Ardizzone, 'Ezra Pound as a
    Reader of Aristotle,' pp. 229–30.
64 Pound uses in the scheme – originally written in Italian – the word 'for-
    tuito' (fortuitous), which he connects with 'inconsequenziale' (inconse-
    quential).
65 Pound has focused on this word in his notes to *Donna me prega*: 'Garbo not
    virtue derives from sensibility'; see Ardizzone, *Ezra Pound e la scienza*, p. 153,
    which reproduces Pound's manuscript.
66 'Dico che per cielo io intendo la scienza e per cieli le scienze' (*Convivio* II,
    XIII, 2). See Ardizzone, 'The Genesis and Structure of Pound's Paradise,'
    pp. 25–8.
67 The following is the fragment of Dante's *Convivio*, III, XIII, 3–8 that Pound
    utilizes: 'Dico adunque che la gente che si innamora "qui," cioè in questa
    vita, la sente nel suo pensiero *non sempre*, ma quando Amore fa della sua pace
    sentire ... avvegna che le intelligenze separate questa donna mirino continu-
    amente, la umana intelligenza ciò fare non può; però che l'umana natura –
    fuori de la speculazione, de la quale si appaga lo 'ntelletto e la ragione-
    abbisogna di molte cose a suo sostentamento: per che la nostra sapienza è
    talvolta abituale solamente, e non attuale, che non incontra ciò ne l'altre
    intelligenze, che solo di natura intellettiva sono perfette ... E così si vede
    come questa donna è primamente di Dio e secondariamente de l'altre intel-
    ligenze separate, per continuo sguardare, e appresso de l'umana intelligenza
    per riguardare *discontinuato*' (italics added).

68 I have discussed this ideogram in 'Pound's Language in *Rock-Drill*,' and in 'The Genesis and Structure of Pound's Paradise.'

69 See Ardizzone, *Pound e la scienza*, pp. 20–1 and p. 153.

70 See Pound, *Confucius*, p. 20, and Ardizzone, 'The Genesis and Structure of Pound's Paradise,' p. 31, n. 54.

71 Donald Hall, 'Ezra Pound: An Interview,' *Paris Review* 28 (1962).

72 See Pound, *Pragmatic Aesthetics*, in *Machine Art*, pp. 155–9, and my discussion on it in the Introduction, p. 14 et seq. See also Ardizzone, 'Per una estetica della techne.'

73 'Tanto segreto e tanta purezza che uomini raccolti come Giotto e come Cavalcanti riuscirono a deporre sulla persona umana, modifica anche per quest'ultimo il concetto delle apparizioni e delle forme che i suoi critici hanno per lo più qualificato dai presupposti platonici della sua scuola' (Luzi, *L'Inferno e il limbo*, pp. 83–9).

Bibliography

Agamben, Giorgio. *Stanze: La parola e il fantasma nella cultura occidentale*. Turin: Einaudi, 1977.

Agrimi, J. Iole, and Chiara Crisciani. *Edocere medicos. Medicina scolastica nei secoli XIII–XV.* Milan: Guerini e Associati, 1988.

– 'Medicina e logica in maestri bolognesi tra due e trecento.' Pp. 187–239 in *L'insegnamento della logica a Bolologna*, ed. Buzzetti, Ferriani, and Tabarroni.

Albertus Magnus. 'De XV Problematibus.' In *Opera omnia*. Ed. B. Geyer. Vol. 17, 1. Aschendorff: Monasterium Westfalorum, 1975.

Alderotto, Taddeo. *I 'Consilia.'* Ed. G.M. Nardi. Turin: Edizioni Minerva Medica, 1937.

Alessio, Gian Carlo. 'Il commento di Gentile da Cingoli a Martino di Dacia.' Pp. 3–71 in *L'insegnamento della logica a Bologna*, ed. Buzzetti, Ferriani, and Tabarroni.

– 'La grammatica speculativa e Dante.' Pp. 69–88 in *Letture classensi*, vol. 13, ed. Corti. Ravenna, Longo: 1984.

Alhazen. 'Le Discours de la lumière.' Ed. R. Rashed. *Revue d'Histoire des Sciences* 21 (1968): 14–64

– *Opticae thesaurus* Introduction by D.C. Lindberg. New York and London: Johnson repr. 1972.

Aquinas, Thomas. *Commentary on the Methaphisics of Aristotle*. Trans. J.P. Rowan, 2 vols. Chicago: H. Regnery, 1961.

– *De unitate intellectus contra Averroistas*. In *Opera Omnia*. Cura et studio fratrum praedicatorum. Vol. 43. Rome: Editori di S. Tommaso, 1976.

– *Liber de veritate catholicae fidei contra errores infidelium seu: Summa contra Gentiles*. 3 vols. Turin: Marietti, 1961–7.

– *On the Unity of the Intellect against the Averroists*. Trans. and intro. Beatrice H. Zedler. Milwaukee, WI: Marquette University Press, 1968.

– *Summa contra Gentiles, Book Two: Creation.* Trans. and ed. James E. Anderson. Notre Dame and London: University of Notre Dame Press, 1975.

Ardizzone, Maria Luisa. 'Ezra Pound as a Reader of Aristotle and His Medieval Commentators, and Dante's Commedia.' Pp. 205–31 in *Dante e Pound*, ed. Ardizzone.

– *Ezra Pound e la scienza: Scritti inediti o rari.* Milan: Scheiwiller, 1987.

– 'The Genesis and Structure of Pound's Paradise: Looking at the Vocabulary.' *Paideuma* 22.3 (1994): 13–37.

– 'Guido Guinizzelli's "Al cor gentil": A Notary in Search of Written Laws.' *Modern Philology* 94 (1997): 455–74.

– 'Love and Natural Law in the Manifesto of the Dolce Stil Novo.' Pp. 35–57, in *The Craft and the Fury: Essays in Memory of Glauco Cambon.* Ed. J. Francese. West Lafayette: Bordighera Press, 2000.

– 'Optics.' Pp. 660–2 in *The Dante Encyclopedia*, ed. Richard Lansing. New York and London: Garland, 2000.

– 'Per una estetica della téchne.' Pp. 27–30, in *Ezra Pound e le arti: La bellezza è difficile.* Milan: Skira, 1977.

– 'Per una lettura del "Cantos LXXII–LXXIII."' Pp. 49–57, in *Ezra Pound a Venezia*, ed. Rosella Mamoli Zorzi. Florence: Olschki, 1985.

– 'Pound's Language in *Rock-Drill*: Two Theses for a Genealogy.' *Paideuma* 21, nos. 1 & 2 (1992): 21–48.

– 'La sapienza del sensibile: Pound (Cavalcanti) Aristotele: Prolegomena.' *Galleria* 35, 3–6 (1986): 155–82.

Ardizzone, Maria Luisa, ed. *Dante e Pound.* Interventi Classensi 13, Ravenna: Longo, 1998

Aristotle. *De generatione et corruptione.* Trans. with Notes C.J.F. Williams. Oxford: Clarendon Press, 1982.

– *Generation of Animals.* Ed. and trans. A.L. Peck. Loeb Classical Library. Cambridge, MA: Harvard University Press, and London: William Heinemann, 1942.

– *Metaphysics.* Ed. and trans. Hugh Tredennick. 2 vols. Loeb Classical Library. Cambridge, MA: Harvard University Press, and London: William Heinemann, 1933.

– *Nicomachean Ethics.* Ed. and trans. H. Rackham. Loeb Classical Library. Cambridge, MA: Harvard University Press, and London: William Heinemann, 1926.

– *On Sophistical Refutations. On Coming to Be and Passing Away.* Ed. and trans. E.S. Forster. Cambridge, MA: Harvard University Press, and London: William Heinemann, 1955.

– *On the Soul [De anima]. Parva naturalia. On Breath.* Ed. and trans. W.S. Hett. Cambridge, MA: Harvard University Press, and London: William Heinemann, 1936.

– *Opere.* Ed. G. Giannantoni. 11 vols. Bari: Laterza, 1984.
– *Physics.* Ed. and trans. P.H. Wicksteed and F.M. Cornford. 2 vols. Loeb Classical Library. Cambridge, MA: Harvard University Press, and London: William Heinemann, 1934.
– *The Works of Aristotle.* 12 vols. Ed. J.A. Smith and W.D. Ross. London: Oxford University Press, 1963–8.
Averroes. *Aristotelis De generatione animalium.* In *Aristotelis Opera cum Averrois Commentariis.* Vol. 6. part 2.
– *Aristotelis Metaphysicorum libri XIV.* In *Aristotelis Opera cum Averrois Commentariis.* Vol. 8.
– *Aristotelis Opera cum Averrois Commentariis.* 11 vols. Venetiis: apud Junctas, 1562–74. Facsimile reprint, 1962.
– *Colliget.* In *Aristotelis Opera cum Averrois Commentariis.* Vol. 10.
– *Commentarium magnum in Aristotelis De anima libros.* Ed. F. Stuart Crawford. Cambridge, MA: Medieval Academy of America, 1953.
– *De substantia orbis.* Ed. and trans. Arthur Hyman. Cambridge, MA: Medieval Academy of America, and Jerusalem: The Israel Academy of Sciences and Humanities, 1986.
– *Epitome of* Parva naturalia. Ed. and trans. Harry Blumberg. Cambridge, MA: Medieval Academy of America, 1961.
– *Middle Commentary on Porphyry's* Isagoge *and on Aristotle's* Categoriae. Ed. and trans. Herbert A. Davidson. Cambridge, MA: Medieval Academy of America, and Berkeley and Los Angeles: University of California Press, 1969.
– *On Aristotle's* De generatione et corruptione: *Middle Commentary and Epitome.* Ed. and trans. Samuel Kurland. Cambridge, MA: Medieval Academy of America, 1958.
– *Sermo de substantia orbis.* In *Aristotelis Opera cum Averrois Commentariis.* Vol. 9.
Avicenna. *Liber canonis de medicinis cordialibus cantica.* Venice: Apud Iunctas, 1582.
Avicenna Latinus. *Avicenna Latinus, Liber de anima seu sextus de naturalibus.* Ed. S. Van Riet with intro. by G. Verbeke. 2 vols. Louvain: E. Peeters, and Leiden: E.J. Brill, 1972.
Bacon, Roger. *The 'Opus Maius' of Roger Bacon.* Ed. John Henry Bridges. 2 vols. Oxford: Clarendon Press, 1897.
Badawi, Abdurrahman. *Histoire de la philosophie en Islam.* Vol. 2, *Les Philosophes pures.* Paris: Librairie Philosophique J. Vrin, 1972.
Baeumker, Clemens. *Des Alfred von Sareshel (Alfredus Angelicus): Schrift De Motu Cordis.* Beitrage Zur Geschichte Der Philosophie des Mittelatters, 23, 1–2. Munster: 1923.
Barolini, Teodolinda. *Dante's Poets: Textuality and Truth in the* Comedy. Princeton: Princeton University Press, 1984.

- 'Dante and Cavalcanti (on Making Distinctions in Matters of Love): *Inferno* V in Its Lyric Context.' *Dante Studies* 116 (1998): 31–63.

Baudrillart, Alfred, A. De Meyer, and Et. Van Cauwenbergh, eds. *Dictionnaire d'histoire et de geographie ecclesiastiques.* Vol. 5. Paris: Librairie Letouzey et Ane, 1931.

Baur, Ludwig. *Dominicus Gundissalinus. De divisione philosophiae.* Beiträge Zur Geschichte Der Philosophie des Mittelalters, 4, 2–3. Munster: 1903.

Bianchi, Luca. 'La felicita intellectuale come professione nella Parigi del Duecento.' *Rivista di filosofia* 78.2 (August 1987): 181–200.

Bird, Otto. 'The Canzone d'Amore of Cavalcanti According to the Commentary of Dino del Garbo: Text and Commentary.' *Mediaeval Studies* 2 (1940): 150–203; 3 (1941): 117–60.

Black, Deborah L. 'The Imaginative Syllogism in Arabic Philosophy: A Medieval Contribution to the Philosophical Study of Metaphor.' *Mediaeval Studies* 51 (1989): 242–67.

Boccaccio, Giovanni. *Decameron; Filocolo, Ameto, Fiammetta.* Ed. Enrico Bianchi, Carlo Salinari, and Natalino Sapegno. Milan and Naples: Riccardo Ricciardi, 1952.

- *Esposizioni sopra la Comedia di Dante.* Ed. Giorgio Padoan. Milan: Arnoldo Mondadori, 1965.

Boehner, Philotheus. *Medieval Logic: An Outline of Its Development from 1250 to c. 1400.* Manchester: Manchester University Press, 1952.

Boethii Daci. *Modi significandi.* Ed. J. Pinborg and H. Roos. Corpus Philosophorum Danicorum Medii Aevi. Vol. 4. 1976.

- *Boethii Daci Topica. Opuscola (De aeternitate mundi, De summo bono, De somniis).* Ed. N.J. Green-Pedersen and J. Pinborg. Corpus Philosophorum Danicorum Medii Aevi. Vol. 6.2. 1976.

Bonitz, H. *Index Aristotelicus.* Graz: Akademische Druck-U Verlagsanstalt, 1955.

Bono, James J. 'Medical Spirits and the Medieval Language of Life.' *Traditio* 47 (1993), pp. 91–130.

Bosley, Richard, and Martin Tweedale, eds. *Aristotle and His Medieval Interpreters.* Calgary: University of Calgary Press, 1991.

Boyde, Patrick. *Perception and Passion in Dante's Comedy.* Cambridge: Cambridge University Press, 1993.

Bursill-Hall, G.L. *Speculative Grammars of the Middle Ages: The Doctrine of Partes Orationis of the Modistae.* The Hague and Paris: Mouton, 1971.

Buzzetti, Dino, Maurizio Ferriani, and Andrea Tabarroni, eds. *L'insegnamento della logica a Bologna nel XIV secolo.* Bologna: Presso l'Istituto per la Storia dell'Universita, 1992.

Calenda, Corrado. *Per altezza d'ingegno: Saggio su Guido Cavalcanti*. Naples: Liguori, 1976.

Calvino, Italo. *Six Memos for the Next Millennium*. Cambridge, MA: Harvard University Press, 1988.

Caroti, Stefano, ed. *Studies in Medieval Natural Philosophy*. Florence: Leo S. Olschki, 1989.

Cassata, Letterio, ed. *Guido Cavalcanti: Rime*. Anzio: De Rubeis, 1993.

Ceard, Jean, ed. *La folie et le corps*. Paris: Presses de l'école Normale Supérièure, 1985.

Cerulli, E., G.C. Anawati, et al. *L'Averroismo in Italia: Convegno internazionale (Roma, 18–20 aprile 1977)*. Rome: Accademia Nazionale dei Lincei, 1979.

Chenu, M.D. 'Spiritus: Le vocabulaire de l'âme au XIIe siècle.' *Revue des sciences philosophiques et théologiques* 41 (1957): 210–32.

Ciavolella, Massimo. '*La malattia d'amore' dall'antichità al medioevo*. Rome: Bulzoni, 1976

Cittadini, Celso. *L'Expositione del Mro. Egidio Colonna Romano degli Eremitani sopra la 'Canzone d'Amore' di Guido Cavalcanti Fiorentino con alcune brevi annotazioni intono ad essa di Celso Cittadini, accademico Sienese*. Siena: S. Marchetti, 1602.

Clagett, Marshall. 'Some General Aspects of Physics in the Middle Ages.' *Isis* 39 (1948): 29–43.

Contini, Gianfranco, ed. *Poeti del Duecento*. Vol. 2. Milan and Naples: Riccardo Ricciardi, 1960.

– *Un' Idea di Dante: Saggi danteschi*. Turin: Einaudi, 1976.

Corti, Maria. *Dante a un nuovo crocevia*. Florence: Libreria Commissionaria Sansoni, 1981.

– *La felicità mentale: Nuove prospettive per Cavalcanti e Dante*. Turin: Einaudi, 1983.

– *Percorsi dell'invenzione: Il linguaggio poetico e Dante*. Turin: Einaudi, 1993.

– 'Quattro poeti leggono Dante: Riflessioni.' Pp. 223–43. In *Ezra Pound: Galleria*, ed. De Rachewiltz and Ardizzone.

– ed. *Letture classensi*. Vol. 13. Ravenna: Longo, 1984.

Couliano, I.P., *Eros et magie à la renaissance 1484*. Paris: Flammarion, 1984.

Dales, Richard C. 'The De-Animation of the Heavens in the Middle Ages.' *Journal of the History of Ideas* 41.4 (October–December 1980): 531–50.

– *Medieval Discussions of the Eternity of the World*. Leiden: E.J. Brill, 1990.

Dante Alighieri. *La Commedia secondo l'antica vulgata*. Ed. Giorgio Petrocchi. Turin: Einaudi, 1975.

- *The Divine Comedy. Inferno.* Trans. with an Introduction by Allen Mandelbaum. New York: Bantam Books, 1980.
- *The Divine Comedy: Inferno.* Trans. with a Commentary by C.S. Singleton. Princeton, NJ: Princeton University Press, 1970.
- *Opere Minori.* Vol. 1, Part 1. Ed. Domenico De Robertis and Gianfranco Contini. Milan and Naples: Riccardo Ricciardi, 1984.
- *Opere Minori.* Vol. 1, Part 2. Ed. Cesare Vasoli and Domenico De Robertis. Milan and Naples: Riccardo Ricciardi, 1988.
- *Rime.* Ed. Gianfranco Contini. Turin: Einaudi, 1980.
- *Vita nuova.* Ed. and trans. Dino Cervigni and Edward Vasta. Notre Dame, IN, and London: Notre Dame University Press, 1995.
- *Vita nova.* Ed. Guglielmo Gorni. Turin: Einaudi, 1996.

D'Alverny, Marie-Therese. *Avicenne en Occident.* Paris: Librairie Philosophique J. Vrin, 1993.

Delhaye, Philippe. 'La Place des arts liberaux dans les programmes scolaires du XIIIe siècle.' Pp. 161–73. In *Arts Liberaux et Philosophie au Moyen Âge*, 1969.

De Libera, Alain. 'La problématique de 'L'istant du changement' au XIIIᵉ siècle: Contribution à l'histoire des *sophismata physicalia*. Pp. 43–81, in *Studies in Medieval Natural Philosophy*, ed. Caroti.

Denifle, Henri, and A. Chatelain, *Chartularium Universitatis Parisiensis.* Vol. 1. Paris 1889; reprint, Brussels: Culture et Civilisation, 1964.

De Rachewiltz, Mary, and Maria Luisa Ardizzone, eds. *Ezra Pound. Galleria*, vol. 35, 3–6 (May–December 1986).

De Vaux, R. 'La première entrée d'Averroes chez les Latins.' *Revue des Sciences Philosophiques et Theologiques* 22.2 (1933): 193–245.

Favati, Guido. *La glossa latina di Dino del Garbo a 'Donna me prega' del Cavalcanti.* Florence: La Nuova Italia, 1952.

- *Guido Cavalcanti: Le rime.* Milan-Naples: Riccardo Ricciardi, 1957.
- *Inchiesta sul dolce stil nuovo.* Florence: Felice Le Monnier, 1975.

Fenzi, Enrico, *La canzone d'amore di Guido Cavalcanti e i suoi antichi commenti.* Genoa: Il melangolo, 1999.

Fontaine, Marie-Madaleine. 'La lignée des commentaires à la chanson de Guido Cavalcanti *Donna me prega*: Évolution des relations entre philosophie, médecine et littérature dans le débat sur la nature d'Amour (de la fin du XIIIᵉ siècle à celle du XVI). Pp. 159–78 in *La folie et le corps*, ed. Ceard.

Freccero, John. 'Ancora sul "disdegno" di Guido.' *Letture classensi*, vol. 18 (1989): 79–92.

- *Dante: The Poetics of Conversion.* Ed. and intro. Rachel Jacoff. Cambridge, MA and London: Harvard University Press, 1986.

– 'Ironia e mimesi: Il disdegno di Guido.' Pp. 41–54 in *Dante e la Bibbia*, ed. Giovanni Barblan. Florence: Leo S. Olschki, 1988.

Gallup, Donald. *Ezra Pound: A Bibliography*. Charlottesville: University Press of Virginia, 1983.

Garavelli, Bice Mortara. *Manuale di retorica*. Milan: Bompiani, 1988.

Giele, Maurice, Fernand Van Steenberghen, and Bernard Bazan. *Trois commentaires anonymes sur le Traité de l'âme d'Aristote*. Louvain: Publications Universitaires and Paris: Beatrice-Nauwelaerts, 1971.

Giles of Rome. *Errores philosophorum*. Ed. Josef Koch and trans. John O. Riedl. Milwaukee, WI: Marquette UP, 1944.

Gilson, Etienne. 'Guido Cavalcanti, Rime.' *Criterion* 12, no. 46 (1932): 106–12.

Gorce, M.M. 'Averroisme.' In *Dictionnaire d'histoire et de géographie ecclésiastiques*, ed. Baudrillart, de Meyer, and van Cauwenbergh, 1931.

– 'La lutte "contra Gentiles" à Paris au XIIIᵉ siècle.' In *Mélanges Mandonnet: Études d'histoire littéraire et doctrinale du Moyen Age*. Vol. 1. Paris: Librairie Philosophique J. Vrin, 1930.

Grabmann, Martin. 'L'Aristotelismo italiano al tempo di Dante con particolare riguardo all'Università di Bologna.' *Rivista di filosofia neoscolastica* 38 (1946): 260–77.

– *I divieti ecclesiastici di Aristotele sotto Innocenzo III e Gregorio IX*. Rome: Typis Pontificiae Universitatis Gregorianae, 1941.

Grant, Edward. *Planets, Stars, and Orbs: The Medieval Cosmos, 1200–1687*. Cambridge: Cambridge University Press, 1996.

Harrison, Robert Pogue. *The Body of Beatrice*. Baltimore: Johns Hopkins University Press, 1988.

Haskins, Charles Homer. *Studies in the History of Medieval Science*. Cambridge, MA: Harvard University Press, 1927.

Hintikka, Jakko. *Time & Necessity: Studies in Aristotle's Theory of Modality*. Oxford: Oxford University Press, 1982.

Hissette, Roland. *Enquête sur les 219 articles condamnés à Paris le 7 Mars 1277*. Louvain: Publications Universitaires, and Paris: Vander-Oyez, S.A., 1977.

Hymes, Dell, ed. *Studies in the History of Linguistics: Traditions and Paradigms*. Bloomington and London: Indiana University Press, 1974.

Ibn al-Haytham (Alhazen) *The Optics*. Trans. with Introduction and Commentary by A.I. Sabra. London: The Warburg Institute University of London, 1989.

Jolivet, Jean. *Multiple Averroes*. Paris: Les belles lettres, 1978.

Jolivet, Jean, and Roshdi Rashed, eds., *Etudes sur Avicenne*. Paris: Les Belles Lettres, 1984.

Kantorowicz, Ernest. *Federico II, Imperatore* (1927). Milan: Garzanti, 1976.

Knuuttila, Simo. 'Modal Logic.' Pp. 342–57 in *Cambridge History of Later Medieval Philosophy*, ed. Kretzmann, Kenny, and Pinborg.

Klein, Robert. *Form and Meaning: Essays on the Renaissance and Modern Art.* New York: The Viking Press, 1979.

Kretzmann, Norman. 'Syncategoremata, Exponibilia, Sophismata.' Pp. 211–45 in *Cambridge History of Later Medieval Philosophy*, ed. Kretzmann, Kenny, Pinborg.

Kretzmann, Norman, Anthony Kenny, and Jan Pinborg, eds., pp. 215–45, *The Cambridge History of Later Medieval Philosophy: From the Rediscovery of Aristotle to the Disintegration of Scholasticism, 1100–1600.* Cambridge: Cambridge University Press, 1982.

Kristeller, Paul Oskar. 'A Philosophical Treatise from Bologna Dedicated to Guido Cavalcanti: Magister Jacobus de Pistorio and His "Questio de Felicitate."' Pp. 425–63 in *Medioevo e Rinascimento: Studi in onore di Bruno Nardi*, vol. 1. Sansoni, 1955.

Larkin, Vincent R. 'St. Thomas Aquinas on the Movement of the Heart.' *Journal of the History of Medicine and Allied Sciences* 15 (1960): pp. 22–30.

Latini, Brunetto. *Li Livres dou tresor*, ed. F.J. Carmody. Berkeley and Los Angeles: University of California Press, 1948.

– *La rettorica.* Ed. F. Maggini. Florence: Olschki, 1968.

Leaman, Oliver. *Averroes and His Philosophy.* Oxford: Clarendon Press, 1988.

Lindberg, David C. *A Catalogue of Medieval and Renaissance Optical Manuscripts.* Toronto: Pontifical Institute of Mediaeval Studies, 1975.

– *Roger Bacon and the Origins of the Perspective in the Middle Ages: A Critical Edition and English Translation of Bacon Perspectiva with Introduction and Notes.* Oxford: Clarendon Press, 1996.

– *Studies in the History of Medieval Optics.* London: Variorum Reprints, 1983.

– *Theories of Vision from Al-Kindi to Kepler.* Chicago: University of Chicago Press, 1976.

Lottin, Odin. *Psychologie et morale au XII et XIII siècles.* 6 volumes. Gembloux: Duculot, 1949–67. Vol. 2.

Luzi, Mario. *L'inferno e il limbo* (1949). Milan: Il Saggiatore, 1964.

Maierù, Alfonso. 'Dante al crocevia?' *Studi Medioevali* 24.2, 1983: 735–48.

– 'Influenze arabe e discussioni sulla natura della logica presso i Latini fra XIII e XIV secolo. Pp. 243–67 in *La diffusione delle scienze islamiche nel Medio Evo europeo.* Roma: Accademia Nazionale dei Lincei, 1987.

– *University Training in Medieval Europe.* Trans. and ed. D.N. Pryds. Leiden, New York, Cologne: E.J. Brill, 1994.

Malato, Enrico. *Dante e Guido Cavalcanti: Il dissidio per la Vita nuova e il 'disdegno' di Guido.* Rome: Salerno editrice, 1997.

Marchesi Concetto. 'Il compendio volgare dell'Etica Aristotelica e le fonti del VI libro del "Tresor."' *Giornale storico della letteratura italiana* 42 (1903): 1–74.

Mazzotta, Giuseppe. *Dante's Vision and the Circle of Knowledge.* Princeton, NJ: Princeton University Press, 1993.

McLuhan, Marshall. *Letters of Marshall McLuhan.* Selected and edited by Matie Molinaro, Corinne McLuhan, and William Toye. Toronto, Oxford, New York: Oxford University Press, 1987.

McMullin, Ernan, ed. *The Concept of Matter in Greek and Medieval Philosophy.* South Bend, IN: University of Notre Dame Press, 1965.

Michaud-Quantin, Pierre. *Études sur le vocabulaire philosophique du Moyen Âge.* Rome: Edizioni dell'Ateneo, 1971.

Murdoch, John E. 'The Involvement of Logic in Later Medieval Natural Philosophy.' Pp. 3–28 in *Studies in Medieval Natural Philosophy*, ed. Caroti.

Nardi, Bruno. 'L'Averroismo bolognese nel secolo XIII e Taddeo Alderotto.' *Rivista di storia delle filosofia* 4 (1949): 11–22.

— *Dante e la cultural medievale.* Ed. Paolo Mazzantini. Bari: Laterza, 1985.

— *Saggi e note di critica dantesca.* Milan and Naples: Riccardo Ricciardi, 1966.

Normore, Calvin. 'Future Contingents.' Pp. 358–81 in *Cambridge History of Later Medieval Philosophy*, ed. Kretzmann, Kenny, and Pinborg.

L'Ottimo commento della Divina Commedia: Testo Inedito D'Un Contemporaneo di Dante. Ed. Alessandro Torri. Reprint with a preface by F. Mazzono. Bologna: Forni, 1995, vol. 1. pp. 171–93.

Pagani, Ileana. *La teoria linguistica di Dante:* De vulgari eloquentia. *Discussioni, scelte, proposte.* Naples: Liguori, 1982.

Pagliaro, Antonino. *Saggi di critica semantica.* Messina and Florence: G. D'Anna, 1976.

Panvini, Bruno, ed. *Le Rime della Scuola Siciliana.* 2 vols. Florence: Leo S. Olschki, 1962.

Parret, Herman, ed. *History of Linguistic Thought and Contemporary Linguistics.* Berlin and New York: Walter de Gruyter, 1976.

Pound, Ezra. *Confucius. The Great Digest. The Unwobbling Pivot. The Analects.* New York: New Directions, 1969.

— *Ezra Pound and the Visual Arts.* Ed. and intro. Harriet Zinnes. New York: New Directions, 1980.

— *Guide to Kulchur.* New York: New Directions, 1938.

— *I Cantos.* Ed. Mary de Rachewiltz, with commentary by Mary de Rachewiltz and Maria Luisa Ardizzone. Milan: Arnoldo Mondadori, 1985.

- *Instigations of Ezra Pound Together with an Essay on the Chinese Written Character by Ernest Fenollosa.* New York: Boni and Liveright, 1920.
- *The Letters of Ezra Pound 1907–1941.* Ed. D.D. Paige. New York: New Directions, 1950.
- *Literary Essays.* Ed. with Introduction by T.S. Eliot. New York: New Directions, 1954.
- *Machine Art and Other Writings: The Lost Thought of the Italian Years.* Essays selected, edited, and with an Introduction by Maria Luisa Ardizzone. Durham, NC, and London: Duke University Press, 1996.
- *Pound's Cavalcanti.* An Edition of the Translations, Notes and Essays by David Anderson. Princeton, NJ: Princeton University Press, 1983.
- *The Spirit of Romance.* London: Dent & Sons, 1910.
Praz, Mario *Cronache letterarie anglosassoni.* 3 vols. Rome: Edizioni di storia e letteratura, 1950.
- 'Due note su Ezra Pound.' Pp. 175–80 in *Cronache letterarie anglosassoni,* vol. 1. Rome: Edizioni di storia e letteratura, 1950.
Quaglio, A.E. 'Prima fortuna della glossa garbiana a "Donna me prega" del Cavalcanti.' *Giornale Storico della Letteratura Italiana* 141 (1964): 336–68.
Quatrième Congrès Internationale de Philosophie Medievale. *Arts liberaux et philosophie au moyen âge.* Montreal: Institut d'Études Medievales, and Paris: Librairie Philosophique J. Vrin, 1969.
Renan, Ernest. *Averroès et l'averroïsme: Essai historique.* Paris: Michel Levy Frères, 1866.
Rosier, Irene. 'Mathieu de Bologne et les divers aspects du pre-modisme.' Pp. 73–108 in *L'insegnamento della logica a Bologna nel XIV secolo,* ed. D. Buzzetti, M. Ferriani, and A. Tabarroni. Bologna: Presso l'Istituto per la Storia dell'Università, 1992.
Ross, William David. *Aristotele.* Trans. Altiero Spinelli, rev. Claudio Martelli. Milan: Giangiacomo Feltrinelli, 1982.
Said, Edward. *Orientalism.* New York: Random House, 1978.
Savona, Eugenio. *Per un commento a 'Donna me prega' di Guido Cavalcanti.* Rome: Edizioni dell'Ateneo, 1989.
Scaglione, Aldo. *Essays on the Arts of Discourse.* Ed. Paolo Cherchi, Stephen Murphy, Allen Mandelbaum, and Giuseppe Velli. New York: Peter Lang, 1998.
Segre, Cesare, Mario Marti, eds. *La Prosa del duecento.* Milan and Naples: Riccardo Ricciardi, 1959.
Shaw, J.E. *Guido Cavalcanti's Theory of Love: The* Canzone d'Amore *and Other Related Problems.* Toronto: University of Toronto Press, 1949.
Siger de Brabant. *Questiones in tertium de anima. De anima intellectiva. De aeternitate*

mundi. Ed. Bernardo Bazán. Louvain: Publications Universitaire, and Paris: Beatrice Nauwelaerts, 1972.

− *Questions sur la métaphysique.* Ed. Cornelio A. Graiff. Louvain: Édition de L'Institute Superiéur de Philosophie, 1948.

Siraisi, Nancy G. *Medieval and Early Renaissance Medicine: An Introduction to Knowledge and Practice.* Chicago: University of Chicago Press, 1990.

− *Taddeo Alderotti and His Pupils: Two Generations of Italian Medical Learning.* Princeton, NJ: Princeton University Press, 1981.

Stewart, Dana E. 'Spirits of Love: Subjectivity, Gender, and Optics in the Lyrics of Guido Cavalcanti.' Pp. 37–60 in *Sparks and Seeds: Medieval Literature and Its Afterlife: Essays in Honor of John Freccero.* Ed. Dana E. Stewart and Alison Cornish. Turnhout, Belgium, Brepols, 2000.

Temkin, Owsei. *Galenism: Rise and Decline of a Medical Philosophy.* Ithaca, NY: Cornell University Press, 1973.

Thillet, Pierre. 'Reflexions sur la paraphrase de la Rhetorique d'Aristote.' Pp. 105–15 in *Multiple Averroes,* ed. Jolivet.

Touati, Charles. 'Le problem de la génération et le rôle de l'intellect agent chez Averroes.' Pp. 157–64 in *Multiple Averroes,* ed. Jolivet.

Trendelenburg, Adolf. *La dottrina delle categorie in Aristotele.* Ed. Giovanni Reale and trans. Vincenzo Cicero. Milan: Vita e Pensiero, 1994.

Van Steenberghen, Fernand. *Aristotle in the West: The Origins of Latin Aristotelianism.* Louvain: Nauwaelarts, 1955.

− *Maître Siger de Brabant.* Louvain: Publications Universitaires, and Paris: Vander-Oyez, S.A., 1977.

− *La philosophie au XIIIe siècle.* Louvain: Éditions Peeters, 1991.

− *Thomas Aquinas and Radical Aristotelianism.* Washington, DC: Catholic University of America Press, 1980.

Van Winden, J.C.M., *Calcidius on Matter: His Doctrine and Sources.* Leiden: Brill, 1965.

Verbeke, Gerard. *D'Aristote à Thomas d'Aquin: Antecedents de la pensée modérne.* Leuven: University Press, 1990.

− *L'Évolution de la doctrine du pneuma: Du Stoicisme à S. Augustin.* Paris: De Brouwer, and Louvain: Éditions de l'Institute Supérieur de Philosophie, 1945.

Vescovini, Graziella Federici. 'Biagio Pelacani a Padova e l'Averroismo.' Pp. 350–8 in *L'Averroismo in Italia.*

− 'La "perspectiva" nell'enciclopedia del sapere medievale.' Pp. 987–98 in *Arts liberaux et philosophie au moyen âge.*

Weisheipl, James A. 'Classification of the Sciences in Medieval Thought.' *Medieval Studies* 27 (1965): 54–90.

– 'Curriculum of the Faculty of Arts at Oxford in the Early Fourteenth Century.' *Medieval Studies* 26 (1964): 143–85.
– *The Development of Physical Theory in the Middle Ages.* Ann Arbor, MI: University of Michigan Press, 1971.
– *Nature and Motion in the Middle Ages.* Ed. William E. Carroll. Washington, DC: Catholic University of America Press, 1985.
– *Tommaso d'Aquino: Vita, Pensiero, Opere.* Trans. Adria Pedrazzi. Milan: Jaca Book, 1994.
Wolfson, Harry Austryn. 'The Internal Senses in Latin, Arabic, and Hebrew Philosophical Texts.' *Harvard Theological Review* 28 (April 1935): 69–133.

Index